IN
WITCH-BOUND
AFRICA

An Account of the Primitive Kaonde Tribe and their Beliefs

FRANK H. MELLAND

" The wildest dreams of Kew are the facts of Khatmandhu
And the crimes of Clapham chaste in Martaban."

NEW   YORK

BARNES & NOBLE, INC.

Publishers · Booksellers · Since 1873

Published by
FRANK CASS AND COMPANY LIMITED
67 Great Russell Street, London WC1

Published in the United States
in 1967
by Barnes & Noble, Inc.
105 Fifth Avenue, New York, N.Y. 10003

First edition   1923
New impression   1967

Printed in Holland by
N. V. Grafische Industrie Haarlem

TO

MY SISTERS

A TOKEN OF GRATITUDE

FOR SYMPATHETIC INTEREST IN MY WORK

AND IN THE NATIVES COMMITTED TO MY CHARGE

WHICH HAS BEEN

A CONSTANT HELP TO ME.

PREFACE

THIS is meant to be a serious study of the ethnography of the Bakaonde and their neighbours inhabiting the Kasempa District of Northern Rhodesia, viewed in the light of comparative religion and social science ; but an effort has been made to record the results of study in such a form as to be readable, and comprehensible not only to the few who live and work amongst these people, but to all at home who may care to get an insight into the habits and outlook of some of the native races who are their wards. For this reason I have endeavoured whenever possible to avoid or explain terms which convey little to the ordinary reader ; I have omitted many minor details which might tend to make the book too " heavy " ; but I have, on the other hand, dealt very fully with those aspects of native life which seem to me to throw most light on the native point of view and on the influences which mould the life of the people. The native point of view as presented here is, of course, only my own reading of it, which may well be prejudiced since one cannot study such a subject without a certain amount of bias. Possibly it is none the worse for that.

I hold the belief strongly that trustees should take an interest in their wards and try to understand them, so that they can follow and—when necessary—check the work of their agents to whom the wards are entrusted. We, the district officials, are not so much guardians of the backward races as agents for the guardians. In the belief that it is possible to write a book which, while recording essentials accurately, is sufficiently interesting to be read, and not too recondite, these notes have been put into book form instead of being filed in the office as " District Notes."

It is hoped that this book may have a secondary use—among all who are going to live and work among similar Bantu peoples, even if far from the Bakaonde ; for, while their customs, habits, and beliefs differ there is, still, a great similarity in these matters as there is in their languages. To acquire an insight into one tribe helps one to understand others.

It may interest students of ethnography to note that the people dealt with here are immediately adjacent, on the north-west, to " the Ila-speaking peoples of Northern Rhodesia," so ably described by Messrs. Smith and Dale in their two-volume work. The points of similarity and of difference are interesting. Many differences are also recorded herein between the Bakaonde and their other neighbours. It was the writer's intention, originally, to confine himself to one tribe ; but this proved imprac- ticable. Their neighbours are, however, only dealt with superficially, and much interesting matter remains to be recorded about them.

As for my qualifications. I have worked for twenty- two years among Bantu peoples : eleven having been spent in the district described in this book. All this time, so far as my work and other occupations per- mitted, I have been studying these things and trying to understand the native point of view. I have not been able to devote as much time as I would have wished to these studies, which accounts for some obvious omissions in the book.

The fact that I was transferred to another district in April, 1922, when the book was still unfinished, has slightly affected the completeness of this work ; and my official position, while bringing me into close touch with some aspects of native life, has also been somewhat of a handi- cap. There is a natural tendency among the natives to

Preface

feel that the knowledge they impart to a magistrate may bring someone into trouble, or may even be used against the informant. To a certain extent I have conquered this fear, but in some degree it necessarily occurs. There is little doubt that an official—as also a missionary—gets a somewhat one-sided view of native life.

Most of what follows is the result of original research. In much of it I have had the benefit (in varying degree) of criticism and suggestions from my colleagues, namely (in alphabetical order), Messrs. V. R. Anley, J. H. C. Griffiths, C. H. Hazell, J. L. Keith, K. S. Kinross, F. V. Bruce Miller, C. S. Parsons, G. A. Taylor, T. R. Williams, and R. E. Broughall Woods. At times I have incorporated work of theirs ; in such cases the interpolation is followed by the initials of the writer ; but I accept sole responsibility for all that is so recorded. These contributions have added greatly to the value and to the interest of the book.

My native assistants are legion, and come from different parts of the country—an important fact since customs and beliefs vary in different areas. I must record a few names in gratitude : My head-messenger Ndirima (from Matavu's country, S.W. Kaonde). Messengers Tapishya (N.W. Kaonde) and Salimu. Chief Kapiji-Mpanga-Mwandwe (N.E. Kaonde) and two of his nephews, Chilolo and Jilapi. Paramount Chief Musokantanda XIII (Lunda), Chiefs Mukumbi-Luwinga, Mukumbi-Katotola, Chiwanza, Kambulungwa, Nyundu, Chilowo, and the late Kalilele and Ntambo, and many others too numerous to mention, including several witch doctors who would probably prefer to remain anonymous. But for their help and confidence nothing could have been done. Donald Chinganga, court interpreter at Solwezi, has also rendered most valuable assistance in many ways ; his knowledge of the people and their language has been a useful stand-by and check ; but (to avoid possible misunderstanding) I must add that none of my information comes from him : it is all drawn from Kaonde sources.

I am grateful for the permission given me to use two photographs taken by my friends. The rest are all my own. For the map I owe my thanks to the Chief Surveyor, Livingstone, who has drawn it from the sub-district maps.

Finally, I owe a great debt to my wife for her help, particularly in carefully correcting and checking the typescript, which has often been typed and re-typed and has needed a fresh check each time, for proof-correcting, and, too, for developing all the photographs. Also more generally for her interest and encouragement, but for which the book would not have been completed : it might, indeed, never have been undertaken.

It is, I think, not necessary to emphasise the fact that I know there are many errors in the book ; but I can affirm that nothing is herein recorded without consider-able cross-checking, and that in no case is guess-work incorporated. There can, however, be nothing approaching perfection in such a work as this.

FRANK H. MELLAND.

Broken Hill,
　Northern Rhodesia.

ACKNOWLEDGMENT

THE substance of Chapter I has appeared in *The Geographical Journal*; a small part of Chapter XVI in *The Journal of the African Society*; and the gist of Chapter XIX was incorporated in an article in *The National Geographic Magazine* (U.S.A.). The material in Chapters XIV, XV, XVI has been used for a paper read before the South Africa Science Association, 1923, and Chapter XXVI is a paper read before the General Missionary Conference at Kafue, 1922.

CONTENTS

LIST OF ILLUSTRATIONS

In Witch-Bound Africa

CHAPTER I

THE COUNTRY

THE Kasempa district of Northern Rhodesia with which this book deals lies to the extreme north-west of the territory, having the Katanga province of the Belgian Congo on its northern border and on the west Portuguese Angola. The Barotse and Kafue districts of Northern Rhodesia form its southern and the Luangwa district its eastern boundary.

The earlier explorers to visit this part of Africa were S. Porto, Livingstone and Capello, followed by Arnot and Gibbons ; much useful work was done by them, but the district was more or less unknown until the late George Grey, guided by the Kaonde chief Kapijimpanga, discovered Kansanshi mine in 1897 or thereabouts (it was first registered in 1898) ; and Edmund Davis (in 1899) pegged the Jumbo and Buffalo mines. Administration came later, and the first record of a resident official appears in 1903, since when there have been government posts at Kasempa, Shilenda (abandoned), Kansanshi (transferred to Solwezi), and Kalualua (transferred to Mwinilunga).

The country is mostly of a gently undulating character, well wooded and watered. The highest point (near Caenby Farm) is about 6000 feet, and the average altitude in the north is about 4500 feet, dropping considerably at its southern border by the Lunga (E.) and Kafue junction, where the country is more tropical and the familiar trees of the north are largely replaced by thorns, baobabs, and borassus palms. The temperature is very moderate, the maximum at Solwezi being 101° F. in October, 1913, and next highest 97° F. in November, 1917 ; the lowest registered there was 28° F., and 25° F. on the ground. Ice is found almost every year, and in the winter the hoar frost remains on the ground till 9 and 10 a.m. in the shade. No records are available of temperature in the south, but the maximum in the shade there is probably about 110° F. I have, however, seen thick ice right on the southern border. The rainfall is good and fairly regular. Early rains can be expected in October, and last till April. The greatest number of days in one year in which over 0·01 inch fell is 138, and the lowest 94. The maximum fall in a season at Solwezi is 69·11 inches in 1916–17, and the minimum 34·81 in the following year, the average being about 50 inches.

The rocks of the district, so I have been told (G. A. T.), are mainly metamorphic and igneous ; owing to the action of carbonic acid the mica, felspar, hornblende, etc., are almost completely dissolved and carried away, leaving behind the less soluble silica, alumina, and iron, which form soil of a clayey nature. The soils are almost entirely residual, the configuration of the district being such that the gradient of the rivers increases rather than diminishes as it approaches the edges of the plateau ; and the rivers have mostly no occasion to deposit their loads of silt and mud in the form of alluvial plains. The rains falling torrentially in their season scour the surface, carrying away much of the soil. The commonest soil is red—varying from 1 to 6 feet—and passing downwards into yellowish brown clay, which in turn passes into a greenish soil, overlying a greenish or bluish rock.

The chief geographical feature of the district is the source of the Zambezi. The river itself rises in the extreme north-west, and its early tributaries, the Kabompo (with the Western Lunga) and Kafue (with the Eastern Lunga), all rise in the north of the district, and all assume considerable volume before joining the main river. Besides these there are the tributaries of the rivers named, many of which are by no means insignificant, notably the Mumbezhi and Dongwe (to the Kabompo), the Mutanda and Luma (to the Eastern Lunga) and the Lufupa (to the Kafue). The rivers resemble all rivers in this part of Africa, and call for little comment. The Zambezi itself rises in a wooded dip, containing several small springs, the water from which unites and forms a small stream; the numerous adjacent tributaries very soon make the parent river a fair size. The Western Lunga and the Kabompo, which are very much of a size at their junction, rise within a mile of each other, and meet some 250 miles to the south. The only real feature of outstanding merit is the gorge on the Kabompo, some 60 miles downstream from its source.

Few places in Northern Rhodesia are more worth visiting; everything is on a grand scale, whereas this country—with all its attractions—has mostly scenery of a monotonous mediocrity. There are of course notable exceptions, such as the Victoria Falls, the Kalambo Fall at the other (north-east) end of the territory, the Chishimba Fall, the Mtinondo and Luchenene Cataracts; but grandeur is the exception, and for the most part " pretty " describes Northern Rhodesian scenery better than " grand." This gorge is undoubtedly one of the exceptions, and it is also quite unexpected. The neighbourhood gives no hint of its existence; it does not advertise itself, and so it has remained unknown and unnoticed except by two or three Europeans. I myself had been six years in the district before I heard of it. The hills, cliffs, and rocks are all on a big scale; the timber is good ; the candelabra euphorbia large and prominent. The river itself, big enough in its lower reaches, is here of small volume ; but even it—save where it hides itself underground—makes the most of itself and looks big enough for its surroundings.

Arriving from upstream one comes on a small spur ; northwards lies a fertile valley, wooded at intervals, the rest—in winter—gold with dry grass. The river enters the gorge through a cleft in this spur, and pauses for a moment in a still pool before rushing on. South of this pool the country rises for several hundred feet on both sides of the gorge, and through this jumble of hills the river tears its way. Proceeding downstream the way is steep and rocky, more up than down at first. Soon one can again approach the river and from a small kopje get a good view—again looking south. The plains are visible, though misty, through a cleft ; on the right is a sheer precipice of 150 feet, and on the left a fine chimney. The total depth here is not far short of 1000 feet. Half an hour on, the ground getting more and more rough, one comes to the top of a precipitous drop of about 800 feet, down which a colleague of mine had descended to the river, and had obtained good photographs of a small waterfall. I followed in his footsteps, and my chagrin can be imagined when, on reaching the bottom, I found the gorge quite dry. The fall was there but not the water ; the river-bed a mass of huge boulders and no more. At that time of the year (June) all the water was underground. The valley here is a magnificent setting, but the setting itself without the river is less effective, especially when one has just scrambled down 800 feet, and has to climb up again, at noon in the tropics. Immediately below the gorge the river is as still as a mill pond, and as it passes through dense woodland it gives no suggestion of the rough and tumble that begins just below, where a series of fine cataracts occurs just before the river reaches the dull quiet of the plains. The whole length from the

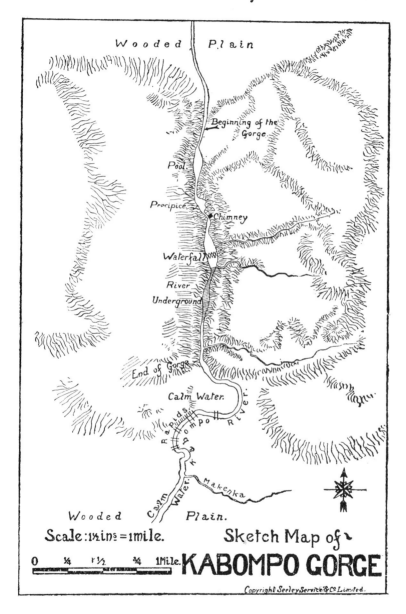

Wooded   Plain

Beginning of the Gorge.

Pool.

Precipice.   ✦Chimney

Waterfall

River

Underground

End of Gorge

Calm Water.

Rapids

Kabompo   River.

Calm Water

Makenka

Wooded   Plain.

Scale: 1½ ins = 1 mile.

0   ¼   ½   ¾   1 Mile

Sketch Map of
KABOMPO GORGE

top of the gorge to the end of the cataracts is about 2½ miles, and were it more accessible there is no doubt that this would be a show place for travellers.

In the south-west of the district are very dense forests known as *mavunda* ; they spread at their worst for about 40 miles from north to south, and 60 to 80 from east to west ; but in a slightly less impassable state they cover a much larger area. I have never seen any forest land so dense and tangled, and from the point of view of the traveller this density is aggravated by the fact that the soil is a fine white sand which makes walking (the only possible means of moving) extremely tiring. At times one can follow an elephant or buffalo track for a short way, which is a relief ; but more often one has to cut one's way literally through the undergrowth. A narrow track is now cut most of the way from north to south, but between east and west there is no traffic of any kind to justify the expense of keeping up a track ; and this forest area is quite uninhabited.

A change from the rolling woodlands of the north and the forest of the south-west is noticeable in the south-east corner, where flat open plains teeming with game (notably huge herds of wildebeeste) spread for a long way on either side of the rivers. The flora here is more tropical, and the ungainly baobab recalls memories of many other hot areas. Immediately north of this is hilly country, with shingly soil, the haunt of kudu.

The Jiundu swamps in the north form a peculiar feature, but they are fully described in Chapter XIX, so need no more than a passing reference here ; and the only other place that calls for any comment is the salt pan at Kaimbwe, a little to the north of Kasempa. This is one of the few deposits of rich alluvial soil in the district, and is an extremely fertile spot. In it is a rich deposit of salt of good quality, and there are also mineralized hot springs, the waters of which have been found, on analysis, to be almost identical with those of Homburg.

Farming of any kind is hardly possible owing to the prevalence of tsetse fly, from which pest only the north-west of the district is free. In this corner there are four or five ranches, which are well placed on the border, near to the populous centre of Kambove in the Congo, and close to the route of the Lobito Bay Railway. Between 1907–12 a few farms existed near Kansanshi, but the cattle eventually succumbed to fly, and the farms were abandoned.

Mining has been the only industry ; and at one time hopes were entertained that many mines would be working in the district. The area enclosed by the Kabompo and the Western Lunga is a reserve—Lewanika used to work a copper-mine there on the Kasanjiko—as is an area near the Dongwe, which also contains copper. Various properties, mostly copper or gold, have been worked experimentally at different times on the south-east and on the north of Kasempa, especially in the area between Kasempa and Kaimbwe, but so far nothing really payable has been discovered. The one mine that has been proved is Kansanshi, which lies only 15 miles from the Congo border : this was worked from 1898 to 1914. There are old native workings about 15 feet deep all along the outcrop, and a considerable amount of copper must have been extracted in the past. The lode appears to be very rich, and the copper ore contains also a good percentage of gold and a little silver. One shaft has been sunk to 250 feet, but a subterranean river then let the water in and work has been at a standstill in it for many years. Other shafts have been sunk down to 100 feet. Limestone is abundant near by at the Chafuguma quarries ; and lime and charcoal (burnt locally) were used as fluxes, for all the copper was smelted on the spot and taken by traction engine to the railway 80 miles away. This mine closed on the outbreak of war, and has not been re-opened ; it is owned by the Rhodesia-Katanga Junction Railway and Mineral Company, to whom it was trans-

ferred by the parent company, Tanganyika Concessions
Limited.

Kansanshi mine was the only industry employing any
Europeans, and the rest of the white population of the
district consists of a few officials, traders, and missionaries. The last named are represented by two societies,
the Plymouth Brethren (Garanganze) Mission, who have
a station, largely used as a sanatorium, at Kaleng'i Hill
in the north-west corner, whence a good view can be
obtained showing Belgian and Portuguese as well as
Rhodesian territory; and the South Africa General
Mission, who are established at Chisalala, east of Solwezi,
and at Musonweji, west of Kasempa.

The natives are dealt with fully in the succeeding
chapters, but it may be stated here that in the west they
live chiefly on cassava and the small red millet. In the
rest of the district the staple crop is kaffir corn, largely
supplemented by maize, with sweet potatoes, ground
nuts, beans, lentils, pumpkins, cucumber, tomatoes, etc.,
as subsidiary crops, tobacco being also largely cultivated.
Fungi, honey, wild roots and fruits, meat and fish are
also used to vary their diet. There are very few industries of any kind; copper was formerly worked, but
now a little iron working is all that is done, and nothing
else in the nature of an industry can be found. Huts are
mostly rectangular in the west, and circular in the east;
in the centre may be seen both types.

The health of the natives is fairly good. Yaws (*fram-
boesia*) is very prevalent and is probably the greatest
scourge in the district. Tropical ulcers also claim a
heavy toll. There is very little scurvy, and what there is
may be due to want of fresh vegetables and potash salts.
Leprosy exists, but each case is recorded, and there is
nothing in the history of any case to point to any influence of fish or fish oil. A few cases of consumption
have been recorded; and scantiness of food, especially of
fat, can be traced in most cases, as it can in the numerous

IN THE KABOMPO GORGE.

This Gorge is quite a feature of Kaonde Land. The Kabompo is one of the principal tributaries of the Zambezi.

SOURCE OF THE ZAMBEZI RIVER.

It rises in the north-west of the Kasampa District of North Rhodesia, flows through Portuguese Angola and the Barotse District to the Victoria Falls.

cases of pleurisy and pneumonia. Small-pox epidemics have occurred ; there is record of one case of tetanus, and one 'of (possibly) tetany. The Spanish influenza of 1918–19 visited the district, and the mortality therefrom was heavy. Insanity is not at all uncommon, mania with homicidal tendencies being distinctly more prevalent than among other tribes known to me. Besides actual cases of homicide and attempted homicide, similar mania is noticeable in assaults, arson, etc. In the many cases I have tried when mania was the apparent reason of the crime, I have found no history of immediate or chronic intemperance in alcohol or any drug. I have only met with two or three cases of idiocy.

In physique the Ba-Kaonde are above the average and are far superior to the Alunda and Andemba. Mentally I am inclined to put the Alunda first : at any rate, they show a more forceful attitude, more strength of will than their eastern neighbours. They give one the impression of coming from a dominant stock, whereas the Ba-Kaonde show indubitable signs of having been harried and oppressed for generations. I consider that all have possibilities and, properly handled, might develop considerably.

Travelling in the district must be done on bicycles, in a machila or a bush car or on foot, accompanied by native carriers. The Ba-Kaonde are excellent carriers. No roads exist as yet, but good scuffled paths for cycles connect not only the different government posts, but almost every village. Except for the south-west corner in the *mavunda* forests, there is no difficulty anywhere ; and even there I have travelled with my wife and young children. My travelling averaged 1000 miles a year, and my wife was always able to accompany me on her bicycle (except in the *mavunda*). There are canoes on the big rivers, and the smaller ones are nearly all bridged ; it is, however, a good plan to carry a machila for use in swamps and at bad crossings, it comes in useful for putting odd things into, and its presence may save trouble. In the cold season mosquitoes are very rare ; tsetse fly is troublesome in parts all the year, but in the winter is not bad in most places. Food for carriers is generally easily obtained from April to September, when it begins to get scarce ; and from November to January it is unprocurable in parts, and must be carried. The water supply is, generally, excellent, and gives no difficulty ; but one should make inquiry as to this in October and November when some streams run dry. Dysentery being endemic in parts, the water for drinking should be boiled.

Before closing this introductory chapter I would give a brief account of

THE WAR RECORD OF THE NATIVES.

It would be unfair to write a book about them and omit this. It is, too, a fact about which people at home are far too ignorant.

The natives of Africa responded marvellously to the calls made upon them in the war (*our* war) between 1914–18, and nowhere was the response more complete than in Northern Rhodesia. The Ba-Kaonde and their neighbours did not have to make quite the same sustained effort as those in the Eastern districts, who were nearer to the scene of war in " German East Africa." *They* fought and worked continuously throughout the war, and the story of their loyalty—yes, and forbearance—is an epic : but this is not the place for it.

In the Kasempa district the natives lived from 400 to 500 miles from the German border. They had no knowledge of the war except what they were told. They had no fear of invasion.

Yet when they understood that their help was needed : that we, their white rulers, called on them, they responded to every call. Granted that the work was " compulsory " and not " voluntary," it still remains a fact that it was cheerfully undertaken—which must be evident to anyone who realises that had it not been so we (with about half our normal staff) could not possibly have enforced it.

Let the figures speak for themselves, remembering that the natives (especially the Alunda and Andembu) were exceptionally wild and not accustomed to go far from home.

In 1915–18 it was estimated that there were 8629 taxable males in the district, of whom 7400 were able-bodied adults.

In 1915 and up to September, 1916, the following did war-work : War transport, 4163 ; six months' work in Katanga (copper production), 932 ; total, 5095 ; percentage of strong adults, 68 per cent. Meanwhile ordinary (civil) work was being carried on.

In four months (to Feb. 28, 1917) 793 more worked on war transport, bringing that total to 4959.

In the next twelve months the figures were : War transport (three months' engagements), 1997 ; total months at work, 5991 ; equivalent numbers in constant employment, 499.1, besides which 4167 natives were civilly employed. From April to October, 1918, another 2000 did three months' work. [In all these cases of three months' work an average of five weeks (additional) was spent going to and returning from work.] The total number written on for war work, 1915–18, was 9888 men.

Add to this an average of 4000 a year (16,000 in all) on civil work—one gets a total of about 26,000 males employed. Divide by 4 *one gets* 6500 *per annum out of* 7400 *able-bodied adults.*

Perhaps the reader will now understand a little why we are rather proud of our natives ; and one reason why we would like to do a little more for them, which we cannot hope to do unless the people at home will take some interest in them. On their war record alone they seem to have earned that interest.

CHAPTER II

HISTORY

THE Kaonde tribe, as at present constituted, appears to be of mixed origin; but there can be small doubt that the main stocks forming it are all parts of the Luba family, and represent some stages of the great migration that swept over all this part of Africa, starting some three to five centuries ago and coming from somewhere in the northwest.

There are, as will be shown, three main divisions of the Ba-Kaonde, or—it may be—three groups of people that have to a certain extent amalgamated or coalesced under the name of Kaonde. It might be more accurate to follow the nomenclature of Messrs. Smith and Dale in dealing with the Ba-Ila, and to refer to these people as " The Kaonde-speaking peoples," but for brevity they will be called the Ba-Kaonde.

The natives themselves seem unable to give a coherent account of their origin, and have practically no idea of chronology; but piecing different " clues " together leaves me convinced that all the Ba-Kaonde are closely allied with, and offshoots of, the Ba-luba. They seem to be most closely connected with the Basanga and the Batemba, both of which are also offshoots of the 'Luba race; but whether the Ba-Kaonde are collaterals of these other offshoots or branches of them I cannot say : I am inclined to the opinion that they are collaterals. I am confident, too, that the different sections seceded from the parent Luba stock at different times, and I think it likely that they sprang from different sections of that stock. They coalesced into " the Kaonde tribe " apparently for geographical reasons and no other ; and the tribe appears to be, in reality, a reunion of scions of an old stock that had split off into different directions and —in the case of two of the scions—having gone further than was consistent with security, returned to what is now the Kaonde country, and formed a kind of loose confederation, being conscious of their common origin, and united by similarity of dialect and customs.

The northern section of the Kaonde tribe, as now constituted, came into the country from the south-east across the Luenge (Kafue) River ; but there can be little doubt that they had had a comparatively short sojourn there, and that it had never really been their home. Before going there they had lived north of their present abode. Chief Kapiji Mpanga Mwandwe tells me that when they came here (roughly the Solwezi sub-district) from the south-east they were " returning to their old home." Chilowo, regent for the present chief Mulimansofu, tells me, however, that this is not so : that they crossed the Kafue because they were overcrowded on the other side (? pressure from the Ba-Ila), that this country was then uninhabited and that they had spied out the land when on hunting expeditions.

I fancy that there is truth in both versions. It seems to me that there is a vague recollection of an earlier migration from the north, through their present home, to the country south and east of the Kafue. That some ancestors of theirs, leading off a colony from the Baluba, migrated in that direction, and, having crossed the Kafue, thought they had gone far enough, so settled down and multiplied there. (Their residence there is confirmed by Mr. Smith in his work on the Ba-Ila, and —be it noted—the Ba-Ila called these settlers " Baluba."[1]). Whilst there they would occasionally come in hunting parties west of the Kafue, always a good place for elephant, and would wander over the country up to the eastern Lunga, and even occasionally as far as the Kabompo. These hunters noted that the country was good ; and when—owing to congestion or pressure of some kind—a move was suggested or provoked they crossed (re-crossed) the Kafue and settled where they now are, between the parent Ba-luba and the Ba-Ila on whom they had trespassed. This migration took place under Chief Kasongo, and his immediate successors (it was not a single movement) : Kasongo was recognised as chief by all this section of the tribe.

Prior to this one Mushima, an older brother of this or of some other Kasongo, had settled on tributaries of the Lualaba River (namely on the Chifwamfupa, Muya-funshi and Mufwa—all in the Congo Belge now) and was chief of another section of the tribe. Some of these people are of the same totem as Kasongo's (*Walonga* = river), but others are of the *Walemba* (=bees). They are still there, and are—I fancy—really the same group as Kasongo's people. I tried to get in touch with the present chief in 1917, through the agency of Chief Musokantanda, but the meeting never took place ; and I have, therefore, been unable to find out more about them.

After Kasongo's and Mushima's people were well established in the country which lies, roughly, between the Congo-Zambezi watershed (spreading a little over the Congo side thereof) down to the Luma River another migration began ; and this came direct from the Luba country (i.e. direct from the north). This split was led either by Kasempa Chiwoko or by one Msake, chiefs of the section of Ba-luba known as Batemba. It is said that they were of equal standing as Katanga, Ngalu and Ntenke chiefs of the Batemba (whose successors still reside over the Congo watershed). They were all of the mushroom totem (*Benachowa*).

Crossing the watershed they came upon Kasongo's

people under a chief Kapiji. Kapiji told the new-comers
that they could not stay there as he had acquired this
country, so Kasempa Chiwoko moved on to the country
by the sources of the Luma and Mafwe streams, where
he settled—right on the edge of the Mambwera country.
Here (apparently) they dropped the name of Batemba
and became known as Ba-Kaonde. I understand that
Kapiji's people were already called Ba-Kaonde. It is
interesting to note that Kasempa's people nowadays,
though living more to the south in what was then Mambwera land, still call this locality near the Luma and Mafwe
sources " The Kaonde country," as if recognising it as
the land of their birth. The late Kasempa told Mr. E. A.
Copeman in 1906 that his forebears were Basanga, who
had left the Sanga country (very closely allied with
Batemba) when Mpandi was their chief, and before the
days of Mwenda (Msiri) ; and that the Mambwera gave
them the name of Ba-Kaonde. It was supposed that this
applied to all the Ba-Kaonde, but I do not think that
it was so. The Ba-Kaonde of Kasongo and Mushima
(probably from the same original stock as the Batemba)
had settled where they now are and were already known
by that name when the Kasempa migration took place
from Mpandi's country to the Luma. The new immi-
grants passing through them (unmolested, be it noted,
as if they were related) were classed by the Mambwera
as being Ba-Kaonde, and so called.

There is another section that appears to have an
entirely different origin, or whose wanderings after a
common origin were quite distinct. This section came
from the south-west. They are the natives under sub-
chief Ntambo on the Kabompo : they call themselves
Ba-Kaonde and state that they have always spoken the
same language or dialect.

They came from the Barotse valley, by the junction of
the Kabompo and the Zambezi ; whence they were
driven by the Ba-luyi. Under the leadership of Ntambo

Chipembe they moved upstream and settled on its upper reaches (tributary Musangeshi). At the time that Musokantanda Ilunga defeated Mushima (*vide infra*) they were so newly settled there that they had not started cultivation, but were subsisting on game and fish.

The late Ntambo informed me that they were not, so far as he knew, connected in any way with Mushima (a little to the north) nor with Kasongo's and Kapiji's Ba-Kaonde (to the east), nor with Kasempa's (to the southeast). The totems of Ntambo's family are *luo* (monkey) and *bapumpi* (hunting dog); and they have not the *walonga* (water) totem of Kasongo, nor the *walemba* (bee) totem of Mushima, nor the *wowa* (mushroom) totem of Kasempa. (They are now much mixed with Alunda, but the different origin is clear from this totemism—for the Alunda have no totems—and from other characteristics.) Intermarriage quickly took place between Kapiji, nephew of Kasongo (or a descendant thereof), who married one of the *Babumpi*, and Kasempa (? the second after their migration) married one of the *luo*—both from Ntambo's. This friendly intermarriage, so soon after their arrival from the south-west, may point to previous knowledge of this section, and I think that before their sojourn in the Barotse valley they had probably lived north of the Congo-Zambezi watershed. Very likely when they retreated from the Ba-luyi and fled up the Kabompo they were merely retracing their steps. In other words, this was a (geographical) reunion with the collateral branch that had sojourned by the Kafue. The language test supports this theory.

It will therefore be seen that the Kaonde tribe, as we call it, comes from three stocks, or from three branches of one stock that had had different experiences.

(*a*) The stock that came, immediately, from the southeast, across the Kafue, and moved north-west under Mushima and under Kasongo.

(b) The stock that came, later, from the north passed through stock (a), and settled south of them under Kasempa.

(c) The stock that came, immediately, from the south-west, by the Kabompo-Zambezi junction, and moved north-east under Ntambo.

There are many minor differences between the sections, as is natural from the different peoples with whom they had been in contact, e.g. in dialect stock (b) has more words the same as in Chi-luba than stock (a) or (c) : in customs, especially as regards the *chisungu* of girls—there is more than ordinary divergence between totems, and seem to belong to different *classes* of totems : in traditions and in religious beliefs : in industries (e.g. stock (b) do not work metals), and so on. When one delves deeply into the ethnography of the people one finds many points of difference, in fact, except for the geographic propinquity, and for the undoubted fact that, except for minor differences, they share one dialect, there seems to be no real connecting link. They do not recognise and never have recognised one paramount chief (except their alien—Lunda—overlord Musokantanda), and group (b)'s recognition of him was *very* perfunctory and intermittent).

The difference in origin of the different branches also makes it more difficult to trace their ancient history accurately. Moreover, there seems to have been a constant tendency to split up, and primogeniture does not appear to have been generally recognised, e.g. (as will be shown later) when the migrating Kasongo died he was succeeded by four nephews who split up his people and were co-equal. (This is not a progressive process, luckily, or it is difficult to say where it would end. What happens appears to be this : Chief A has in his hand the powers and titles of the chieftainships of A, B and C. In fact, his full name is " A-B-C."[2] On his death he is succeeded by his brothers or nephews, one taking the rank and

style of " A," another that of " B," and a third that of
" C." Later the new A dies, and B as next heir becomes
A-B. If C dies next he then becomes A-B-C, as was his
uncle ; but if he predeceases C, then C becomes A-B-C.
So it goes on from generation to generation.)

It is small wonder, then, that—broken in origin and
with nothing to bind them—the Ba-Kaonde with hardly
a show of resistance became a subservient race, paying
tribute to the Alunda, a tribe among whom descent is
regular, and which recognises primogeniture. (The
Alunda were also better armed, having guns.)

Before considering further the different divisions of
the Ba-Kaonde it will be necessary to try to trace the
history of these Alunda in so far as it concerns the paramount chief Musokantanda. Some of what follows is
probably mythology, more is on the border between
mythology and history : I can only say that the first
account is that given me by Musokantanda XIII (according to his reckoning)—formerly called Kazhi. He
told me this in 1916, and has never varied in the telling
on subsequent occasions, nor will he admit any other
version. I think it can safely be accepted as the tra-
ditional history of the Musokantandas, as handed to each
one at the time of his installation, and memorised by
each in turn.

MWACHIAMVU AND HIS SONS. [The spelling of this
name varies greatly : Muato (or Mwata) Yamvo being
common in old books—*Mwata* is a title meaning " Lord "
or " King "—Mwachiamvwa, and so on. The spelling
used throughout by me represents as near as I can get it
the actual pronunciation of Musokantanda.]

At some date (probably, I think, in the seventeenth
century) a woman called Lukokeshya Mang'anda was
living, unmarried, in her own village on the Kazhilezhi
stream. (This is a tributary to the Lulua, one of the
main affluents of the Kasai, and is said to flow into the
right of the Lulua at, I fancy, about 7° S. and 23° E. I

cannot trace the stream on any map to which I have access. Musokantanda knows nothing of the antecedents of Lukokeshya Mang'anda, nor anything about her family, except that she had had a brother called Kasanzhi ; but, as among the Alunda succession goes direct from father to son, it is reasonable to suppose that some chief had died leaving no heir male, and that his daughter Lukokeshya succeeded him as chieftainess of the Alunda in those parts.

A man called Chivinda wa katele came from " Kasongo" and stayed at Lukokeshya's village, and the chieftainess married him. When she married him she gave him the *lukano* (hereditary insignia) as a sign of chieftainship, and named him Mwachiamvu. Apparently the children of this union were a daughter, Mang'anda Kalazhi (possibly some other daughters), and six sons, born in this order : 1. MUTEWA. 2. CHIEMBE-EMBE, subsequently called Kazembe Mutanda. 3. KAZEMBE PA NCHINDA. 4. MUSOKANTANDA (Chipaiya). 5. SHINDE. 6. KANONGESHA.

In due course Lukokeshya died and was succeeded by her daughter Mang'anda Kalazhi, who became Lukokeshya II, married, and passes out of this story.

Then Mwachiamvu died, and was succeeded by his eldest son, Mutewa, who became Mwachiamvu II. He also married, and from him there is a direct line to the present Mwachiamvu.

The remaining five sons then came to Kasanga, a country spreading between, approximately, 8° and 12° S., and 25° and 27° E. They settled on the Mukulezhi, a tributary of the Luji which feeds the Lualaba. Chiembeembe, the eldest of them, then developed cannibal tastes, used to cut off people's hands and mix them with game meat ; and eat them with gusto. He told his brothers to eat this mixture too, but they refused. Chiembeembe also had another habit which made him unpopular : he would approach people who were taking tribute to

Mwachiamvu, armed with a big hook, by means of which he used to grab their offerings. Owing to his tastes in diet the brothers returned to Mwachiamvu rather than live with him ; and at the same time they renamed (or nicknamed) him Kazembe Mutanda.

Mwachiamvu II received them and gave them different countries. To Kazembe Panchinda he gave the country of the Wa-Uzhi (Ba-Usi) and told him to rule there (by the Luapula, about 29° E.). His successor is still there and still called Kazembe. Musokantanda was given the country of the Ba-Kaonde, on both sides of the Congo-Zambezi watershed between about 24° and 28° E. (With him went Mukumbi, Kakoma, Shamarenge and Sakabinda.) To Kanongesha fell the Andembu and Mambwera, west and south-west of Musokantanda's country. (To this day Musokantanda and Kanongesha are paramount chiefs of nearly all the natives in the Kasempa district, and the former has also a large following in the Congo, and the latter in Angola—in fact the present Kanongesha is the first to live this side of the border.) Shinde (accompanied by Katema) was given the country called Ikondo, west of Kanongesha by the upper Kasai (about 20° E.) and Kazembe Mutanda settled on the Lukozhi a tributary of the Kasai. This gives some idea of the great size of the " Empire " of Mwachiamvu, a potentate with whose greatness all the early travellers were much impressed.

All the sons and their successors looked and look to Mwachiamvu and his successors as their overlord : appealed to him in trouble, and took tribute to him. Tribute is still taken regularly by Musokantanda and Kanongesha. I cannot speak for the others. The late Mwachiamvu (who died in 1919) visited part of the domains of these two chiefs the year before his death—in fact, I believe his death is attributed to the fact that he crossed some stream which no Mwachiamvu was supposed ever to cross—a sign that though the old " Empire " has crumbled, it is not yet extinct ; and I believe that the chief himself still holds a position of exceptional importance and influence in the Belgian Congo.

MUSOKANTANDA AND THE BA-KAONDE. As stated in the previous section, Musokantanda received from Mwachiamvu the country of the Ba-Kaonde. As far as the present Musokantanda knows this " gift " was more in the nature of a decision by Mwachiamvu of the direction in which he could go and establish himself, by carving out a kingdom ; for Musokantanda had to conquer the country allotted to him. In fact, the whole " partition " seems to have been in the nature of establishing buffer states, under his sons, around the real kingdom of Mwachiamvu.

At that time, as now, there was no paramount chief of the Ba-Kaonde : the principal chiefs (or most powerful ones, for the Alunda would not concern themselves with precedence among the Kaonde) were Kasempa, Muwambe (Mushima), Ingwe and Kalasa. Shiwukinga appears to have been the leading Lamba chief.

The first Musokantanda settled on the Kazhilezhi stream, downstream from Mwachiamvu, nearer to the Lulua. The others have been established mostly on affluents of the Lualaba as will be seen in the following list of the Musokantandas :

List of the MUSOKANTANDAS.

1. Chipaiya, settled on the Kazhilezhi, tributary to Lulua.
2. Ilunga J settled on the Luji, tributary to Lualaba.
3. Chikwanza settled on the Nyampalala, tributary to Mumbezhi.
4. Mutombo I settled on the Luji.
5. Kasongo settled on the Luji.
6. Chipola I settled on the Mivunza, tributary to Lualaba.
7. Mutewa settled on the Luji.
8. Kasanza settled on the Luji.

9. Kanembu[3] settled on the Luji.
10. Mutombo II settled on the Luji.
11. Ilunga II settled on the Katontola, tributary to
    Lueya, tributary to Luji.
12. Chipola II settled on the Muzhila, tributary to
    W. Lunga.
13. Kazhi settled on the Lueya, tributary to Luji, till
    1916, when he crossed the border into N.
    Rhodesia. In 1920 he returned to the Congo,
    and at present (1922) is still there. He succeeded
    not later than 1902, possibly some time before
    that.

No. 2 seems to have been the first definite move to the
east, for No. 1 lived about 22° 30′ E., whereas the real
sphere of this dominion was, and is, from 24° to 28° E.

No. 3 and No. 12 were the only two to live on the
Zambezi side of the watershed until the present ruler
moved across in 1916. All the others lived on Congo
waters (now the Belgian Congo); but controlled also
the country well south of the watershed—to an average
depth of 120 miles south of it.

(Musokantanda-Kazhi has died just as this book is
going to the press, 1922.)

As already stated the above is the story as told me by
Musokantanda XIII, and which I believe to be fairly
accurate. It is impossible within the space of a chapter
to give other versions in full, but the following discre-
pancies (among others) enumerated by the late Sailunga
and the present Kakoma deserve to be chronicled. I
need only add that Musokantanda ridicules them : that
Kakoma's corroboration may be valueless as he has never
been installed as Kakoma, and therefore (I believe) would
not have been instructed in history—moreover, I have
proved him inaccurate in some points ; and that the late
Sailunga was not distinguished by intelligence.

They say that Chivinda wa katele had two wives,

Lukokeshya Mang'anda and Mwachiamvu (making the first Mwachiamvu a woman and not a man). That Lukokeshya was the principal wife and her children were : 1, Sailunga; 2, Kakoma; 3, Mukumbi, 4, Sakabinda. The children of the second wife (Mwachiamvu) were : 1, Chiembe-embe (Kazembe Mutanda) ; 2, Kazembe Panchinda; 3, Shinde; 4, Kanongesha; 5, Katema; 6, Kakeng'i.

According to them there was no Chipaiya, and Ilunga was the first Musokantanda, being the son of Sailunga (the name means " father of Ilunga ") and grandson of Chivinda wa katele by Lukokeshya. In the lifetime of Chivinda he gave the present Lunda country (in this district) to Sailunga, and Sailunga was reigning there when Chivinda died ; so—though he was the eldest son of the senior wife—he did not succeed his father, but founded his own dynasty. Sailunga was followed into these parts by his brothers (or their descendants) Kakoma and Mukumbi, by his half-brothers (or their descendants) Mwanachikunko, Shinde, Kanongesha, Kakeng'i, Katema; and by Sinyama Chang'ambo—who became chief of the Achokwe, Valuena and Balovale (not to be confused with the Mrotsi " induna " Sinyama).

The list of Musokantandas which these chiefs give varies considerably : they say that Mtombo, Kasongo and Kasanza were only pretenders who were defeated by Kanyembo before he succeeded. The last four in Musokantanda's list agree with theirs, but their total is seven (and three pretenders, all contemporary) against thirteen. Musokantanda's list agrees more in length with the known chronology of Kazembe on the Luapula.

The following is typical of Kakoma's evidence. He says he has been to Mwachiamvu's capital, but says that he has never heard the name of " Musumba," given by many authorities for this capital. He says it is called, " Ng'anda." Musokantanda and others all say " Musumba " is correct. [Parenthetically the following may

be of philological interest. *Ng'anda* in Lunda means
the chief's house or quarters (same as *Isano* in Wemba :
ng'anda in Wemba being " hut "). *Musumba* used
(apparently) in Lunda for chief's " town " in Wemba
means the chief's household or personal following.]

Having now explained how it was that the Ba-Kaonde
came under the sphere of influence of a Lunda chief we
will return to their own history.

Musokantanda II (Ilunga) seems to have come into
the country about the same time as Mushima, the " elder
brother " of Kasongo and the first Kaonde to settle in
what is now Kaonde-land. Ilunga, backed by Mukumbi
and Kakoma, called on Mushima to pay him tribute.
Mushima had called himself " Mushima Ilunga," which
roused Ilunga's anger and led to the demand for tribute.
Mushima refused the demand ; and, helped by Musompo
and Chitowo, fought Ilunga for two days on the Lualaba.
The battle ended in a victory for Ilunga, and Mushima
paid him a slave and other tribute in token of submission.
He also dropped the assumed title of Ilunga and called
himself Mushima Kaonde thereafter. The number of
casualties in this fight is not known, but it was fought in
the days before guns were introduced, the sole weapons
being bows and arrows.

Apparently at this time Kasongo had already entered
the eastern part of the country now known as the
Kaonde country, crossing the Kafue from east to west
and moving in a north-westerly direction, seemingly in
the footsteps of Mushima ; but he never penetrated as
far as his " brother," probably because he heard of his
defeat by the Alunda. Kasongo, in fact, never came into
contact with Ilunga nor with any other Lunda chief and,
so far as can be ascertained, died an independent chief.
His fourth nephew (and one of his successors later),
Kapiji, quarrelled with him at the Kafue, and with his
section of Kasongo's people pushed on to the Kam-

funshi, a tributary of the Lualaba. Here Ilunga placed him under Sailunga, telling him that he was " an independent chief," but must send tribute to him through Sailunga.

A little later Ilunga, who was carving out his kingdom and seeing how far he could extend his power, sent Sailunga Jikundu ahead as his *kalala* (tribute collector) ; and Chinemba was sent on before him as his *mwajamvita* (advance guard or warden of the marches). He met Ntambo Chipembe—who had come up from the Barotse valley (*supra*)—and made him pay tribute to Sailunga. About this time Ilunga divided up the country, Mukumbi being appointed *mwajamvita* (warden) on the Mumbezhi, Kakoma on the Jiundu, while Sailunga Jikundu appointed Katambi as his *kalala* (tribute collector). In consequence of this last appointment Ntambo began to pay his tribute through Katambi to Sailunga.

Sailunga Jikundu then died, and Katambi meant to get himself elected as Sailunga ; but a quick succession of deaths in his family caused him to come to the conclusion that the omens were adverse, so he secured the succession of Luseng'a, son of Sailunga, as the new chief ; but hereafter he kept Ntambo's tribute himself, and forwarded none of it to Sailunga, who, however, retained the tribute of Kapiji and others.

The Ntambos are said to have been contemporaries of the Musokantandas in this order :

Ntambo Chipembe with Musokantanda Ilunga I.
Ntambo Katwamuloa with Musokantanda Ilunga I and Chikwanza.
Ntambo Chipwerere with Musokantanda Mutombo I.

(There then appears to be a gap, which may be accounted for by the fact that a period of exile ensued for this branch of the Kaonde. Musokantanda V (Kasongo) fought with Kakoma, Chinyimba and others at the source of the W. Lunga owing to their refusal to pay tribute; and scared by this Ntambo and his people left the Kabompo and fled to Kanongesha's country, where they stayed for some time. They returned later.) Ntambo Kamukoyo was deposed and fled, he was succeeded by:

Ntambo Kajansono, contemporary with Musokantanda Kanembu, Mutombo II and Ilunga II.

Ntambo Chikondo (d. 1915), contemporary with Musokantanda Ilunga II, Chipola II and Kazhi.

Ntambo Kawundula (d. 1920), contemporary with Musokantanda Kazhi.

Ntambo Swanamumi (suc. 1921), contemporary with Musokantanda Kazhi.

To come back to Kasongo's group of the Kaonde. Among the Ba-Kaonde, as amongst most of these Bantu tribes, succession does not go from father to son (the Alunda are an exception, and reference to this will be made later, see note to this chapter), but is matrilineal, that is to say, it passes through the female side—a brother by the same mother can succeed, or a sister's son.

So when Kasongo died he was succeeded by the sons of his eldest sister, Ng'onyi. These sons were—in the order named—Nyoka, Kayindu, Mushima and Kapiji. (N.B.—This Mushima is not to be confused with Mushima the elder brother of Kasongo—present successor Katupishya—in the Congo.) These four nephews set up independent chieftainships, thereby breaking up the " kingdom " of Kasongo.

Kapiji, who had quarrelled with Kasongo in his lifetime, had gone north-west in the footsteps of Mushima (Katupishya); but Nyoka, Kayindu and Mushima stayed near to the Luenge (Kafue).

At this time there were also other chiefs among the Kaonde-speaking peoples, the chief of whom appear to have been Mwape (Kalasa), also near the Luenge; Muwambe at the source of the E. Lunga, in what is now Mulonga's (Lamba) country on the Solwezi–Elisabethville road; and a little later Kasempa came from the north and marched to the Luma-Mafwe sources. Ingwe was either at, or came a little later to, the upper Solwezi, near the present Mwatula's country (quite close to the Congo watershed).

I have already related that Kapiji had to pay tribute to Musokantanda (through Sailunga): he was also ordered by Musokantanda not to go west of the Mutanda. He agreed to the tribute and to the limit of his sphere without fighting. The explanation given by his successors, Chief Kapiji Mpanga Mwandwe and Regent Chilowo, is interesting:

" Mushima had tried to resist Ilunga, had fought against him and had been defeated. In the end he had to pay tribute. If Mushima could not resist satisfactorily, how could we? We (i.e. our ancestors) thought it better to be content with the country east of the Mutanda (roughly between Mutanda and Kafue) and pay tribute to Ilunga, so we did so. It was the same later—when we heard that the white man had conquered Mwenda's (Msiri's) country, and Mutitima's we said in our hearts, ' If the white man can defeat Mwenda, how can we Ba-Kaonde resist him? So we made no resistance and paid tax to you without fighting."

According to his present descendants one Kapiji (I cannot be sure of the number) was succeeded by Chiwanza, Chiwanza by Kapoa Mulimanzovu. This last amalgamated in his person also the chieftainships and titles of Chiwanza, Kapiji and Mpanga. On his death he was succeeded by Katutamwiulu (the present Mulimansofu, who is about a hundred years old,[4] and for whom Chilowo is regent), but one Jing'amba, grandson of

Kapoa, led a rebellion against Katutamwiulu and succeeded in wresting from him the chieftainships of Kapiji and Mpanga, which he took for himself (i.e. the present Kapiji Mpanga) and that of Chiwanza, which another took. This Chiwanza died in 1909 and was succeeded by Mulilambonge in 1915.

Kapiji Mpanga (the addition of Mwandwe to his dignities is quite recent) is the next most powerful Kaonde chief (numerically) to Kasempa; but Kasempa and many others look upon him as a junior, because he was but a usurper.

The chief Chiwanza, who preceded Kapoa Mulimanzovu, was a contemporary of Musokantanda Kanyembo and of Msiri (called locally Mwenda or Musiji). This interesting historical figure does not figure very largely in Kaonde history. He and his Bayeke, as is well known, were a great power a little to the north (Sanga country), and they raided a considerable distance to the south. They appear at one time to have had a good chance of becoming overlords of the Ba-Kaonde, and of ousting the Alunda from that position. Chiwanza certainly paid tribute to Msiri (his descendants euphemistically say that he " took him a present of ivory "), but the power of the Bayeke was fleeting, and Kapoa once more paid tribute to Musokantanda (Ilunga II) as his predecessors had done.

The varying fortunes of different Kaonde chiefs would be interesting to work out and record before it is too late, but even if I had the information now I do not think it would be of sufficient interest to record here. What has been recorded already tends to become tedious; but it has, I think, a value in that it shows the extraordinarily broken nature of this " tribe " from its beginning until to-day.

To conclude the chapter it may be well to record the neighbours of the Ba-Kaonde at the time when Kapiji was settled between the Luma, the Mutanda, the Congo

watershed and the Kafue : Kasempa had just settled on
the upper Luma (north of it) and Ntambo was on the
upper Kabompo.

1. On the north-east they were adjacent to the
   Balamba, and the boundaries were the upper
   Kafue, the E. Lunga and the Luswishi Rivers.
2. On the south-east they touched the Ba-lenge, their
   boundary being the Kafue (Luenge) River.
3. On the south their neighbours were the Mambwera,
   who came as far north as the Mufwashi and Luma
   Rivers. These Mambwera were divided into
   three branches : (i) The Mankoya ; (ii) Masasa ;
   (iii) Balukolwe. The chief of the former was
   Mutondo, of the second Kahari, who lived on the
   site of the present Kasempa " boma," and of the
   third Fumika and Pumpola.
   To the south also was a small swamp tribe, the Ba-
   Usanga (*usa*=swamp), under chief Jimbo : apparently a branch of the Wa-Twa who came there
   long ago, but owing to the drying of their swamp
   (on the Lufupa River) they lost their sanctuary,
   and have been reduced now to insignificant pro-
   portions.
4. On the west came the Alunda, and the border
   varied—from the Mutanda to the Kabompo. At
   present there are but few Alunda east of the
   latter river.
5. On the north came a few Baluba and the Basanga,
   Bayeke and Batemba. The Batemba (from whom
   Kasempa came) were under Katanga, Ngalu and
   Ntenke : they were by the source of the E. Lunga
   and Kafue Rivers. The Bayeke were north of
   them, and between them and the Basanga (if any
   of the latter were independent) the Lufira was
   the boundary.

As time went on the Kaonde races spread further. Especially was this so in the south. Kasempa's natives pushed the Mambwera further and further, and came in contact with the Barotse. The old Mambwera country is now entirely Kaonde.

Note on Succession. As stated above, succession among the Kaonde is matrilineal, and among the Lunda it is filial (direct from father to son). This needs qualification. Lunda succession is, so I am told (F.V.B.M.), *usually* from father to son, but occasionally is by the female side, e.g. a Katambi, whom we will call Katambi A, had several sons, yet on his death his sister's son succeeded as Katambi B. When Katambi B died, the eldest son of Katambi A succeeded as Katambi C. The present Katambi D is the grandson of Katambi B, so succession has again reverted to the female line.

The late Ntambo explained to me that there has been a great " mix-up " in the Ntambo succession. Originally, as with the rest of the Ba-Kaonde, the succession followed the female line, but in the time of Ntambo Katwamuloa, Sailunga, his Lunda overlord, made them adopt the method of succession followed by the Alunda, i.e. from father to son. This changed the totem of the rulers, for totems follow the female line ; but that would not have worried the Alunda, who are totem-less. This section of Ba-Kaonde has now reverted to the matrilineal succession, and the late Ntambo succeeded his uncle (of the *bapumpi*), but a considerable section objected and supported the senior representative of the *luo*. I believe the present chief, Swanamumi, is accepted by all. This unusual conduct of Sailunga seems to have been extraordinarily tactless or overbearing, and not in accord with the general high level of statecraft that that tribe has shown. It may have been to show contempt, for the Alunda are apt to consider themselves the salt of the earth, but if such contempt had been general I doubt if they would have attained or retained such power as was theirs.

¹ These notes were written, in more or less their present form (for further enquiries have modified them but little), five years before Messrs. Smith and Dale's book was published, and our information obviously came from opposite sources.

² e.g. Kapoa-Mulimanzovu-Kapiji-Mpanga-Chiwanza and Kapiji-Mpanga-Mwandwe.

³ The human sacrifices referred to by Pereira and Livingstone continued with the Mwachiamvus and the Musokantandas to this reign, but no later.

⁴ Died 1922 while this book was in the press.

CHAPTER III

FROM BIRTH TO DEATH

CHILDHOOD

IN these chapters a brief description of the Kaonde native's career from birth to death will be given, followed by notes on succession.

Birth. When a woman's confinement arrives she is attended by other women who go into her hut when the pains begin. After the birth the placenta is buried on the verandah of the hut, and a little warm water is dabbed on the baby's arms and legs to make it strong.

When the navel is dry the people in the village have to take all guns and spears out of their huts and leave them outside while the baby is brought forth : then a fire is made and a piece of old cloth is rolled on the leg into a spill and lighted. A bit of the infant's hair over the right temple is held in the fingers and burnt off with this spill. The hair that is burnt off is then rolled into another bit of cloth-string and tied round the baby's neck. After this the mother can begin to carry the child on her back and return to her ordinary occupations. The father cannot touch the child for about a month (until it laughs and shows that it is strong).

When the child does this the father has to find some beads and two small wooden charms made from the root of the *mulembalemba* tree. He strings the two together and puts them in his hut. That night sexual intercourse is resumed between the parents. (It will be noted that there is no long period of taboo until the child is weaned,

KAONDE MIDWIVES.

These are typical of their class. Witchcraft (originally a fertility cult) and midwifery are closely connected. Their methods are primitive and unhygienic, but they are by no means devoid of knowledge.

as with some neighbouring tribes.) After the first resumption of cohabitation the father when rising for any purpose must not leave the baby but must take it in his arms until he lies down again. Similarly the first time that the mother rises she has to take and hold the baby. Then the mother takes out the hairs from the arm-pits and pudenda of her husband and hands them to him. After receiving them he lies down and covers his head : then rises, claps his hands and says " *Mutende.*" The woman claps her hands and the husband says, " *Eyo ! Mkazhami, eyo !* " (Yes ! My wife, yes !)

In the morning the string of beads and charms is tied round the baby's waist, and the mother takes the child to her mother. She (the infant's maternal grandmother) takes away the beads, replacing them by others, but not changing the charms. The original beads the grandmother keeps. This change, however, should not be made until two months have elapsed from the baby's birth or the husband will suspect his wife of having been unfaithful during her pregnancy.

This day the wife (and occasionally the husband, too) is forbidden to walk about in case she should hit a stump, which would be a bad omen. The next day all in the village touch the baby and life resumes its normal course.

Twins. Twins (*mapasa*) are not common. When they are born the routine is the same as at an ordinary birth, but each of them must receive identical presents : e.g. if one has *white* beads or *blue* cloth given it, the other must have *white* beads or *blue* cloth too. At the next new moon the mother of the twins and the other women of the village carry them round the village dancing the while. They carry with them a flat basket and sing obscene songs. Everyone they meet has to put some small gift into the basket (tobacco, grain, meal, beads, etc.). Of the meal a thin gruel is made for the babies : the beads are for them, too ; and tobacco, etc., for the parents.

After some days the father, with as many friends as he can collect, visits their big chief, with presents (in some parts tusks of ivory, guns, cloth, etc.; in others only baskets of meal, bark-cloth, strings of beads). The chief has a mat produced and sits on it, dressed up in his best, with his shells on his forehead, etc. He provides beer and food, and all the elders eat and drink. The chief then gives a present to the twins and says : " Now that this is done they will be able to visit me, and I can eat food cooked by their mother."

Infanticide and Infant Mortality. If a child cuts its upper incisors before its lower ones (known as *lutala*) it is thrown into the river. (I have been informed that the Ba-Kaonde throw such a child into the bush, and that throwing it into the water is only done (locally) by the Ba-lamba ; as, so I was told, the Kaonde women believe that if thrown into the water the child's spirit will become hostile. I have, however, met with no case of a child being thrown into the bush, but have met cases of such infanticide by drowning among Ba-Kaonde and Ba-luba.) After the child has been thrown away the mother returns without mourning. No one asks any questions.

The reason for this custom is as follows : With a *lutala* child it is believed that every time one of the milk teeth comes out a person dies. Similarly if a nail comes off someone dies. If a woman allowed her *lutala* child to live, hiding the irregularity, she would be constructively guilty of murder of many people, a risk she dare not attempt to take.

There is one way in which the saving of a *lutala* child's life is at times permitted. The mother may be allowed to put all the teeth as they come out, all loose nails, all nail-parings, all hair as cut, into one calabash and keep it. After the last milk tooth has come out the calabash is taken and carried on the mother's back, like a baby, in the same cloth that she has been wearing to carry the

child. She goes to a river and drops the calabash off her
back into the water (as she would have done to the baby—
in all such cases of infanticide by drowning the mother
just loosens the cloth and lets the baby fall off, without
looking round). As the calabash splashes into the water
she calls out " Here is the *lutala*." But this " reprieve "
is rare.

A child who does not walk at the proper time is called
Chisheta and is also killed. This again is done by drowning ; and if the mother does not do it voluntarily her
relatives order her to do so : she cannot refuse. The
reason for this is that the child is supposed to be waiting
to walk until all its relatives are dead. To save hurrying
the death of so many people the child is drowned.
There is no reprieve for this.

If a girl be confined before her first menstruation
(*Katangwa*) she has to stay in a shelter in the bush for the
event. No one can approach her except her grandmother
or some other woman who is past child-bearing, and even
they can only approach near enough to put down food
where the woman can fetch it. When the child is born
it is thrown away, and the woman moves from the shelter
she has occupied and goes to another where she stays
a full month. After this her relatives go and wash her
with medicines, then take her towards the village. She
is then bathed in a bark bath, with special medicines in
the water, and has a fresh cloth given her to wear. Spots
of *pemba* (white clay) are placed all over the upper half
of her body. She then sits on a mat, and gives beads to
the women who have washed her. Then all do the
mikunda (shrill trilling). The reason for this is that if
such a child be born in a village, or if it be not killed, all
the elders in the village will die.

A baby born feet first is not killed, it is only called a
mwika.

By our law, of course, all these cases of infanticide are
murder. The woman and her accessories stand their

trial on that charge and are punished. I am glad to say that great severity is not usual : e.g. in one case of *lutala* the mother " got " six months, and her husband, who had been very casual in his behavour, " got " twelve. In one case of *chisheta* the mother " got " six months, and the maternal uncle who had instigated the murder " got " two years. It is open to doubt if even these sentences can be justified before we have educated the natives out of these ideas. We are punishing the mother (and her relatives) for a distinct sacrifice to which they have submitted in order that they might not commit constructive murder on a large scale. Until we eradicate those beliefs I doubt if we are right in convicting.

On other grounds, too, it seems extraordinary illogical. We set the law in motion because of the death of one child—in one *chisheta* case I remember the child was not only a cripple, but was an idiot and a mute ! We have no infirmaries, asylums or hospitals where such a child could be cared for, yet we make no effort to check the death of thousands of normal children healthy at birth ! Until we do that I think we might close our eyes to the rare cases of infanticide of abnormalities. The Rev. E. W. Smith in *The Ila-speaking Natives of Northern Rhodesia* (neighbours to the Kaonde), puts the infant mortality at 75 per cent in the case of cattle-owning natives, and as high as 90 per cent in the fly areas where there is no cow's milk ! I have made careful investigations among the Kaonde and neighbouring tribes in the Kasempa district, and I think that in the worst corners the infant mortality is about 75 per cent, and the average is not less than 60 per cent. Cases of *lutala, chisheta* and *katangwa* are probably not one in a thousand. Surely we would do better by medical assistance and instruction to reduce the ordinary infant death rate, before we bother about the extraordinary cases.

I think that very few people at home realise the facts

about this death rate. When we hear of a *temporary* death rate among babies in, say, Moscow amounting to 75 per cent owing to famine, columns appear in the home papers, and funds are raised to help the sufferers. Most excellent and humane, but one cannot persuade editors to give space to record, nor people to subscribe, to reduce the equally high *normal* death rate in our African protectorates . . . yet we are directly responsible for these people : we are their trustees, they are our wards ! We have had charge of them for about a quarter of a century and have done nothing to check this—except to imprison a few unfortunate mothers who, acting rightly as they believe, have killed their children.

It may be said by some that charity begins nearer home. Yes, but we have assumed direct responsibility for these natives, and we have only the general responsibility of humanity for the others. And as regards their " civilisation " (if that be a factor), judging from books on Russia, or even nearer to us (e.g. Knut Hamsun's *Growth of the Soil*), it can be emphatically stated that in some ways some Europeans are less civilised than these Bantu races—even judged by our own standards of " civilisation."

One of our very first duties in Africa is to tackle this question of infant mortality seriously. Not only on the grounds of duty and of humanity, but also because nothing retards progress so much as a sparse population ; and we can help the evolution of our wards in no better way than by speeding up the increase of population a little. The births take place all right : all that we have to do is to save life.

Naming the Child. The name given to the child, which is always that of a deceased relative, is chosen by the method of divination called *kansheku* (*vide* chapter on Divination).[1] The name given in infancy is kept until puberty when he (or she) chooses a name for him-(her-) self.

The custom known as Teknonymy holds good ; that is to say, that when the first child is born the father calls himself Shanjia Kananga (the Father of " Kananga "), and the mother is called Ina Kananga (the Mother of " Kananga "). When the first grandchild is born the grandparents are called Wankambo Kananga (the grandparents of Kananga).

Circumcision. Circumcision is not practised by the Ba-Kaonde, but it is practised by their neighbours the Alunda, and the following is a brief description of the rites.

(Condensed from notes by F.V.B.M. and J.L.K.)

Circumcision (*mukanda*). Among the Alunda all males are circumcised, and the ceremony takes place in the dry season. Meetings of elders are held, at which central villages are chosen for the ceremony. The men (and youths who have been circumcised) then build large leaf shelters about a quarter of a mile away from the village, and several elders appoint themselves guardians of the camp. *Makishi* (dancing men : singular *ikishi*)[2] are dressed up in elaborate costumes and masks : they are sometimes called in from Angola and are paid a fee of 10s. or £1, but more often they are local youths skilled in the *mukanda* ritual dances. When all is ready the *makishi* make ceremonial entries into the villages as a sign that the shelter is built : the women all hide, as the whole of the *mukanda* is considered a thing of shame (*nsonyi*) to females ; and the young boys who are ready for circumcision join up with the *makishi* and proceed to the camp. These boys are generally from about ten to thirteen years of age, but sometimes younger. The *mukanda* is under the direct supervision of the family spirits, and the *makishi* take the names of several deceased elders who were reputed to have been skilled in the operation. The dancing is in order to propitiate these spirits.

Songs and dancing are sometimes kept up for as much

as two months, until the wounds are entirely healed, during which time all concerned keep strictly within the camp, which is on a site near water so that it need not be left unnecessarily. The women at the village provide food, making porridge and beer, etc., which is placed by them at a convenient spot, whence it is fetched by the men. There is no mixing whatever between those in the camp and those outside. During this time the whole country-side is denuded of men : so many participate in the ceremony. The operation itself is performed with a special little knife, just like an ordinary native knife, and often results in sores which cripple a man for life. The attendants who hold the boys are called *Ilomboshi*. The great event in the ceremony is the exodus from the camp, when the newly circumcised are carried on the backs of their elders, being disguised with leaves and white chalk (*mpemba*) : the mothers have to rush out and try to recognise their offspring.

Once a boy has been circumcised he " puts away childish things," and thenceforth it is " shameful " for him to sit with his mother, or with any women. He sleeps in a hut with other circumcised, and no longer lives in his mother's hut.

The first boy to be operated upon each year is called Kambanzhi : the second is named Kasalantanda. The boy who first suggests the *mukanda* for the year is known as Mwatawamukanda. Kambanzhi gets his portion of food first all the time that they are at the *mukanda*, while the last to be circumcised gets his last. Both at the morning and evening meals each boy keeps a little of his porridge to which is added some ash from the fire : at the morning meal they sing " Kang'ere weze " and throw the mixture to the east, while at supper they sing " Kang'ere waye " and throw it to the west. This is to ward off leprosy.

Nyachimbanda is the name of the woman whose child was first (originally) circumcised. Legend says that it happened thus : the woman was going to draw water, and placed her son on the river bank whilst she went down to the water's edge. The child started to crawl after her and the sharp grass cut him. When the wound healed it was found that he was circumcised. When the chief heard of it he thought it good and gave orders that all males were to be circumcised. Another story is told to the effect that many years ago the son of the Lunda chief was out hunting, he wounded a buck and gave chase : a thorn with which he came in contact performed the operation, so the chief, his father, ordained that all males must be similarly circumcised. The former story seems the better known of the two.

Except for circumcision the customs of the Alunda as regards birth and childhood are very similar to those of the Ba-Kaonde.

[1] The divination is not merely to choose a name : it is undertaken to find out of which deceased relative the baby is a reincarnation, for they believe that everyone who dies is born again in the person of some infant of the same family. Thus a baby called Mbonge is considered to be the reincarnation of, say, his great-uncle Mbonge ; *vide* chapter on RELIGION.

[2] Care should be taken to distinguish between (s.) *ikishi*, (pl.) *makishi* dancing man (men), and (s.) *mukishi*, (pl.) *akishi* spirit (s.). But it may be noted that women and children are supposed to believe that the *makishi* are *akishi*, and come from a hole in the ground to take away naughty little boys from their mothers to the mysterious ceremony. This is a pious fraud like " Father Christmas " or the " Bogey man," but, nevertheless, the *makishi* have a real religious significance, in praying to the spirits of the departed upon whose favour rests the success of the *mukanda*.

" YOUNG AFRICA."

A fair specimen of a Lunda baby.

CHAPTER IV

FROM BIRTH TO DEATH

MARRIAGE AND DIVORCE

THE Ba-Kaonde are polygamous (strictly speaking they are polygynous, for polyandry is not recognised).

Polygyny, however, is not particularly common—being restricted by several causes. In the first place the proportion of women to men is only as thirty-seven to thirty-one so that there are not many superfluous women. Secondly, the custom known as matrilocal residence, i.e. that the bridegroom has to reside in the village of his wife's mother, tends to check plurality of wives. As the residence at the mother-in-law's need not be continuous it is not an absolute veto ; but, coupled with the obligations to be fulfilled, it certainly does tend to limit polygyny.

The actual figures,[1] according to our census, as regards married people in the tribe, are : Men with one wife, 4778 ; with two wives, 1110 ; with three wives, 100 ; with four wives, 15 ; with five wives, 4 ; with six wives, 2. The above figures include women married *and women inherited*, for the custom of inheriting through the levirate (i.e. when a man dies his brother succeeds to his wives) is locally observed. It is regretted that the proportion of inherited wives cannot be ascertained. Most of the real pluralists are chiefs or important headmen. Generally speaking the wives get on fairly well together (each has her own hut) though, naturally, jealousy and bickerings are not unknown. When the

57

older and less well favoured wife is neglected on account
of the attractions of a new acquisition a good deal of
trouble may occur ; but on the whole things go quite
smoothly. *Kusongola mpaji* is the phrase for " to marry
an additional wife." The first wife is known as *mwaji* :
the second and each subsequent one *ntemena*.

There being no *lobola* here the marriage customs are
more similar to those of kindred tribes in this part of
Central Africa than in those in South Africa. The chief
difference in this group of Bantu tribes rests in the degree
of freedom that is given to the young to arrange their own
marriages ; and the Ba-Kaonde appear to have as much
freedom as any.

A man, having found a likely girl, approaches her
parents or her maternal uncle, or her maternal grandmother . . . and marries the girl. A small present is
given, two or three cloths being the accustomed amount.
Formerly bark-cloth (*mwemba wa nkolwa*) stitched and
oiled, with a few beads in addition, formed the gift.

There is very often a probationary period of cohabiting
before the marriage ; and this may be before or after
the parents have been approached. In some cases the
probationary period is spun out for a considerable time,
possibly with a view to postponing the obligations that a
man has towards his wife's relations. During this period
the man will build a rough hut (or borrow a hut) in his
" fiancée's " village and will live there openly with her.
If it comes to nothing he gives her a small present and
moves on to try his luck elsewhere.

A slave wife in the old days cost much more than a
proper wife. In cases that have come to my knowledge
goods value £4 or £5 have been paid (e.g. in one case—
7 cloths, 5 blankets, 1 gun, 1 packet of gun-powder and
3 strings of beads). This price was paid for a girl to be
selected by the payee. (The man who paid did not
choose a particular girl.) The reason for the higher
price is simple. A slave wife became a man's actual

property : she could not divorce him, and the children from the union were his and his family's, not his wife's family's. Further, she lived with the man where he chose to live ; and her parents (or former owner, for that matter) had no claims on him, nor on his services.

Far different is the case with an ordinary marriage. The bridegroom has to live in his wife's village (except when marrying a widow). The chiefs and others disagree as to how long he had to reside there, but in more cases than not it was (even if it is not now) for ever. In other cases after a period of from three to ten years the man could return to his own home. In this, as in many other things, there is a great divergence in different localities.

As a general rule a man married a girl long before puberty (see Note 1 at end of this chapter) and had to live at her village until she grew up and had born him a child —some say as many as four children. Then he could return to his own village, provided :

1. That his mother-in-law did not refuse, which she might do for (a) no special reason ; (b) because he had married her only daughter—a very common reason ; (c) because she did not think him likely to be constant if he went away from her supervision.
2. That his wife agreed.
3. That his wife's other relations agreed : e.g. her maternal uncle could veto his departure.
4. That he did not mind leaving his children with his mother-in-law ; for the children belong to the wife's family and they (the man's " in-laws ") can and do claim the right to bring them up. When the wife dies her family has a prior right to the children over their own father.

In these circumstances there is no doubt that a man generally remained permanently in the village of his parents-in-law. There he lived and worked. (It may be noted, in parenthesis, that while living there he had to obey the headman of that village in small things and assist him in small things : but in the major events of life—notably in witchcraft trials—he owed his allegiance to the headman of his own village.)

(*All the above has been written in the past tense, because in parts of the tribe especially the custom is becoming modified ; the whole matter is somewhat in a state of flux ; and to describe it in detail in the present tense would not be in every case accurate.*)

If after a reasonable time, say when some children had been born and had left babyhood behind, the mother-in-law refused to accede to the man's request that he could return to his home, he could, if he wished, claim a divorce and the restitution of his marriage gifts ; but nothing else—he could not insist on removing his wife.

The reason for this is quickly apparent. Amongst all Bantu races the female child is considered a great asset. Where the *lobola* is customary each girl fetches a high price—so many cattle as a rule. The man who marries her, having paid the price, takes her to his home—to his people's kraal—they probably " put up " the cattle. In the Kaonde land, however, the marriage gift is of but small value ; but the girl is still looked upon as an asset. The price her parents get is represented by the residence at their village of the girl's husband, and by the work which he does in gardening, hut-building, etc., as by the children which he begets. (As will be explained more fully later under Succession, the children of any union belong to the wife's side of the family.)

The actual ceremony of betrothal and marriage is as follows :

1. A man chooses his own bride, approaches her parents and suggests marriage. If they agree
2. He returns to his own home, and sends his mother and sisters with the marriage gifts.

3. On their arrival they go to the girl's parents and ask if she be of good character : the answer being in the affirmative the marriage is arranged.

4. These ambassadors then return to their home and tell the man, who then goes back to the girl's village with his brothers, sisters and brothers-in-law (if any).

5. The girl's people provide a spare hut—or, if none be available, her grandmother's hut.

6. At night the girl is taken to this hut and then the man is fetched and is taken there too. The first night is called *kulajika*—no connection takes place.

7. At dawn the bride's mother cooks a big bowl of porridge (called *chipununa wukala*, signifying that the bridegroom can possess his bride) and takes it to the bridal hut. The bride thereupon leaves the hut : the husband remains, but does not eat.

8. The following day the marriage is consummated.

9. The man is never allowed to look his mother-in-law in the face.

Nowadays the marriage is also registered by the Native Commissioner, an important matter, as the slight ceremony necessary for a native marriage is apt to grow less and less : which might result in marriage degenerating into haphazard concubinage, were there no registration.

Marriage of Chiefs. When a chief married matrilocal residence did (and does) not hold good. The bride resides in her husband's village.

A chief can marry anyone (not being within a prohibited degree) whom he wants, even if she be already married. Nowadays, such a custom would not be encouraged, but it is still legal according to native custom. If the chief wished to marry a married woman he sent an ambassador with some lion's fat with which he anointed the woman on the shoulders. This done, all the people, including her husband, ran away ; and her parents took her to the chief who had so honoured her. The chief then married her, but did not compensate the husband with another wife, or in any other way, owing to the " legal fiction " that he had run away from her.

Prohibited Degrees. These are very complicated, and do not appear to the writer to be sufficiently valuable to give in full. They may be summed up as follows :

   1. A man may not marry within his own totem.
   2. A man may not marry one whom he calls his mother, his sister, his daughter or his niece.

These terms, however, are very different from those of European races, and if taken literally would lead to error. The following (in European terms) covers approximately all prohibited degrees—apart from the general totem prohibition—(reversed for a woman) :

A man may not marry his

Grandmother (paternal or maternal).
Sister of grandmother (paternal or maternal).
Mother.
Mother's sister.
Father's sister (*a*)
Mother-in-law (*b*)
  (*a*) & (*b*) have a kind of *hlonipa*. The man may not even look at them.
Sister.
Brother's daughter.

Sister's daughter.
Wife's brother's daughter.
Wife's sister's daughter.
Daughter.
Father's brother's daughter.
Father's sister's daughter.
Mother's sister's daughter.
Sister's daughter's daughter.
Stepdaughter.
Wife's sister (in her lifetime).

But he can marry his

| Mother's brother's daughter. | Brother's daughter's daughter. |
| Brother's son's daughter. | Sister's son's daughter. |

Duties of Husband and Wife.

The Man.	The Woman.
(*a*) In building the hut.	
Cuts the trees for hut; builds it; thatches it; makes the door and bed.	Fetches the thatching grass; muds the walls and the floor.
(*b*) In the low ground garden (black soil).	
Cuts trees (if necessary); fences (if necessary).	Does everything else from the preliminary hoeing to the reaping.
(*c*) In high ground gardening.	
Cuts trees, collects and burns them; fences.	Weeds; reaps.
Both hoe (till) the ground.	
(*d*) General life.	
Collects firewood; makes *mukeka* mats; makes *musansa* baskets; tends fowls; cuts men's hair; hunts and fishes; and, generally, has to do the same kind of work for his mother-in-law; has to earn money for tax and cloths, etc.	Threshes; winnows; grinds and pounds the grain; draws water; makes cookpots; makes *chilalo* mats; makes all baskets except *musansa*; makes beer; makes castor oil; cooks; sweeps; dresses husband's hair in tufts; does the washing, but can refuse if busy pounding grain, in which case the husband does it.

The Man.   The Woman.

(e) On a journey.

The man will carry an elder child if necessary, otherwise he carries a spear and an axe to protect the party. As the women say : " What would I do, if we met a lion and my husband were carrying a load ? " In camp he makes a shelter, if necessary, and collects fire-wood.

The woman carries any load (cookpots, food, etc.) and the younger baby if more than one, or the only baby if an infant or toddler. The load is on her head and the child on her back or hip. In camp she cooks, draws water, etc.

Some further details will be found in the chapter called " All the year Round."

Divorce. Divorce is fairly common, and seems always to have been common. If there is a tendency to greater frequency it is probably only in cases of " mutual consent " with no special grievance : or, at any rate, with none that is quoted. The Ba-Kaonde have very clear and well-defined rules as to what constitutes grounds for divorce (apart from the mutual agreement referred to).

A man may divorce his wife (if he chooses to) :

(a) If, after a reasonable time—variable, her parents refuse to allow him to take her to his home.
(b) If his parents-in-law abuse him continually.
(c) If she does not cook food for his friends.
(d) If she does not make beer.
(e) If she does not do her other work properly (unusual).
(f) If she commits adultery, especially in her own village. (For further details as to the law concerning adultery see Note II at the end of this chapter.)

GOING ON A VISIT.

As is usual, the man is practically unencumbered in order that he may be free to protect his family in case of danger. The party is passing through a garden of sweet potatoes.

(g) If she is barren : he proves this by marrying a second wife and begetting a child by her.

(h) For leprosy, syphilis (but not for yaws), bad legs (caused by elephantiasis, or tropical ulcers or other sores bad enough to prevent her working), or for blindness.

(i) For excessive quarrelling and bad temper.

(j) Because he has got tired of her, in which case he usually trumps up some such reason as c, d, e or i.

A woman can divorce her husband for :

(a) Impotence.

(b) Failure to do his garden work.

(c) Failure to clothe her.

(d) If after the death of a child of theirs it be indicated by divination that he, or some member of his family, is to blame ; and if when so indicated he refuses to pay the customary compensation.

(e) For communicating syphilis, gonorrhœa, leprosy or yaws to her.

(f) For excessive beating.

In such cases as absenting himself and failure to maintain her for a long time, or obstinate refusal to live in her parents' village, the man practically divorces himself.

In all cases the divorce is arranged as a family matter : failing friendly settlement it is carried to the chief and settled by him.

After the divorce, no matter which party is the petitioner,

i. The man gets back his " dowry," and often damages (e.g. if adultery be one of the grounds for divorce) sometimes from his parents-in-law as well as from the co-respondent.

Formerly he also got a slave, and frequently killed someone at his wife's village.

ii. The children stay with the wife's mother, but are
   allowed to visit their father and take him meat ;
   and (if girls) on marriage to take him bark-cloth, a
   hoe or an axe. In a few cases the daughter of such
   a broken union may be married from her father's
   village.

NOTE I

Marriage of Immature Girls

[In the course of our official duties the question of
marriage of immature girls was investigated by all the
District Staff, and the results were carefully collated.
The following note is, in my opinion, the best account of
the practice and the best balanced judgment thereon.
There is one more point that should be emphasised :
namely the danger of underestimating a young girl's age
among such people. While admitting, as all acquainted
with these people do, that girls are carnally known at
an extremely tender age, it remains a fact that the girl is
not as young as she looks. Maturity among them comes
slowly. Of any two children—white and black—born
at the same time, all through childhood the black looks
far the younger. So when a native girl appears to be about
six one may generally reckon her age as ten : if she appears
to be but ten, she is very likely thirteen or fourteen. This
must be born in mind besides the fact that " they are
adapted for marriage both mentally and physiologically
far earlier than " among European races.]

 " Native girls are courted and wed between the ages of
eight and thirteen : i.e. always before they have attained
puberty and often as many as three or four years before
menstruation. It is not uncommon for them to be wives
for two years before they are even capable of coitus. The
reasons for this are :

(a) A girl's parents are disposed to realise her marriageable value as early as possible : her being unfit to

perform the duties of a wife does not appear to detract from her value.

(b) In a polygamous country there is no plethora of marriageable girls : men are, therefore, inclined to secure their wives in advance of their (the wives') full capacity for wifehood ; i.e. as soon as they have passed safely out of infancy and its dangers, and are in a fair way to developing into normal women.

(c) Men marry child wives as being more tractable for training to their duties and to a proper appreciation of the dignity that is in man.

It must be born in mind that native children begin at a very tender age to probe the mysteries of life. Sexual pleasure, or rather performance, is an everyday affair to urchins from the age of six—out of sight, as a rule, of their elders. It follows that by this early practice girls are adapted for marriage both mentally and physiologically far earlier than they are in societies where practical sexuality among children is effectually discouraged.

The following aspects of the custom are worthy of consideration :

1. "Though a girl usually contracts her first marriage at an age at which she is completely at the disposal of her parents, she does not require much persuasion, I fancy, to wed the most eligible wooer. Marriages between young girls and old men are extremely uncommon. When an adult man marries a child wife he does so with the intention of accustoming her to him, and waiting until later for his sexual satisfaction. Such marriages are particularly common between cousins " [on the non-prohibited side. F.H.M.]. " It is not unusual for a girl to ' sleep behind her husband ' for as much as two years— he studiously refraining from frightening or alienating her——" [These two years are really somewhat of a

formal betrothal. F.H.M.]" nor, I believe, are unnatural practices—intercrural, etc., indulged in during this period." [According to the Rev. E. W. Smith the Ba-Ila differ in this. F.H.M.] " A girl would be free to refuse to sleep in her husband's hut, and he would become an object of aversion to her family were he to ignore her immature sex or manifest any salacity before she reached sufficient development." [I fear that as regards a man other than a husband this does not apply. Grown men do have complete carnal knowledge of even such young girls and, in Kaonde eyes, this is not wrong unless the girl suffers physically therefrom. Nor, except when injured, is a girl supposed to complain of the " assault." Either alone or " hunting in couples," adult men have connection with such children—in gardens and elsewhere : sometimes after an assignation, sometimes the result of a casual encounter. Such intercourse when sought is very rarely refused by the girls, who—apparently— consider it natural : public opinion entirely endorses this view. F.H.M.]

" About two years before menstruation " [the writer adds " at ten or twelve . . ." Two years before men- struation would probably be twelve to fourteen . . . for reasons stated in my preliminary note. F.H.M.] " girls are said to be ready to show their readiness for coitus with their husbands, and from that time on there is neither restraint on the one side nor any risk of aversion on the other." [In a case that came to my knowledge a girl, thus married, cohabited fully and regularly, and admittedly with pleasure, with her husband for at least three years before her first menstruation. F.H.M.]

2. " No complaints have been made indicating disgust or horror on the part of the girl. Nor is any marriage registered or recognised without the girl's personal appearance and oral agreement." [Cases of refusal by the girl are not unknown, and absolutely veto the registra- tion. F.H.M.]

3. " Native public opinion is that (*a*), a girl married young and carefully trained makes the best wife ; (*b*) a man who undertakes to train a girl and is then carried away by his passions is a fool and will have to abandon the girl ; (*c*) to postpone coitus until menstruation is " no better than the beasts of the field do."

4. Whatever tendency there may be at the present day towards the emancipation of women it does not appear to affect the local feeling in favour of girls marrying before they are mature.

5. Native opinion is cordially in favour of the present custom, abuses of which must be very rare indeed, and which, if it is to be condemned at all, must be condemned on grounds eugenic. From this aspect I am not competent to offer criticism. It may be said, however, that in this tribe the standard of physique is good, and where in certain localities it is not maintained hunger and unhygienic habits are the rule." (T.R.W.)

The above note has been inserted because the custom of early marriages is one that is very largely misunderstood ; and it is of sufficient importance to justify careful examination. In many ways (according to our ideas) the custom is repugnant and indefensible. The only way to eradicate it would be by education, and by the elevation of the native to higher ideas. To legislate against it would result in the concealment of many such marriages, and would remove the very real protection that is now afforded to an unwilling girl-bride.

NOTE II

Native Law as Regards Adultery

In tribes such as this, where sexual intercourse has been well described as the " chief pursuit " of the adult, adultery is very common. The woman's sexual attributes being considered the personal property of her husband, it follows that adultery is regarded as a form of larceny.

Except when either party is a chronic offender (and so becomes a social nuisance) no stigma attaches. It is quite impossible to regard the subject from the European point of view, and it must be considered, soberly and without sentiment, from the point of view of the natives themselves.

" I know of no reason," says one careful observer, " to think that chiefs, headmen, or the people generally, attach much importance to adultery as an offence." (C.S.P.)

" The local opinion" (Alunda), writes another, " is that the husband should be compensated for the damage done to his property." (F.V.B.M.)

" It is commonly averred by the senior natives that the marriage tie is less well observed than it was before the coming of the white man. Though the influx of money and the absence of husbands at work are not spontaneously mentioned as reasons for this, yet there can be no doubt that they are to be counted among the causes of deterioration in native morality. Those who were questioned were unanimous in attributing the deterioration to the fact that in these days summary punishment of the offenders is forbidden by the white man, though their summary punishments, which they boasted had been so effective a deterrent, were somewhat disappointing when minutely examined." (T.R.W.)

The following represent the ancient customs of these people. (Kaonde—or a majority opinion of Kaonde—except when otherwise stated.) (Compiled by T.R.W.)

I. ADULTERY BETWEEN A COMMONER AND A CHIEF'S WIFE

1. *Where the man takes the initiative.*

(a) If the offender were a stranger, i.e. not one of the chief's own subjects, he would be made to pay heavily and would then be expelled from the realm. He would not be enslaved—nor would he be killed. " The woman would be an object of derision for falling to the charms of a mere stranger."

Variant. Among the Ba-lamba it appears that the stranger would probably be killed. To kill him would be the first inclination of the chief and of his loyal young men, and only if he were a *rich* stranger might a council of elders persuade the chief to spare his life and enrich the community with his goods.

(*b*) If the offender were one of the chief's subjects he would be made to hand over his sister, or some female relative, who would then become the chief's wife. He might, as a favour, be allowed to pay goods, and these would amount to about five guns (say £5). The offender would not be enslaved or killed.

Variant. Among the Ba-lamba the chief would receive the offender's sister as his slave, not as his wife.

(*c*) If the offender were a relative of the chief's he would be expelled from the realm. After a while he might collect goods and, so redeeming his citizenship, be allowed to return. If he were a very near relative of the chief, or in the possible line of succession, the presumption against him would be that in tampering with the chief's household he intended to bewitch the chief and " eat up " his estate. In this case he could never return during the lifetime of the chief whom he had insulted.

In no circumstance would the chief take an active part in arresting or killing the offender. This would be done by his loyal people.

The woman would not be beaten except to elicit confession : nor would she for a first offence be divorced unless she were already unpopular.

If the offender fled before being arrested he might find sanctuary with some powerful chief hostile to him whom he had insulted (if this chief were not powerful he would be afraid to shelter the offender : if he were not hostile to the injured chief he would send back the offender under arrest).

For a second offence—or for a first offence after warning—where the same parties were concerned (or with a different woman) anything might be done to the offender. He would certainly be put out of the way, either by expulsion or death. Payment would not be demanded, the idea of self-enrichment being incompatible with the white-hot purity of the chief's wrath.

2. *Where the initiative is with the woman.*

This would make no difference to the male offender's liability.

Variant. Chief Kapiji Mpanga (Kaonde) says that this would make *all* the difference to the man's liability; " for," says he, " a chief must be just or his people would leave him "—an illuminating sentence. [It may be noted that this chief, one of the biggest, is a usurper ; and obtained his chieftainship by " right of conquest " (successful rebellion). F.H.M.]

The woman would be beaten, but not in public nor officially, nor by any but the injured husband and by him in wrath. She would not be dismissed for the first offence unless she were already disliked. The chief could not demand from her people a substitute, but he could—at his pleasure—demand from them compensation in goods, whether he divorced her or not.

Variant. Musokantanda (Paramount chief—Lunda) says he could do this even when the woman had only yielded to the advances of the male offender.

A second offence by the same woman, whether she were the prime offender or not, might be visited with any or all of the above punishments, and dismissal would be certain.

Variant. Only among the Ba-lamba, it appears, was

A CHISUNGU GIRL BEING LED OUT FOR THE KUYEWOLA.

She is walking on all fours, covered by a blanket. A young girl guides her.

A CHISUNGU GIRL RETURNING TO THE VILLAGE.

She is covered from behind by a mat, and from the front by a woman holding the mat. The *chisungu* girl's head is just visible behind this woman.

mutilation of the woman practised, and among them
it must have been rare. No optical proof of mutilation
having ever been practised is now extant in the district.

II. ADULTERY BETWEEN A CHIEF AND THE WIFE OF ANOTHER CHIEF

No instance known. Though natives interrogated
do not hesitate, on occasion, to answer with the conviction of eye-witnesses concerning conditions that,
they later admit, have never arisen; yet the circumstances in which a chief would commit adultery
with another chief's wife appear to be beyond the
scope of their imaginations, and the fountains of their
inspiration run dry.

III. ADULTERY BETWEEN A CHIEF AND A COMMONER'S WIFE

A chief might possess himself of a commoner's wife
and pay the husband compensation, and all would be
well. But if he ignored these facilities and seduced
the woman by guile, then her husband might make an
attempt on his life. The offending chief might
appease the man with goods, or by giving him one of
his own wives to wed.

(This is the only case, it seems, where the wife of
the offender—instead of some other female relative—
was handed over in compensation for the adultery.
Answers on this subject were not satisfactory : they
seemed to be founded less on tradition than on sur-
mises of those questioned.)

IV. ADULTERY BETWEEN COMMONERS

The injured husband might, in anger, kill the
offender out of hand. But as a rule the case would be
settled by payment. Goods might be refused and a
slave demanded. Payments in goods would be upwards of one gun . . . 20s. to 30s. in value.

The community always discouraged killing for adultery as that led to endless vengeance between families. If the husband killed the offender he would have to take sanctuary, otherwise a relative of the adulterer would kill him, unless authority intervened. If the relatives of the dead adulterer did not kill the avenging husband they might kill one of his wife's family, " for she caused the trouble."

[It is interesting to note in this connection that in either case mentioned above, i.e. if the husband kills the adulterer while his anger is fresh, or if the dead adulterer's relatives kill the avenging husband while their resentment is fresh, the spirit of the deceased does not become *mutala* (an adverse spirit. *Vide* Chapter on RELIGION) to the slayer " just the same as with a man who steals in a garden " (*vide* Chapter on CHARMS); but if the killing be done after the blood has had time to cool, after brooding over the grievance, then the deceased does become *mutala* to the slayer. F.H.M.]

For a man to seduce the wife of his relative was a heinous offence, and he would probably be charged with witchcraft in addition.

[It may be noted here that whereas a man may lend a wife to his *mulunda* (friend or blood-brother), the *mulunda* may not take the privilege for himself : if he does it is adultery. F.H.M.]

Variant. It seems that only the Alunda were in the habit of making away with the troublesome Lotharios by bartering them as slaves. The Ba-Kaonde, Ba-lamba, etc., did not do so.

It will be seen from the foregoing how irregular was the procedure in the old days in dealing with adultery. There was little or no stereotyped official method of punishing the offenders and salving the husband's wounded pride : everything depended on the personality of the parties most intimately concerned and the composition of the council before which the case was brought. In one or two points, however, there may be noted a certain vague stability :

(*a*) Unless she had flagrantly provoked the offence the woman suffered no censure for her first frailty. Even in repeated offences the presumption was generally that she was the victim. [It has also been put this way to me : that the woman, before marriage, was always accustomed to an unlimited variety in her caresses, so that it is not natural to expect her to be content with the attentions of one man after being wed. F.H.M.]

(*b*) The case was generally settled by payment of goods or a slave or a relative. Violence was the exception, and corporal punishment, except as administered by the husband in anger, unknown.

(*c*) Goods paid to the injured husband might be valued at from £4 up if he were a chief : from £1 up if he were a commoner.

(*d*) Where there was so little stereotyped procedure, and so much depended on the character and temper of the parties there was invariably a degree of uncertainty as to how the matter would end ; and that must have acted upon the normal docile native as a natural deterrent from giving offence. [So far, that is, as anything can act as a deterrent on a sexually uncontrolled people in a matter of strong sexual impulse : aggravated by the ease with which a woman is persuaded—one of the commonest answers made by women in such cases being, " How can a woman say ' No ' to a man ? " The uncertainty as to the penalty might deter a man from a deliberate, but hardly from a spontaneous, offence. F.H.M.]

---

[1] The figures include a small percentage of other tribes, chiefly Ba-lamba, Ba-luba and Alunda ; but are sufficiently accurate as pure Kaonde.

CHAPTER V

FROM BIRTH TO DEATH

Puberty, Pregnancy, Etc.

PUBERTY. The *chisungu* or initiation ceremony of Kaonde girls takes place not at puberty, but before it. It is considered very dangerous to leave it until menstruation has begun, and the usual time is two or three years before the first menstruation. [There is an exception to this : among two totems, the *Benachowa* (mushroom) and *Benambuzhi* (goat), the *chisungu* is after the girl is known to be pregnant.]

First of all the girl herself has to do some preliminary stretching of the vagina ; and when this is accomplished the real *chisungu* begins. She is taken and laid down by a *mwenge* tree, being wrapped up completely in a blanket, and the women all dance round her, chanting, until 5 p.m. The men dance in the village at the same time. I have not actually witnessed this among the Ba-Kaonde, but in 1913 I saw precisely the same procedure at the *chisungu* of the daughter of the Kandembu chief Ikaleng'i.

At 5 o'clock she is taken to her hut, where she spends the night perfectly nude : not even a bead on her. On the following day girls, walking backwards, lead her by pulling gently at the hair above her forehead, or alternatively the girl is covered with a blanket and walks on all fours, the guides taking hold of the blanket and walking slowly (the girl herself stoops as she walks) to a place in the bush for further stretching (*kuyewola*), which continues for two or three months. She is given porridge to eat, and her husband partakes of the same porridge (*kusumisia*). All this time she sleeps in a different hut from that occupied by her husband. (It will be noted that it is taken for granted that she is married before the *chisungu*, and therefore long before puberty, and though this is not invariable, it is usual.) During this period no one sees her except small girls, who bring her her food, etc.

At the end of this period her husband is told to get beads for the people, after which dancing takes place from about 5 to 7 p.m. This done the girl is taken to her husband's hut. He arranges a string of beads in a circle in the doorway, over which she has to step when entering the hut.

Then the husband is called and he, too, steps over the beads ; and, entering the hut, finds her already lying on her back. When she lay down she placed four small strings of beads (about the size of a finger ring), one at her head, one at her feet, one in front of her and one behind her (*mishinga ya bana*) as a sign of children. The people who have accompanied her then go a little way away. On their departure the husband lies by the side of his wife and pretends to have connection with her (*kusawa chisungu*), then rises and knocks at his door, whereupon all the people give the shrill trill (*mikunda*) and rush off to the hut of the girl's mother and sing about it. After the singing they scatter to their own huts and the couple resume marital relations. Following the first intercourse the wife pulls the hairs out of her husband's armpits and pudenda, and hands them to him. She then wraps herself up in her blanket, while the man rises and throws away the hairs ; after which his wife gets up and claps her hands.

On the following day the man and the wife are taken into the bush in opposite directions and wash all over : the girls also adorn her hair with beads. The populace drink beer, meanwhile. The couple are then fetched and are brought into the village, the man walking, the girl carried on a woman's back, or walking behind a woman, both being surrounded by a long mat held up by half a dozen men. They are thus escorted to a spot opposite the hut of the girl's mother. Here a mat and a stool are ready and the girl is placed on the former, while the man sits on the latter. They are then covered with blankets and the encircling mat is withdrawn. The father and brothers of the man place a present by him and remove his blanket: similarly the girl's father and brothers present her with a gift and remove hers. Then all present add a few beads and greet them with the trill. This done the girl is carried by a woman and the man is led by the hand to his hut: he enters it, but his wife has to walk round it once before entering. They stay in the hut until about one hour before sunrise the following morning, when the girl goes to the river and takes some of the black earth from the river-side and places a little in the doorway of each hut in the village. After this she cannot talk to anyone except in a whisper for fifteen days. (Others say that the silence begins from the time that she is taken to the *mwenge* tree: the custom may vary in different localities.) After the fifteen days her mother calls her by name early in the morning and she answers back, aloud. She then removes the beads from her hair. This finishes the *chisungu*—all of which has to take place in her mother's village.

First Menstruation. When the first menstruation takes place the girl goes and lies down in her hut and has to eat (also called *kusumisia*) two pumpkin seeds. Otherwise there is no ritual of any kind. The first menstruation is called *kalume ka chisungu*.

Puberty of Boys. When nearing adolescence boys receive medicine from their brothers-in-law: this they eat and rub what is left on their breasts. Then the boy who has done this looks for a place where the root of the *chikole* tree crosses a path, and cuts a section of the root at this point. He puts this section in the fire (*kukanda*) until it is warm, and then places it against the penis until a state of erection ensues. Then the root is cut up and mixed with a little beer in a calabash and hung up at the top of his doorway. He leaves it there all night and drinks it in the morning. When he finds signs that he is maturing he applies to an unmarried girl (preferably his mother's brother's daughter) and sleeps with her. If she tells him that she likes him and asks him to repeat the visit, he then says that he is grown up and old enough to marry.

Pregnancy. When the bride becomes pregnant the husband is sent to find a small piece of bark-cloth and to make a belt of it (*kayemba*). On this he rubs wet clay, then dries it and removes the clay and gives it to his mother-in-law with some beads wrapped up in it. In the evening the bride's sisters bring a calabash of water with the opening stopped up with grass. At night the sisters take this calabash a little way outside, and call the bride. Then they fill their mouths with water, and as she comes they spit the water on to her, saying, " You have conceived." They then tie the *kayemba* round her waist. After this they bring her back to the village and have a dance. In the morning the pregnant woman is placed on her sleeping mat in her mother's hut, and everyone who has any beads puts a few on the mat. Then the woman and her husband are anointed with castor oil. After this all return to the ordinary routine of life.

The reasons for these different customs are not very clearly defined. The *kayemba* is supposed to ensure a satisfactory confinement.[1] The spitting of water by the sisters is said to be done because if strangers were to be the first to comment on the pregnancy a miscarriage would ensue. This spitting is referred to as *jimi ja wuwedzhi* (or *bubedzhi*). The anointing with oil of husband and wife is done as signifying their joint parenthood of the coming child.

There appears to be no taboo whatever in the Kaonde tribe for a pregnant woman. So far as tribal law is concerned she can eat anything she fancies. A woman in this condition, however, refrains from such food as she finds disagrees with her. There is one custom which has no sanctity as a tribal custom, but which is, nevertheless, freely practised : if the pregnant woman dislikes anyone, especially if she does not like their looks, she will tell the offending person not to pass behind her back, for fear that if she were to do so, the child—when born—would resemble the object of dislike.

One more point may be mentioned in this connection. Young girls (before their *chisungu*) are not allowed to scrape the pot containing their porridge, nor to scrape the ladle, the belief being that if they do so their parts will become closed (or unnaturally small), thereby preventing them from having intercourse with men and from bearing children.

Miscarriage, etc. In the case of miscarriage, or of a child being born dead, the woman is said to be *kafunga*, and cannot touch any fire but her own, nor any dishes or other household articles. A shelter is made for her on the outskirts of the village, wherein she has to sleep, her food being supplied to her in old and broken pots. (The fear of pollution by one unclean is the cause of all this.) When the breasts are dry the shelter is set on fire, with the woman inside it, and she rushes out. Then the people take a large piece of bark from a big tree and place certain herbs inside it, and take it and the woman to the river. Arrived there she is put, quite naked, into the bark bath, and has to wash herself all over with the water and herbs, her husband being a spectator of the ablution. After this purification she is handed new clothes to wear, and returns to the village. The first night in the village her husband resumes marital relations with her, and the next morning he gives her two strings of beads to wear (*mutozhya*), and a blanket or piece of bark-cloth. The woman then cooks some porridge, and collects the necessary things for tatooing, after which she calls all the people together, children included. The woman then tatoos the assembled women, and the husband tatoos the men (in small parallel lines of dashes, between the breasts). This done the woman places a pinch of porridge, dipped in salt, in the mouth of each tatooed female, and her husband does the same with each tatooed man, which removes any chance of evil that might ensue from the unfortunate event.

[1] The *Kayemba* is often a strip of white cloth about a foot wide. The husband buys it and hands it to his mother-in-law. On it the mother-in-law sews two cowrie shells (*miwere*) and a pendant of white beads. The belt is given to the wife about the third month of her pregnancy; she wears it day and night for from three to five days and then returns it to her mother. If any person removes the *Kayemba* from the woman it is a very serious offence, to be wiped out by compensation paid to her mother or uncle. Of old the compensation was a slave. This compensation is high, because the removal of the belt is supposed to cause miscarriage (*Kupulumuna*) or to cause the baby's death soon after birth, and to cause the death of all subsequent children born by the woman.

There is a variant of the *Kayemba* among the Alunda and among some Ba-Kaonde. No belt is worn, but the *miwere* are suspended from the neck by a chain of white beads, so as to hang between the breasts.

(K.S.K.)

CHAPTER VI

FROM BIRTH TO DEATH

DEATH AND BURIAL
(With Notes on Taboos)

(For supposed origin of death *vide* Chapter XII, RELIGION, paragraph on the Creation.)

THE Ba-Kaonde believe that death can come in many ways.

1. Death by *Lesa* (=Act of God, and death from natural causes). This can happen as a direct act of God, by thunder or by accidents, which are supposed to have been arranged by *Lesa* for his own inscrutable reasons. Also *Lesa* can kill by disease, and when divination does not show the disease to have been caused by witchcraft nor by adverse spirits it is presumed to have been sent by *Lesa*. *Lesa* also can kill by inciting a person to commit suicide.

2. Death by direct human action, i.e. by homicide, assault, warfare, and so on.

3. Accidental death (as we would call it) can be due to (*a*) *Lesa ;* (*b*) *mitala* (adverse spirits); and (*c*) *bulozhi* (witchcraft) ; especially is it believed that *tuyewera* (*vide* Chap. XVI) can cause death by accident as well as by sucking out a person's breath.

4. Suicide. This, the Ba-Kaonde say, can be caused by (*a*) *Lesa ;* (*b*) *mitala ;* and (*c*) witchcraft—the promptings of *tuyewera*.

5. Death by *mitala*. The adverse spirits (*vide* RELIGION) can cause death by accident, by suicide, by

82

sickness ; and of all forms of death this is probably considered to be the most common.

6. Death by witchcraft. This is the next most common cause of death ; and—besides accident and suicide as named above—death can be due to *bulozhi*, as the result of the many forms which are enumerated in the chapters on WITCHCRAFT.

7. Death as the punishment for breaking taboo. This occurs for the breach of the greater taboos. (*a*) Sleeping with a *munshengwe* woman (see Chapter on WITCHCRAFT) ; (*b*) incest, if with mother, aunt or sister. (If only with a woman of same totem, the penalty is only barrenness of the guilty woman. If with the man's mother-in-law his wife will die, not he himself. Entering a mother-in-law's hut, or looking at her is only a cause of shame (*bwumvu*), and does not cause death or sickness ; (*c*) sleeping with a widow who has not been " cleared."

As death for breaking the major taboos has been recorded it may be convenient to record here the

MINOR TABOOS.

Taboos[1] are not so common among the Ba-Kaonde as among many neighbouring tribes ; and, except for those recorded above, most are of personal significance only.

Some will not eat one kind of meat, and others will not eat another kind, because—after a cure—that particular meat has been declared taboo by the doctor who attended.

Some will not eat bush-buck for fear of rash, but this is not universal as with the Wawemba and other tribes : in fact, it is exceptional.

Ex-lepers [*sic*] will eat neither pig, nor hippo, nor zebra, nor mud-fish ; and those suffering from goitre will not eat mud-fish either.

Small boys cannot eat the fish called *jilemba*, or they will grow up impotent.

The taboo of porridge-pot scrapings (*makolwelwo*) for young girls was recorded in the last chapter.

When a person dies, one of the chief events is the divination that ensues to find out the cause of death ; but this is dealt with under RELIGION and DIVINATION, so need not be referred to here.

On the death of any individual, man or woman, the brothers of the deceased are called, and they say that they want to fight everyone. They are, however, prevented from doing so, and the people give them two presents : one for the death, and one for the burial. The corpse is then taken to a place where the paths branch, and is laid across the " fork," and everyone throws leaves on it and says " good-bye." After this the corpse is carried away for interment, which takes place (as a rule) in a regular burial area, generally by the side of an anthill. [The burial may be in an isolated place where no others have been buried, but generally the grave is close to others. In some cases—even with commoners—the body is buried in the hut of deceased : this was more common when the people lived in isolated huts, but still occurs now that they live in villages. In some cases the burial is in a *jitu* (grove of swamp timber), but whether this takes place in any other case, except when the body is of a *wusangu* man (*vide* Chapter XI, RELIGION : REINCARNATION) I cannot be sure.]

Anyone can attend at the funeral (any adult, that is : children do not attend), but except in certain cases women do not attend. A man's mother would probably attend if she were alive, or some other elderly female relation. As regards the adult men there appear to be no restrictions, neither of totem nor of anything else. The bearers are volunteers, and are not specially chosen. The corpse is carried head first. On arrival at the selected spot everyone present takes a hoe and scuffles a little bit, but the actual digging of the grave is started by the man who was in front (i.e. at the head) when carrying the body.

The grave is made in the shape of an L—like a shaft with a drive at the base. The corpse is put in the drive facing east. This is so that the spirit (*mukishi*) of deceased will be favourable when an emanation from it enters some baby (i.e. becomes the soul of a new person—*vide* chapter on RELIGION). The corpse is oiled, and wrapped in clean cloths : the head and all is covered, no hole being left over the ear or elsewhere as with some neighbouring tribes. It is roughly fenced in, so that no loose earth will fall on it. The position is prone, lying on one side, with the knees bent up, and the arms bent so that the elbows are by the abdomen and hands by the neck. When the body is in the grave everyone sits at the top of the opening, with their backs to it, and sweeps in a little earth backwards into the grave. They then turn round, rise and hoe in the rest. After the burial they go and wash (*kuwoa malomba*), and then proceed to the forked path where the body had rested. Then a man (any one of the same totem as deceased, *or* alternatively, the father of deceased) comes from the village with a little porridge and salt, and a lighted torch of grass taken from the roof of the deceased's hut. With this torch he runs round the funeral party and throws the torch on the ground. The burial party stamp out the fire, and then the new-comer puts a pinch of porridge and salt in the mouth of each, which they eat ; and each then anoints himself on the chest with a little castor oil.

They then return to the village and enter the hut of the deceased backwards with hands clasped behind. Eating and dancing follows in the evening. If the deceased was an important person the dancing may last from five to ten days. On the last day the people lie down in front of the hut occupied by the departed, and on the last night the feasting and dancing is continued throughout the night. The widow or widower (if deceased left one) is put in a very small hut (*kasamvu*)

which is set on fire, and she (or he) escapes therefrom
Presents are then given to the mourners, one for sleeping
by the hut of deceased, one for washing and one for
shaving the head of the " relict." The next day the
widow (or widower) is given bark-cloth to wear, and all
her (or his) old clothes are thrown away. (This is a
custom more honoured in the breach : it is a formula and
not a real act, for clothes are too precious : even in the
case of a man dying from highly infectious disease, the
clothes he had are " inherited " and are not destroyed.
The same kind of thing may be observed with offerings
to the spirits : once made they may be taken back by
the giver.)

The following day a mat is placed on the ground and a
young boy (generally a boy, it may be an older person)
is called and placed thereon. All the deceased's portable
property, such as his belt, guns, spears are given to him,
and he is told that he is the *mumbelunga* (= in this case
something between executor and trustee ; a *mumbelunga*
is also in a way a regent), and he is ordered to watch over
the property and the widow (when there is one) until
someone succeeds to the deceased. As succession may take
an indefinite time, the reason for a *mumbelunga* is apparent.

No sign of mourning is worn, e.g. no band of bark or
banana fibre as often worn by neighbouring tribes on the
forehead.

In the above I have tried to portray an average
funeral. There are many minor differences, and rigid
observance of many of the details is not necessary.
Within certain limits a great deal is left to individual
tastes. The following account by an eye-witness of an
actual, and ordinary, Kaonde burial is, therefore, of
interest. With old customs being undermined an eye-
witness's account is always of particular value. The
" generic " account that has been given (carefully compiled from different sources) is quite independent of the
following " specific " description.

A Kaonde Funeral

The following is a brief account of a native funeral ceremony witnessed by me in March, 1918, near Bukonde's village. It is possible that the funeral was not a typical one, also that formalities were omitted which would have been observed had not a European been present.

Early in the morning after the day on which the man died, the body was brought out of his hut and placed, entirely wrapped in a white cloth and well-covered with blankets, on a rough machila or stretcher of bark-rope. Only six people seemed disposed to go to the burial, namely the deceased's father, his elder and younger brothers and one brother-in-law. No resentment or surprise was exhibited at my desire to attend the funeral. One of the six went first to ask the headman where the body should be buried. On his return he indicated the direction and the two men quickly picked up the stretcher and marched off with it (deceased's father and younger brother). Deceased was a bachelor. No women came to the burial, and no notice was taken of our departure from the village. The place selected was about a mile from the village, out through the gardens and across a stream, to the foot of an anthill in bush country, where there was evidence of only one previous interment. It did not seem to be a regular cemetery and the place was quite unmarked in any way, and might have easily been passed by in the bush.

The machila was deposited on the ground close to the old grave and a space in the long grass was quickly trodden down. The father (who acted throughout as chief mourner) then took a hoe in his right hand, and the remaining five men also grasped the handle with their right hands and together they cut the first sod. The father then set to work and began to dig a pit. After he had dug several feet down the others took their turn with the hoe for a short spell each. Finally a grave about five feet deep was excavated, all the earth being thrown up in a heap on one side only of the pit. About three feet down a lateral excavation or " pocket " was made on the side next the anthill, more or less as shown in the diagram, and large enough to have contained a couple of good-sized coffins. This cavity and the whole of the pit was cleaned out and stamped down with much care, no loose earth being allowed to remain on the floor. The father then got down into the grave and very carefully laid and arranged two grass mats in the side cavity, pressing them well along the floor and walls of the cavity. Upon this he then made a sort of bed of two blankets. The body was then lowered into the grave and there received by the father, who spent a considerable time in placing it in position and covering it with the blankets. It was still wrapped in the white cloth, and as far as I could see was arranged on its side with the knees drawn up to the chin. Two men had in the meantime cut a large sheet of bark, and when this had been whittled down to a convenient size (about 4 ft. by 5 ft.) it was placed against the lateral cavity, as a shutter or screen, thereby enclosing the body entirely in a separate chamber and preventing the earth subsequently thrown in from touching or falling upon the body. The interstices between this shutter and the wall of the grave were closed with grass and pieces of bark. The father then came out of the pit and he and the elder brother immediately sat down on the heap of excavated earth, with their backs to the grave, and simultaneously gave one big shove backwards with their buttocks, thereby pouring a considerable quantity of earth back into the grave. They at once stood up, and the whole party then set to and filled in the pit as speedily as possible, using their hands, hoes, axes, etc. The grave was soon filled in and the slight mound resulting well stamped down with their feet.

The machila on which the body had been carried was

KAONDE MEN MAKING MIKEKA MATS FROM RAPHIA.

These mats are plaited in strips and the strips then sewn together.   Only men make these.

LUNDA AND KAONDE WOMEN MAKING COOKING POTS.

A finished pot is seen in right foreground.   The scene is a village on the Kabompo River.

then broken with an axe and carried off a little way
into the bush and hidden.

There appeared to be no further ceremony or formality
at all. No pots, dishes or other property belonging to
deceased were placed on the top of the grave, nor were
any buried with him (as is done by some tribes, and quite
possibly sometimes by the Ba-Kaonde). The father was
the last to leave the grave, and he carelessly threw a tuft
of earth on the grave as he left, but this may not have
been a matter of ritual.

Little solemnity was observed during the interment,
and no sorrow exhibited. The burial took about three
hours, and the whole affair was carried through in a
brisk and business-like manner. Throughout the proceedings the grave diggers conversed without restraint
and occasionally cracked a joke with each other.

On the way back from the grave to the village all
thoroughly bathed (the entire body) in the stream,
washing themselves with much care. This may have no
ceremonial import, as it was certainly rendered necessary
by the dirty and perspiring condition of those who had
dug the grave.

Mourning. This is, of course, quite a distinct custom
and has nothing to do with the burial. Drums, beer,
dancing and songs had proceeded during the whole
night prior to the burial and would continue, possibly,
for three weeks or so. I saw drums inside the hut where
deceased had lain during the night, and little fires were
placed in a semicircle around the door of the hut (? presumably to avert evil spirits, but I did not enquire into
this).[2] The mourning ceremony is a bigger affair alto-
gether and a far more important matter in connection
with a man's death than the actual burial. (R.E.B.W.)

A Chief's Burial. The burial of a chief varies considerably, and the body is not *interred*. The corpse is
placed in a *chitala*, a kind of coffin raised on piles, well
off the ground, within the hut of the deceased. The

floor and walls of this " coffin " are mudded, and the
body is placed therein and covered with cloths. The
hut is then closed and the door mudded up, and a small
white flag (of calico) placed on the roof. The body
remains there to decompose. The hut stands till it falls
down from decay, fire, etc. Sometimes the village is
deserted when the chief dies, but not always. Sometimes
a live fence of bamboos or other plants is planted round
the hut. (I have seen this round a Lamba chief's hut,
but have not myself seen one round a Kaonde chief's
hut.) Sometimes there is no embalming at all, in other
cases the body is covered all over with porridge made of

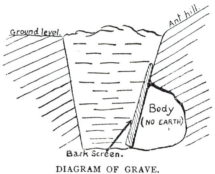

DIAGRAM OF GRAVE.
(Described on pp. 87, 88).

the small red millet (*luku*). This is known as *kuchina
kuwola* (to ward off decomposition). I cannot find out
that it has any special significance, and I am assured that
nothing else is used, nor are any other ingredients having
special preservative powers added to the porridge.
There may, however, be more to be learnt about this,
for I was assured several times over a period of some years
that *no* embalming was *ever* practised ; and I only discovered that this was incorrect by accident.

I give the following note on Lunda burials (F.V.B.M.)
as their custom differs in some essentials from that of the
Kaonde.

" When a person dies, first of all the body is washed and

anointed with oil. A pole is cut from the bush and the body is wrapped in a blanket or cloth and tied to the pole; it is then carried away, and on arriving at a cross-road the assembly sit down. Late-comers then arrive and find the funeral party waiting. They then address the corpse, saying something as follows :

'Someone has been responsible for your death—you must now revenge yourself on him.' The grave which has been prepared is made in a circle with a straight piece projecting from it. The first few loads of earth which have been excavated are placed carefully near the side of the grave. Famous hunters only are buried in a sitting position ; all other people are placed in a prone position (this includes chiefs). The body is untied from the pole on arrival at the grave and buried, completely covered in the blanket or cloth. If the deceased is a man of importance his friends and relatives place offerings such as beads, etc. in the grave; it is then filled in and the earth, which was formerly placed near the opening, is used for making the mound. For a man of wealth the grave is fenced round and pieces of calico are tied to the top of the fence or palisade—sometimes plates, hoes and other articles are placed on the mound inside the fence (mostly the deceased's own property); the reason for this seems to be that the relatives think that people will say that they are glad the man has died if they take possession of all his property—hence they place some of it on the grave. On return the funeral party again stop at the cross-roads and a fire is made and one of the number takes a torch from the fire and lightly touches with it the feet of all the people who were present at the graveside. This prevents any harm being done to them by the spirit of the dead man. Each one also anoints himself on the chest with oil, they then go to mourn outside the hut of the deceased, where a feast is held and beer drunk. The period of weeping and waiting lasts a long or a short time, according as the rank of deceased is high or low—the usual time of mourning is ten days or so for a commoner and generally a month for a chief or more important headman. At the death of a chief all cultivation at his village is stopped for six months. The latter is a harmful practice which fortunately is being abandoned now as the result of persuasion on the part of the Government."

Mourning. The mourning ceremonies (dancing, feasting, etc.) take place to appease the spirit (*mukishi*) of the deceased, to show the *mukishi* that it is respected, and that the dead person was well loved. It is believed that if the ceremonial signs of respect be omitted the *mukishi* will become a *mutala* (an adverse spirit : *vide* Chapter XI, Religion).

One of the songs is sung by the burial party inside the hut of the deceased : it is known as *Lwimbo wa majima* and is as follows :

Solo

" *Mukwenu wafwa*   " Our companion is dead.
   Wayiya ku kalunga."   He has gone whence there
Chorus is no return."

Treble : " Iyo, yo, yo, yo,
Bass :   Yo, *Yo*, Yo.
Treble : Ya, yaiya, ya, ya.
Bass :   Ya, *Ya*, Ya."   Repeated *ad lib.*

On emerging from the hut another song is sung, to the accompaniment of beating by axe on hoe (the axe and hoe which were used in the interment—after which the hafts are thrown away).

Solo

" *Kumilenda takupita*   " To the grave none may go,
   weleli."   none but the bearers may
    pass there."

Chorus

" *Wamufupikabyo.*"   " If one does he will be
Repeated *ad lib.*   killed."

More interesting is the following, a specimen of the
Wadya Wanji song (lit : " He ate the life of his companion ") which is sung at the death of anyone who is
supposed to have died from the witchcraft or other
machinations of someone. This is a song often sung,
with variations, and the example given was sung at the
death of headman Kakoshe, when one Kimu was supposed to have bewitched him.

" *Iyo, iyo, iyo !*
Kimu adya Mateu !
Iyo, iyo, iyo !
Kimu adya Mwanza !
Iyo, iyo, iyo !
Witupwizhya :
Kimu apwizhya bantu.
*Mwaji kumukwata lukelo
  kampe muntu wusha-
  kunyema !*
*Kimu achina kwilembera
  muchi,*
*Nanchi Kimu wapwishya
  kuipaya wakwenu.*"
Etc., *ad lib.*

" Oyez, oyez, oyez !
  Kimu ate Mateu !
Oyez, oyez, oyez !
  Kimu ate Mwanza
Oyez, oyez, oyez !
  He has finished killing
  us :
  Kimu has finished off
  the people.
  You should catch him,
  perhaps he will run
  away in the morning!
  Kimu is frightened
  to tatoo himself,
  That is why Kimu has
  killed off his rela-
  tions." Etc.

(Poor Kimu was sung about on so many occasions like
this, that finally he felt the limit of endurance had been
reached, and speared one of his traducers and killed him.
He spent the last months of an old life in gaol, as a
lunatic ; and they were—I fancy—the happiest months
of his life. I mention this to show what effect this kind
of song can have.)

On the morning after the dancing has been completed
a basket of meal and some beads are placed in the doorway of the hut of the deceased. From the basket each
of the bearers takes a little meal and puts a smudge

thereof on his forehead (from the bridge of the nose vertically up to the hair). Each also takes a bead and ties it with a thread to his forelock, so that it hangs down as far as the base of the meal-smudge. This is a sign of purification.

After this (when all the mourning is well over) a final washing takes place. A bark bath (or small boat) is made, and certain medicines called *mwanzambalanga* or *kulakazhi* are placed in it. It is then put in the river (floating) and the bearers all wash therein. Then they sink the bath till it floods, after which it is turned over. This completes the purification.

The front bearer keeps the hoe, and back bearer the axe (which were used at the interment) as perquisites.

It is interesting to note that of old beer was *not* drunk at the mournings : only porridge (*nshima*) was eaten. Beer was considered unlucky at such times. Nowadays the younger generation has come to the conclusion that they cannot get " happy " without beer ; and they, therefore, do not attend " wakes " when it is lacking. So it has become customary to ensure a big gathering and much dancing at the mourning by providing adequate supplies of beer. The bigger the attendance the bigger the honour to the dead. This innovation is now completely sanctioned and adopted. It is the only case within my knowledge of a deliberate change in custom with the Kaonde, and shows that though " the laws of the Ba-Kaonde alter not " is a safe maxim, yet the people *will* depart therefrom when it suits them : a fact that may be of great assistance in the future, if we take care to have some attractive feature in any advisable change.

---

[1] There appears to be no word in Chikaonde for " taboo," but it is implied by the verb *Kuchina* to fear ; thus *Kuchina bwumvu* (of looking at one's mother-in-law), *Kuchina moyo* (of approaching a grave).

[2] I gather that one fire is inside the hut for the bearers, and that the little fires outside the hut are for the other mourners to sit by and cook at, and that the fires have no other significance. (F.H.M.)

CHAPTER VII

INHERITANCE & SUCCESSION

THE first point to make clear is who succeeds whom. This will be most clearly shown by means of a genealogical table. In this the capital letters *A, B* represent males and the small letters *a, b* females.

The man who dies and for whom a successor has to be found is " A."

His first and most natural successor is his brother *C,* if not too old, nor otherwise unsuitable.

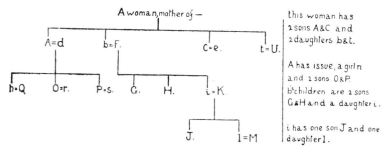

The next heir would be *G,* i.e. the elder son of his sister *b,* and after him *H,* the younger son of *b.*

Supposing that these predeceased *A* he would be succeeded by *J,* the son of his niece *i* (niece, the daughter of his sister : not daughter of brother). Failing all these the succession would lie first with the children of *A's* younger sister *t ;* or, failing such, with the descendants of one of his maternal aunts.

This is called matrilineal descent, and is the antithesis

of filial descent as we have it in England : from father to son.

A's own children, *O*, *P*, by his marriage with *d* would succeed to *d's* brother, so would the children of *A's* daughter *n*. They all belong to *d's* family : not to *A's* ; which is why at marriage *A* has to go to—and generally settle with—*d's* family. Thus although *A's* family loses *A* and *C* when they marry, they gain *F* and *U*. So the more daughters a man has the more he gains (see MARRIAGE).

Succession. The succession of a chief may be taken first as it is more detailed than that of a commoner ; and, once the former has been followed through all its intricacies the latter is easy to follow. As a rule, a year or more (sometimes as much as three years) elapses between the death of a chief and the installation of his successor : the period of waiting is dragged out if not many births have taken place. In the interim the *mumbelunga* reigns, if he is old enough, and is treated as a chief. If he be too immature the *mumbelunga's* uncle or elder brother acts as regent for him. All customary chief's presents, food, share of game and so on are given (used to be given, or should be given) to the *mumbelunga*, who is (was, or should be !) honoured as a chief during the time that he holds office.

When the proper time has elapsed the person who is to install the new chief is sent for, a present and some sign being sent to him by the heir—for there is not often much doubt as to who is the heir—and then comes the first preliminary : the heir has to undergo the hunting test. Put briefly this means that he has to go out hunting and, if he has been in any way responsible for the death of the late chief by killing, witchcraft or any other means, or has slept with his wife, he will kill a male and will be unable to succeed. In such case the next heir has to undergo the test and so *ad infinitum*. This is the idea in theory, but in practice it never gets to anything

A CHIPANDA OR ALTAR FOR THE FAMILY SPIRITS.

This consists of an inconspicuous stick leaning against a tree in a village. At the base will be seen the offering of flour.

A CLAY SNAKE, WHITE WITH RED SPOTS, ON A PATH OUTSIDE A VILLAGE.

This is to ward off malaria, attributed to evil spirits. Note the broken pot and forked stick,

like that. If the heir kills a female it signifies that he has done no wrong to the deceased chief and is a fit successor. Among many tribes this test is done by driving game into a long net which has the merit of being impartial, but among the Ba-Kaonde, apparently, the heir goes forth to the test with his gun (or, more rarely, with a bow and arrow) to decide his own fate. One would feel that he could be sure of killing a female, but the Ba-Kaonde say—and in my opinion they believe—that if he be not a worthy successor the spirit of the deceased is too strong, and even though he aim at a female he will not kill her, but will eventually kill a male. I have met a few sceptics (? disappointed next heir-apparents) who do not believe this.

The giving of the leaf. The night after the female animal has been successfully slain and the heir confirmed in his " heirship," the meat is given as food to the assembled people. That night a man who is called the *chimankata* catches the heir and salutes him, saying, " You are the heir." At the salute the *chimankata* places a *mulemba* leaf in the heir's mouth. After this he is the heir-designate, and can inherit the wives of his predecessor.

The inheritance of the wives. This takes place the following night. The widows (or some of them, if they be numerous) are taken to a shelter and the successor is also taken there. Each gives the successor gifts, which are known as *via u tuzhi* (contraction for *vintu vya utuzhi*, gifts of widowhood—the singular being *chia u tuzhi* contracted from *chintu chya utuzhi*). The matter of *via u tuzhi* is a complicated one and, to simplify the present description, is dealt with in a foot-note to this chapter. Sometimes the widow herself gives the present, at other times her relatives produce it : at times it may happen that she has nothing ; and, if such be the case, she makes an admission that she owes it to the heir-designate and states that she will pay it when she is able to do so.

That night the widow stays in the shelter with the heir (if there be only one widow : if there be more than one the senior widow stays, unless she is too old, in which case any other younger one is chosen and is called the *Kafwana*). The heir-designate cohabits with the *kafwana* and, having inherited her, has inherited all the widows. Old widows are frequently allowed to return to their homes after giving the *via u tuzhi* ; and it may be added that if the sole widow be very old the heir need not actually cohabit, but goes through a brief ceremony in lieu of it : cutting her abdominal string of beads and placing his hand lightly on her private parts. This is said to have the same effect as actual connection, namely, it is supposed to free the spirit of the deceased. The whole of this affair is based on the absolute necessity for freeing the spirit of the dead man ; and any hasty effort to interfere with this custom (on the grounds that it is indecent or immoral) is considered sacrilegious. More than that (as will be understood better when the chapters on religion are reached, a man simply *dare not* take the risk of so offending the spirits. No one but an absolutely irreligious native would evade this ceremony, and—in the writer's opinion—we have no right to expect that any should. The inherited wives have precedence over the successor's own wives.

The formal appointment or installation. This occurs on the morning after the inheritance of the wives, and is somewhat similar to the anointing of a king at his coronation ; and, though it does not actually finish the succession, it is the principal part of it. The heir has already proved his fitness to succeed by the hunting test : he has been acclaimed chief, and has proved his actual succession by inheriting the wives, all of which combined show that his succession is not in dispute : but the installation is necessary before he is chief. There is always a special person who has to install him. (To succeed is *swana :* to appoint as successor is *swanika*.)

The man who has to *swanika* the heir is generally (but by no means invariably) a chief. There is, however, always one person whose sole right it is to do this. For the sake of brevity this " installer " will in the next paragraphs be called " the chief," and the person to be installed will be referred to as " the successor."

The chief, with the relatives of deceased, elders and other people, gather before the door of the successor's hut. The successor is present. The chief takes the *lukano* (an heirloom, generally a bracelet) and very often a gong, called *luonge*, which is shaped something like a carpenter's square). There are other insignia varying in each succession, e.g. Chiwanza has the feathers of the *kalong'o* bird, from the Luba country. These the chief hands to (*a*) the *inamfumo* = sister of deceased chief ; or (*b*) to a man known as the *chifinganyundu* ; or (*c*) to a man called the *chifwikankano*, who takes them to the successor, and places the *lukano* on his arm. She (or he) then takes two small iron hammers, and, bending over the successor, strikes them together above his head. She also puts *mpemba* (white clay, chalk, or lime) on the centre of his chest and on his forehead. This practically amounts to anointing, and is done (in Chiwanza's case, anyhow) by the sister of the deceased chief. Kasempa has a *chifinganyundu*, Kalela : Katotola Mukumbi's is Mateu : Mushima is installed by one of his own family : Mulimanzovu by one of the Wayanga totem, and so on.

The inheritance of the goods. Immediately after this installation the successor takes over the goods of the deceased. The successor is led into an open space, and is placed facing the east. The *mumbelunga* (regent) stands to the south of the successor, looking at him. The *inamfumo* (or *chifinganyundu*, etc.) takes a gun (formerly a slave) and hands it to the *mumbelunga*, receiving at the same time the goods of the deceased from him. She (he) then hands over these goods to the successor.

The acclamation. Then all the people trill (the

mikunda) and beat the *luonge* (gong) : they give beads to the successor and fire off their guns. The *chimankata* (the man who originally hailed the successor and gave him the leaf) carries the new chief upon his shoulders to his hut. Beer drinking follows, and the new chief is given a chair or stool whereon to sit, his brother bringing a mat and sitting by him. The chief (i.e. the installer) then returns to his own home, receiving from the installed chief a gun (formerly a slave) in return for his services. The new chief also hands out beads to all his headmen.

The State visit to the installing chief : the final recognition and second anointing. After a few days (apparently to give time for the brewing of beer) the successor calls together his men, and they go to visit (*kusanga*) the chief who installed him ; and also to give him a second gun (formerly slave). On approaching the chief's village the visitors beat the *luonge*, and the small two-ended drums that are hung from the neck (*tushingi*). As they draw near the chief's people come out with guns and pretend to fight against the visitors. When they are still closer to the chief his people line up in front of him and hide him. The successor's brother then " makes peace " by presenting beads to the members of this human screen, whereupon they draw aside, exposing the chief to view. The successor then approaches and hands the second gun to the chief, whereupon he rises, goes away to fetch a blanket which he places on the successor, putting also some white chalk on his chest (not on the forehead this time) saying, " Now art thou a big chief even as I am ! "

Beer drinking follows, and in the morning the new chief and his party return home. The appointment is now complete.

(The above is a typical succession of a chief. Each one will be found to have variations, but the general routine varies but little.)

Succession of a Commoner. This is, naturally, far less elaborate. The leaf of the *mulemba* is not given, and a brother-in-law or a cousin takes the place of the *chimankata*, hailing him with the words, " You have succeeded." Dancing, with drums and much " *mikunda* " follows. That same evening comes the inheritance of the widow or widows. The *via u tuzhi* having been given the heir enters the shelter with a widow, and before he " inherits " her he removes the hair from her armpits and pudenda. The following morning he is placed on a mat with the inherited wife and both are oiled. He then gives her two strings of white beads (*mutozhya*).

After this the *mumbelunga* is called, and the successor's sister or mother takes a cloth or some beads, which she gives to the *mumbelunga* in return for which he hands over the property of deceased, and she gives the same to the successor. Then all the people trill (*mikunda*) and give beads (*kwanuna*) to the successor, after which he and the inherited wife are led to his hut—he is not carried.

He is then called " the inheritor of so-and-so " (*Swana Kananga*). If he is fully grown himself he remains *Swana Kananga* until his death, and does not drop the prefex " *Swana*." When he, in his turn, dies *his* successor is called after his original name. Thus Kapiji dies and is succeeded by Muloa. Muloa is called *Swana Kapiji* until his death. Mulapwa succeeds him and is called *Swana Muloa*. If the successor be a young boy he is called *Swana Kananga* until he grows up, when he chooses a name for himself and drops the succession name entirely.

The above refers to the Ba-Kaonde. The following is a résumé of notes on " Succession among the Alunda " (condensed from notes by F.V.B.M.).

Succession usually runs in the male line, i.e. is filial, not matrilineal. All things being equal the eldest son succeeds, next the younger sons, then the sons of a brother, failing which sons of a sister. There are a good many exceptions to these rules : a headman's nephew, if popular, will often succeed to the exclusion of a son.

The following is given as an example : the succession to the chieftainship of Sailunga, the most important resident Lunda chief.

A year, more or less, elapses after the death of the old chief, during which a *mombailunga* reigns. He looks after the property of the chief, receives tribute, carries on the chiefly duties, but can, himself, never succeed. When the elders have decided on a successor the *chifwikankanu* takes a *mulemba* leaf and places it in the mouth of the heir, who promptly gives gunpowder to several hunters and instructs them to go out and kill a female animal. Should they shoot a male he cannot succeed, but if they shoot a female he is then formally elected, unless the female shot is hartebeeste, warthog or zebra, which are *kahenga* and count as males. The following day the chief-elect is taken to a shelter and washed, has his hair dressed and is re-clothed. He is crowned with a crown made of the feathers of the *kalong'o* bird. This done the *chimankta* carries the new chief on his shoulders to an appointed place where the crowd awaits him ; and on arrival the *chifwikankanu* hands him the *lukano ;* and, taking some *mpemba* from his mouth, rubs it on the chief's forehead and chest. Presents are now given by the successor's relatives to all who have danced all night without sleeping. Everyone then files past the chief and drops some presents on a mat near him (which presents are a perquisite of the *chimankata*). At this present-giving there is a formula used by the donors, " You must now know me, and if at any time you settle my cases you must treat me well."

Then the *chimankata* leads the chief (who walks behind the *chimankata* holding on to his shoulders) to the shelter, where the night is spent. It may be noted that at the time that the *chifwikankanu* presents the *lukano* he also gives his daughter to the chief in marriage, and she is henceforth called " Lukano."

Alunda chiefs do not succeed to the wives of a dead chief; they are returned to their homes after being cleansed. This marked difference between them and the Ba-Kaonde is easily explained by the fact that succession is filial. If the succession falls to a grandson he does the cleansing (by cohabiting) himself, but if son succeeds father his son (deceased's grandson) does this. If the widow(s) are very old the spirit is released by their being touched by another woman.

NOTE

(*VIA U TUZHI*)

The following notes on *via u tuzhi* (by C.S.P.) are worthy of record.

" *Via u tuzhi* means the goods paid by widows or their relations to the successor so that he will clear or whiten the widow(s) and release the spirit of the dead man from them : it also refers to the goods paid by a widower to the relations of his deceased wife so that they will provide her sister or some other woman that he may release himself with her of the spirit of his dead wife.

" The ceremony of releasing the spirit is as follows : When the successor is appointed the widows of the deceased or their relatives approach him with goods, so that he may release the spirit. This may be done by sleeping with a widow for a night or so (the most usual way), or, if the woman be too old or ill-favoured, he takes her before the people and rubs a little white flour on her body or puts some white beads on her. Should this successor keep any one of the widows as wife the *via u tuzhi* is sometimes (not always) less than it would be if he freed her to return to her own home. In the case of a widower he approaches the relations of his dead wife with goods and asks for her sister, or—failing her—for some other woman with whom he may pass the night, so as to release himself from the spirit of his dead wife. If he wishes, and if the woman agrees, he may marry her. If the widower be old or unattractive, the woman chosen may content herself with entering a hut with him and cutting her abdominal string, which is sufficient to release the spirit, but in such case a part of the *via u tuzhi* paid by the man is refunded.

"The great objection to *via u tuzhi* lies in the fact that at the present time many men refuse to clear the widow or widows unless they are paid an exorbitant amount (£2 to £4). Meanwhile, the widow is not free to marry, and, strictly speaking, cannot leave the village of her late husband. Then it happens some man is implicated in a scandal with her and has to pay, say, 20s., as it is considered a great offence to have connection with a woman who has not been cleared. This may happen several times. I have known women wait in this way for over five years, and the original demand abating not more than 10s., while the successor may have made £2 or £3 by her intercourse with other men.

"Widowers can usually look after themselves, but the same exorbitant demands are often made before the customary woman is produced; and, should the man marry or cohabit elsewhere, he is then liable to pay compensation on both sides : to his new wife's relatives for having married before being cleared (because it is believed that the spirit of the dead wife will become adverse to the new one if any formalities be omitted), and to the relations of the deceased for not doing as he should.

"So far as I can ascertain, before the arrival of our administration a gun and some beads sufficed for these payments, and earlier a slave and 20 lb. mixed beads. Also then the clearing *had* to take place before the ripening of the next but one kaffir corn crop, after the death. This prevented the abuses that now exist."

The above notes give an aspect that would not appear from the text of the chapter, and I think it merits considerable notice, because no custom has greater ramifications.

Will the reader try to grasp this fact ? *Whenever a person dies there is a case of via u tuzhi.* Each case concerns many people, so that *u tuzhi* is practically everpresent in every family.

I know of many cases in which a family has up to three *u tuzhi* claims pending simultaneously. (Let me be quite clear : three is by no means a maximum, but up to three claims at once is common.) Sometimes these claims occupy so much time that the family has no leisure for anything else. To illustrate this more clearly I will give a concrete example. A family " X " owes *via u tuzhi* for two members by marriage who have died, and is owed for one member also recently deceased. The claims for the former amount to four long guns, two blankets, five double cloths and some beads. The third one was settled at one long and one short gun and three cloths, none of which has yet been paid. The creditors are clamouring for the payments due so that the clearing can proceed. The family has two guns in hand, but they are rejected as not good enough : they try to collect what is due to them in the third case and to exchange their two guns for one good one, and to make up the balance by borrowing, or in some other way.

The above is a *fair* example. The following are illustrative, and it is not to be imagined that one family would have the misfortune to meet with all at once ; though " misfortunes never come singly " holds good with black as with white, and *chanswe* (ill-luck) dogs many a man.

One member of the family has just collected a good

gun towards his *u tuzhi* debts when it is claimed in friendship (see Chapter VIII), so he has to start again. Another lends a gun he has ready to B, who accidentally kills himself with it. The owner is responsible for the accident and pays the gun as the handiest compensation available. A third neglects cultivation and everything else as he wanders about seeking goods to pay : by his wandering he forgets his tax, and on arrival at his home finds he has to sell his hardly cadged goods to pay tax and fine. Here is an actual case which would seem fanciful if it were not on record. A man having had no luck in his search for *u tuzhi* goods is abused by a female relation as a helpless ass. He retaliates with some personal remarks about her chastity. She keeps the ball rolling by saying she would not have a cripple child like his, anyhow ; whereupon he retorts that a cripple is better than none (she was barren). This enrages her so that she calls her husband to protect her and shouts a grossly exaggerated account of the abuse she has received. The husband becomes abusive, and the man can stand no more and hurls his spear at him : result, a sojourn in gaol that puts the *u tuzhi* payment still further back.

This also often happens. " A " has just succeeded by great efforts in paying for two *u tuzhi*, when he becomes liable for a third, and is mulcted extra heavily *because of his recent payments*, i.e. there have been so many deaths among his " in-laws " that if he does not pay up handsomely people will talk of witchcraft. Quite recently a respectable headman divorced a wife for this reason : if she had died it would have been the third death, and he told me he could not afford to risk that.

Now this custom is classed by Europeans as " repugnant to morality and to natural justice " (chiefly because of the " taking the death off the body "). Morality is relative ; and I know of no authoritative definition of NATURAL justice ; but apart from this there is no doubt that there is a great deal to be said against *via u tuzhi* as it stands to-day. The preceding notes show that.

What can be said for its retention and against its prohibition?

Firstly, it is bound up with religion. A person pays his *u tuzhi* debts owing to moral coercion, fear of creating an adverse spirit (*mutala*). We cannot eradicate this custom without undermining the religious belief of the people, for to tamper with moral coercion in one thing tampers with it generally. In the writer's opinion the greater need is to reform, purify and build on the existing religion. One needs to tread warily before interfering with any part of religion. To do so carelessly is to invite chaos, and to put the natives back in their evolution: nearer to the beasts of the field; whereas, surely, we aim at elevating. Not only should we avoid pulling down before we are in a position to build up, but we should start building before we begin to destroy; and this we can only do by building on to the existing structure. To change the metaphor, let us graft on to the existing stock instead of pulling up and attempting to plant anew.

Secondly, among the natives life is not valued highly. This custom is one of the few things that gives any protection to life. Murders for insurance money are not unknown at home. *Via u tuzhi* acts in diametrically the opposite way to insurance-temptation. As a death always mean payment it protects and prolongs life. Even when a man and his wife are bitter enemies the man dreads her death because it will affect his pocket. Personally, I should feel very chary about removing this check. Natives can be extraordinarily callous, and it seems dangerous to remove what is (with fear of *mutala*-making, *vide infra* RELIGION) the sole, or chief, check on their callousness.

Thirdly, it is a very important part of the social

fabric, and we are not in a position to substitute anything for it yet. We are undermining the social fabric too fast as it is, and need not speed up deliberately.

Fourthly, I doubt if we could do more than attempt to remove the custom even if we decided on such action. And an abortive attempt would result in aggravating existing abuses and removing existing checks : it would drive the custom underground.

Although many disagree, it seems to me that the custom is sound in origin. Any custom, until it be codified by statute law or proved and declared by judiciary law, tends to get debased by variations and excrescences. In our own history feudal tenure, the guild system, etc., were sound enough (or suitable enough) originally, but became vicious through abuses. Many native customs are sound at the root and quite suitable for the local stage in evolution ; but they have become or are becoming vicious partly because they are not written or codified, and also partly because *our* advent has hastened evolution unduly.

This seems to me one of the cases in which our help and guidance are needed. To purge the custom rather than reject it. To codify and then support the improved version rather than to penalise it. (Granted we need to purge ourselves of a bit of prejudice to recognise such a custom at all, but since we are supposed to govern in the interests of the governed, why not ?) We have been a destructive force in Africa, and surely we should try to counteract this by helping the natives in such a matter as this.

Because we do not understand the real meaning of such a custom : do not appreciate its importance : do not see what would be the consequences of its removal : in a word, do not grasp the native point of view, we often step in too hastily to prohibit where it would be better to accept, purify and enforce.

CHAPTER VIII

BLOOD BROTHERHOOD OR FORMAL FRIENDSHIP

BULUNDA IN KAONDE ; *UBWAMBU* IN LUNDA

THE custom or civil contract of *bulunda* is, apparently, a very ancient one, the origin of which is now unknown. It ranks next to (possibly equal to) marriage as a civil contract, and has definite obligations on each side.

Commonly translated " friendship," it seems to me that " blood-brotherhood " is a better rendering, especially as the contract is sealed in blood.

My own enquiries among the Ba-Kaonde elicited the invariable reply that no one knew whence this custom came. A colleague (R.E.B.W.) has informed me, however, that " it is said to have reached the Ba-Kaonde via the Alunda, but that it does not owe its name to this circumstance." Another (J.L.K.), investigating the matter among the Alunda, states " the custom is reputed to have come from ' our elders,' and it seems to have originated from an instinct of insuring oneself against misfortune."

One of the innominate contracts known to Roman law found expression in the phrase, " Do ut des." This appears to be the main idea underlying the contract of *bulunda*. Part performance, i.e. the gift of something of material worth, is (as with the Romans) accepted as evidence that such a contract has been made ; and sooner or later the recipient is expected to reciprocate gifts of equal value to those received.

The reasons why A seeks B as his *mulunda* are various, but the evidence seems unanimous that the contract is not, in essence, a disguised form of cadging. A does not seek B as a *mulunda* for the sake of his immediate help in some known difficulty, but as a future ally in possible time of need. It is said that the obligations of a *mulunda* originally were assistance in warfare, in times of famine, in litigation; and that a prudent man would seek, in the hour of his prosperity, for desirable and suitable allies upon whom he could rely in emergency; and with such he contracted *bulunda*.

Besides this, at times, the two who make this contract may be influenced by physical attraction and by community of interests; but this is not a common feature, since *bulunda* is often extra-tribal, and even among fellow-tribesmen is frequently entered into between those who were complete strangers immediately before entering into *bulunda*. Like many customs it appears to have become debased of late—possibly owing to the disintegrating influence of European rule—and while it seems so popular as to be almost universal, it is possible that the " sanctity " of the obligation is looser than of old. Other observers concur in this conclusion. Thus R.E.B.W. :

" Present day *bulunda* is *possibly* (his italics) a debased form of the original conception and probably less binding. It is extremely common and seems to exist among all the local tribes. One gathers that it arises largely from caprice and personal, social or mercenary considerations. Many cases that have come under my notice show that *bulunda* is frequently of only a few years' duration and may be dissolved by a civil suit brought by one of the parties who happens to be dissatisfied with the material benefits that have accrued (or failed to accrue) to him. This dissolution of *bulunda* occurs without any manifestation of regret or animosity on either side."

J.L.K. writes : " It cannot be described as open cadging but, as with many white friendships—through the weakness of human nature—it frequently descends to it." (In my own experience this seems to sum it up admirably.) " In its elements it appears to be a wise custom, also one which adds much to the amenities of local social life, besides being a providence for the unprovidential ; but it is, or should be, entered into according to local law with a sense of responsibility."

When A seeks a *mulunda* he seeks one of his own sex. This is invariable. Man and man : woman and woman ; but if A is *mulunda* to B, A's wife is *mulunda* to B and B's wife to A.

Among the Alunda I myself know, and have had it confirmed by others, a chief can contract *bulunda* with commoners, and a commoner can seek and obtain a chief as his *mulunda*. Mr. Keith says, " In theory anyone can contract *ubwambu* (*bulunda*) with anyone ; but *in practice* it works out, as with Europeans, that those equal in station and interests are usually friends. The seeker need have no precedence in age or position (of this I am certain) : young boys will *kwata* elders as having property or influence ; and an aged man will sometimes *kwata* a boy." Among the Ba-Kaonde the evidence is more conflicting, and different rules may hold good among different sections of the tribe. Mr. Woods writes : "*Bulunda* may exist between a chief and an ordinary native," but chief Kapiji Mpanga (supported by others) emphatically states that it cannot. He told me that he could be *mulunda* with Kasempa, Kalilele (both chiefs) and so on, but not with any except his peers.

As regards the method of contracting. A comes to B's village, meets and likes B. He decides to *kwata* him in friendship. [A note on " *kwata* " is necessary. The verb in its general sense means " catch," but in this connection this meaning is absent. I have had it paraphrased as " ask for." One cannot be " caught into " friendship without at least nominal consent, though—of course—B in a weak moment may agree to contract with A and regret it afterwards ; as we ourselves might say, " I could not help making his acquaintance : he practically forced it on me." Besides this there may be a certain amount of social stigma to one who refuses *bulunda*. He may be considered a bit of a bear, or stingy ; and (among the Álunda) he may be laughed at as *mukung'-kurayo* (empty) for such refusal. R.E.B.W. translates *kwata* in this sense as " to make," " to bring about " ; and he instances for comparison *kwata mambo*, *kwata muzhi*, *kwata bukende*—though the last might equally well be translated " catch " or " contract." The evidence seems unanimous, however, that *kwata* in this sense does not imply a snare or compulsion.]

Having made up his mind, A gives B a dowry-gift just as he would to a woman whom he was seeking as his wife —only in this case it goes to B and not to B's relatives. This gift generally takes the form of a shilling, a cup, or some other small article. After this has been accepted either party can begin the serious obligations, although it is generally A (the seeker). This stage may be represented by a gift of cloth or a gun or any other article(s) of value ; and it may be almost simultaneous with the first small gift or it may follow later. The other party subsequently returns the compliment.

The contract is " sealed in blood." Each of the contracting parties (Kaonde) makes a slight incision in the wrist or arm of the other and drinks a drop of the blood therefrom. This is just before the gift of substantial value is given. Among the Alunda blood is taken from the chest and mixed with beer and drunk with solemn affirmations of eternal *ubwambu*.

Once the contract is sealed each must support his " friend." As to how far this obligation goes opinion differs, and no doubt a great deal depends on the individual idea as to the obligation ; but, generally

speaking, a man will come to the aid of his *mulunda* so
far as can be reasonably expected. I have been informed
on many occasions that (among the Kaonde) the totem
invariably has precedence over *bulunda*, i.e. A would help
C of his own totem against B his *mulunda* should there
be a quarrel between C and B. There is, however
(says R.E.B.W.), a local saying " *Bulunda mukoka* "
(" the *bulunda* is the totem ") which is taken to mean
that the ties between " friends " are as close as those
binding members of a totem ; and I think we may take
it that these ties are as close (or " sacred ") when not in
conflict with totem. The Alunda have no totems, but
family ties among them have precedence over *ubwambu*
(*bulunda*) ; but, on the other hand, *ubwambu* has precedence over tribal ties.

In both tribes hospitality and friendship to a *mulunda's*
relations are imperative. I know of a case where a man
paid the debts of the wife of his brother's *mulunda* (the
debts were big to set her free from slavery). In both
tribes, too, A besides giving shelter and food to his
mulunda B, may allow him access to his wife (generally
if A has more than one). It would appear, however,
that while among the Ba-Kaonde this is recognised,
among the Alunda it is done but not recognised. Probably this was originally foreign to Lunda ideas, but as
many Alunda have *bulunda* with Ba-Kaonde, occasions
arose in which this hospitality would be given by a Kaonde
host to his Lunda guest and *mulunda*. When the Lunda's
turn came to be host he might naturally feel bound to
extend the same privilege to his friend. Thus the custom
would spread, and would be practised even between two
Alunda. However, it is not yet recognised by Lunda
law. " When B comes to stay," writes J.L.K., " A
removes his wife from the bed, and B sleeps thereon :
the host (A) and his wife sleeping on the floor. The wife
does not always sleep on the floor, but that is not talked
about and is contrary to local law." And again : " It is

strictly against Lunda custom for A to offer his wife to B ; but when A has more than one wife he frequently extends this hospitality," i.e. the practice is the same among both tribes : the law alone differs.

Among both tribes a man has no right to approach the wife of his *mulunda* without his permission : to do so is ordinary adultery—neither more nor less than in a case where there is no *bulunda*. In such cases, however, A—if a " gentleman "—would not make much fuss about it, and B (if he also answered to that description) would be expected to settle the matter with some suitable compensation. If A were to bring an action against B for the adultery the *bulunda* between them would probably cease (and so with any claim for goods, if it " comes into court " the contract of *bulunda* is at an end . . . this is sometimes deliberately done to wind up a *bulunda* which has become tiresome. Really the natives are not so unlike Europeans at times !).

As regard sisters there appears to be a distinction. Among the Alunda, if A sleeps with the sister of his *mulunda* B, action would lie against A by the woman's husband if she were married ; but if she were single she would very naturally be suggested as a temporary companion for A, and no one would think anything of it. Among the Ba-Kaonde, however, a man must treat his *mulunda's* sister as his own sister—even to the extent of sexual exclusion.

The form in which *bulunda* comes before us (officials) is generally with reference to claims, which may be recent claims, or old ones or inherited claims. It is important, therefore, to get an idea of native law on the subject.

Bulunda debts rank with any other debts, e.g. A gives B a gun in *bulunda*. B, therefore, automatically owes a gun or its equivalent to A. This is just as much a debt as if B had bought a goat, or had received some service, and had not paid for it, the fact that the gun was given him as an entirely unsolicited gift being considered irrelevant. Mr. Woods says that he does not think that such cases were submitted to chiefs' courts in former times, but I cannot agree to this. I am credibly informed that chiefs often settled such cases, and that even when A and B were of different tribes living far apart such cases would be judged in a chief's court (always before the defaulter's chief), and that he had full power to adjudicate. This is a good proof of how binding the *bulunda* contract appears to the native. A Mulamba native, for instance, would cheerfully sue a Kalunda, living 200 miles away, before the defendant's own chief, knowing well that, if his claim were just, he would get the verdict. In such case the chief not only found for the plaintiff but forced defendant to pay. The " force," I am informed, was moral : nominally no penalties attached for failure to obey the order of the court. As with other debts among these tribes, *bulunda* obligations are hereditary, not personal. The debts do not die with the debtor. If A owes B a gun under this contract and dies with the debt unpaid, B or B's heirs can sue A's heirs.

This part agrees more or less with Lunda ideas, which I give in Mr. Keith's own words :

" The crime of lese-*ubwambu* was considered only second in importance to breaches of the marriage customs. In the old days if A did not receive anything from B after due lapse of time (presuming he himself had fulfilled his obligations), he would consult with his elders about the strength of his case and then go to the headman of B's village, before whom he would lodge his claim. His case proved, the headman would order B to pay. If B said he would do so later on, A would then return to his home, and if the promise did not materialise he would apply again in due course. Then unless B were morally forced by his elders to pay, A would return again to B's village and would seize the first child he could catch and make off with it. From his home he would send a message to B's village saying that B was responsible for this abduction, owing to his falseness, and that the parents of the child had better proceed against B. (In smaller cases a gun of C's, a fellow-villager with B, would be seized instead of a child.) In any case the parent of the child, or owner of the gun, would have no claim against A : only against B."

With regard to *bulunda* among women it seems that the procedure is similar, but that everything is more trivial. Their presents generally consist of honey or a little food, and the obligations and duties amount to no more than mutual help in looking after each other's children and so on.

As regards the etymology of the words. No one seems to know the origin of the words " *mulunda*," " *bulunda*." There is no relevant verb " *ku-lunda*." The word *mulunda* takes an irregular form of the possessive pronoun *Mulundnami* (*mulunda nami*) instead of *mulunda wami*. " A friend with me," and not " my friend," so in the other persons :

> *Mulunda nami* not *mulunda wami*.
> *Mulunda nowe* not *mulunda wowe*.
> *Mulunda nanje* not *mulunda wanje*, etc.

Turning to the Lunda words *Ubwambu* (friendship) and *Ibwambu* (friend) there is a verb *kwambula* " to divide into two equal parts," which has the same root, so *Ubwambu* seems to mean "Equality." " *Ibwambu dyami*," " my equal " and so " my ' friend.' "

In conclusion, it may be said that the custom is very old and exceedingly popular, as it proved by its general use. As with many old customs (excellent in origin) abuses are creeping in. Some people, such as alien natives, occasionally get *bulunda* with the less sophisticated locals and take care to burden them with debt until they are nearly enslaved. Even between local natives I have met with several cases in which the *bulunda* has been made an intolerable burden. This is not the fault of the custom but of abuse in practice : it should not be difficult to eradicate (or penalise) such examples without hurting the general idea.

A little sidelight occurred not long ago. A chief who has a perennial stock of grievances was talking to me, and after a bit I said " I wish you would drop this attitude. I would like, as representing the Administration, to make *bulunda* with you, as a chief. Then we could support and help each other, without so much bickering and mistrust." He promptly replied :

" We chiefs would gladly make *bulunda* with the *Boma* (Government), but we cannot, for with the *Boma* it is all take and no give ; and that is contrary to the spirit of *bulunda*."

Of course, he was wrong ; but it tends to show that so far we have failed *to show the natives* the benefits which our Administration has conferred upon them : wherefore they see only the irksome restrictions, the tax and other disadvantages which we have to impose. Although I do not believe that we have done all we could or should for the native races over whom we rule, it is a fact that they have benefited considerably, and in many ways, by our government, only we have been curiously lax about explaining the benefits of our rule to them. We take these benefits for granted : they remain ignorant of them. If we made them a little more patent we might yet get some kind of *bulunda* with the chiefs, to the benefit of the whole community.

CHAPTER IX

ALL THE YEAR ROUND

IN trying to sketch a Kaonde year it is only possible to detail the occupations that a native would have if he were at home all the year ; but it must be borne in mind that he is not.

Many natives go away for at least three months' work, besides a month spent going to and from the place of employment—four months in all : some may be away much longer ; but, on an average, we can say that a man is away for two months in the year at work. (If not actually at work he will spend at least as long going round trying to borrow money for his tax, or hawking a gun about the country on which he hopes to realise sufficient money to meet his liabilities.)

Besides work the ordinary native will be absent from his home for a considerable time on his own affairs— ordinary visiting, generally to a village where there is mourning and, *ergo*, beer and dancing ("wakes") : going to his mother-in-law's village (if he does not live there) to work for her. (*Vice versa*, going to his own people's village if he lives at his mother-in-law's) : doing possibly a bit of tree-cutting or fencing for his chief ; and, above all, journeys in connection with *via u tuzhi* and *bulunda* (q.v. Chapters VII and VIII). Both of these necessitate (*a*), trying to collect goods due to him, and (*b*), trying to collect goods which he has to pay to someone else. It is no exaggeration to say that some natives spend six months in a year on this kind of thing ; for though one man will probably only have one *bulunda* collection in hand at a time, he may easily be connected with two or three *u tuzhi* simultaneously. It will be a conservative estimate to say that an average native will spend ninety days a year on visits of one kind and another. Added to the two months spent away at work we have a total of five months a year absence from the village, which means that he has to put in the year's home work into seven months, or (as is often the case) leave much of it undone.

Then, again, if he has neglected his cultivation, he will spend all the more time hunting game with his gun, hunting small game—such as cane rats—with his dog ; collecting honey, wild fruits, roots and other food ; or visiting villages where he can cadge food. The lazy man will often " work " as hard in this way as the industrious cultivator : just as the chronic " work-shy " will spend more months in raising 10s. on his second-best gun (which no one wants) than he would in earning £1 or £2 at work.

Another cause of lengthy absence is getting married, or courting. In practice it generally amounts to short periods of experimental marriage, called " trying the woman " (not, I believe, unknown in village life at home). He will wander over the country for a year or more, so engaged, before finally considering himself settled.

Last, but perhaps not least, one must allow for sickness in a country where illness has to take its own course to a large extent, and time is the chief healer. In sickness one can include, too, " that tired feeling " and lack of application (except when convenient) which is endemic. Much time, moreover, will be taken over matters concerned with divination, births, *chisungu* and other affairs that are dealt with elsewhere in this book. [It will be obvious to any reader that these must absorb considerable time.]

One realises, therefore, that it would be an exceptional (probably unique) man who carried out the complete programme sketched in the following pages ; but, if this be borne in mind, it can be taken as an accurate summary of what some natives are doing throughout the country at the different seasons.

The actual day's work is not a very long one. It might be from 7 to 11 a.m. (sometimes only from 7 to 9) which accounts for the extraordinary time taken to complete a job, be it preparation of a garden, building a hut, or what not—and the prevalence of uncompleted jobs, e.g. when a native has worked steadily, and has got his hut sufficiently advanced for it to be habitable, he is tempted to live in it and rest from his toil (or from that particular toil), postponing the completion till the morrow—the morrow that never comes. Again, while many natives—especially if the headman be a good one—fence their gardens really well, others find their energy exhausted after preparing the fields, with the result that the bush pigs and other crop-thieves take a large percentage of their food.

The rest of the day will be spent sitting, and talking, and smoking, or "just sitting": doing odd jobs like mat-making, sharpening a spear, whittling down a new haft for an axe, or a porridge spoon: scraping and softening a skin, or patching an ancient garment. There are always little things to be done; and, except in the case of the aged, a native's hands are rarely idle. It must be remembered that every tool, utensil, gadget, has to be made at home—from Nature's raw material, and repaired at home—with home-made tools; e.g. if natives want a bit of wood for any purpose they must not only cut a tree to obtain it, but must make the axe to cut that tree, and find the stone whereon to sharpen the axe.

With these preliminary remarks we will detail the year's work. The preliminaries doubtless seem rather long, and very petty; but they are necessary to realise the actual life of natives in primitive self-supporting communities like these, and to prevent the common error that " the native never does anything." True, he fritters away a lot

A CHISUNGU GIRL.

The beads in her hair are a noticeable feature. (The tribe is Kaonde).

of his time : the results of his busyness are often disappointing ; but he does do a lot one way and another. Sometimes—when one finds a really well-built village, with fine large cultivations, enclosed in strong fences of great length, and so on—one wonders how the inhabitants have found time for it all. The answer generally is a strong-minded active headman. *Per contra* the dirty, ill-built and ill-kept village, scanty crops, etc., betoken the weak headman, and a shiftless, cadging population.

The following are Kaonde seasons (the rains, which average about 50 inches, fall from mid-October to end of April) :

Summer (*Mayo*), roughly from December to May.

Winter (*Mwera*), roughly May to July.

Spring (*Chisalo* or *Milemba*), roughly August to October.

Beginning of Rains (*Chiwundo*), about November.

The seasons (likewise the months) depend on the changes of Nature rather than on a calendar, so the times are approximate only.

The year is divided into thirteen moons, and the following is a list with the nearest English month inserted. The year seems to start best with August-September, and to end with July-August. For simplicity's sake I give two Septembers, thus bringing the months to thirteen like the moons.

Month	Name	Description
September	*Kanyinganyinga*	Good green leaves on trees.
September	*Kafuketo*	
October	*Ntundwe*	Too hot with sun.
November	*Kapande*	Start sowing.
December	*Kavumbi*	Heavy rains.
January	*Kakubo*	Rain ; old food finished.
February	*Chisaka*	Early new crops ready.
March	*Kasafia*	Rivers full (like " February fill-dyke ").
April	*Ndolo*	Eat corn, beans, etc.
May	*Kapepukachi*	Cold starts.

June	*Chishikana*	Leaves burn and dry with cold.
July	*Kapyantoto*	Grass fires start (an onomatopœic word).
August	*Kasarakanduba*	Leaves replaced by red spring leaves.

(In compiling the above lists I have used largely notes by C.H.H.)

The Year's Routine

In giving, month by month, the occupations of the Ba-Kaonde, two things should be borne in mind : (1) The men and women spend the day almost entirely apart. Except for a few things like weeding and hoeing each has his, or her, own appointed task, and generally these tasks lie in different directions. When not working it is the same : they feed apart, sit apart, talk apart ; (2) the *mebele* (kaffir corn) is the staple crop, and it is this that is grown on the biggest scale, and entails most work in preparation : in sowing, reaping, threshing and grinding. The method of growing it is that used over large parts of Africa. Big areas of the woodland are cut down—the Ba-Kaonde being poor climbers do not pollard the trees as do the Wawemba and other tribes, but cut them low down and then lop off the branches—the branches are gathered together in heaps, and, when dry, are burnt, which action destroys the roots of grass and weeds, and lessens the subsequent toil of cultivation : incidentally it also enriches the ground. The seed is sown in these patches, and the large acreage containing several of the patches is then fenced to keep out pig and other animals. The other crops (maize, sweet potatoes, beans, etc.) are grown as subsidiary crops ; and in varying degrees : some villages having much variety, and others but little.

The everyday tasks (which will be found enumerated for each sex in Chapter IV) are not repeated here, e.g.

fetching water and firewood, cooking, mat-making, washing, mending, pot-making, etc.; but it must be borne in mind that they are going on continuously.

Kanyinganyinga. THE MAN has an easy time this month. He may be helping his wife in the garden work, or may be out hunting, or getting honey, or merely staying in the village. THE WOMAN is busy hoeing the low-ground gardens, and sowing the early mealies and beans. GENERAL: Honey beer season begins and lasts about three months. This is a favourite month for hippo-hunting.

Kafuketa. THE MAN: the same as last month, plus salt making if near a pan. For THE WOMAN a continuation of last month's work.

Ntundwe. THE MAN: same as last month, also collecting the following wild fruits: *makusu, mpundu, fungo, sokomene, makonkola, mawingo,* as they ripen. (Note. The Ba-Kaonde do not eat caterpillars, but with other local tribes collecting the edible varieties begins now.) He will also begin hunting the cane rat (*nzenzhi*), which is a great delicacy, and will also be spearing fish in drying up pools. THE WOMAN is occupied much as in the previous months, sowing more mealies, beans and pumpkins, and watering the seedlings already sown.

Kapande. THE MAN: much the same, but the following additional wild fruits should also be ready now: *nsole, nsafwa* and *mindu.* He is getting busier now as an agriculturist and has to hoe in the high gardens, and begins fencing the low gardens, and planting ground nuts. He will also have to set fish traps (generic name *muvuwa*) of the kind called *yamba.* THE WOMAN sows mealies on higher ground gardens than hitherto, and at the end of the month starts sowing kaffir corn. She is busy weeding the early gardens as the grass is growing fast, and helps her husband sowing ground nuts.

Kavumbi. For THE MAN collecting wild fruits continues and the *musongwasongwa* is now also ripe. He has to dig the sweet potato beds. Starts fencing the high gardens. THE WOMAN plants the sweet potato slips in the beds prepared by her husband. She also collects mushrooms this month. BOTH sow the small red millet (*luku*) this month (in the high gardens : prepared similarly to the kaffir corn gardens). They also join in hoeing and weeding the kaffir corn.

Kakubo. BOTH MAN AND WOMAN are fully occupied hoeing and weeding during this month. UNMARRIED WOMEN go to live in shelters called *katungu* in the low gardens to look after the crops. The following are beginning to be ripe : mealies and pumpkins.

Chisaka. THE MAN is stacking mealie cobs on a scaffold (*nkalanga*) to dry, and also has to be cutting poles for any hut-building that is necessary. THE WOMAN gathers mealies (*mataba*), pumpkins (generic name *myungu* : there are three varieties called *vilenge, misungu, machimpa*), cucumbers (called *vyakala* or *viwimbi*), beans (*nkunde*). She is also busy storing food. This is the month, too, when she must collect the swamp grass called *malalo*, from which she makes the *chilalo* mats. GENERAL : this month and the next month are the months for mealie beer. Also, as food is plentiful, this month is the time for the first stage in *chisungu* ceremonies.

Kasafia. THE MAN's chief work is to fence the sweet potatoes and nuts, and to place the poles in position for hut-building. THE WOMAN continues to store food, and gets busy pounding grain. She muds the walls of the huts which her husband has put up.

Ndolo. THE MAN goes on building huts, and makes scaffolds for drying the *luku*. He has to smoke it (*kufita*) by burning fire under the scaffold. He cuts thatching grass, and starts thatching. THE WOMAN reaps the *luku*, digs sweet potatoes and nuts. At the end of the month THE CHILDREN go bird scaring (by day) in the *mebele* gardens. BOTH MEN AND WOMEN go trapping fish in the kind of fish traps (*muvuwa*) known specifically as *chiwinji* or *wa ngwashi*, and in a smaller kind known as *musalala*.

Kapepukachi. THE MAN : tree-cutting for the next year's gardens—continuous. WOMEN AND CHILDREN : bird-scaring in *mebele* gardens, all through daylight. Even the grain-pounding is done in the gardens. GENERAL : There is *luku* beer this month, and much *mebele* beer : the latter is plentiful for three months. Road-cleaning generally starts now, the women scuffling and the men building and mending bridges : this is not " indigenous," but done for the Government.

Chishikana. THE MAN : tree-cutting as last month. Also fish poisoning (stupefying) by means of the *wululu* or *bubwa* starts this month and continues next. In this THE WOMAN joins : her main work is reaping the *mebele*.

Kapyantoto. THE MAN starts building temporary grain stores (*vitala*) for the *mebele*. This and the two preceding months iron smelting (where practised) : also in the month of *kapande* (these months are chosen because beer is then plentiful). THE WOMAN is busy threshing *mebele* and taking it to the *vitala*. GENERAL : *Chisungu* ceremonies end.

Kasarakanduwa. THE MAN builds permanent grain stores (*matala*) for the *mebele* and cuts the *jitambo* (trees in the *jito*, or swamp groves) for early mealie gardens. The woman takes the *mebele* from the *vitala* to the *matala*.

General Notes. From choice a man would choose *Kanyinganyinga* to *Ntundwe* as the months during which he would be absent at work, earning money for tax and other things ; returning in *Kapande* when his share of work gets strenuous.

Of old, *Chisaka* was the month for a campaign, as food was then plentiful among the enemies, and also easily obtained on the march.

Kanyinganyinga is a favourite month for elephant hunting, as the natives have then plenty of food to take with them into the bush : also (for the same reason) *kapepukachi* and *chishikana* (and, as regards *kape-pukachi*, because honey is then plentiful in the bush).

Visonga (raphia) for the *mukeka* mats can be got all the year round, as can bark for bark-cloth. Hunting also takes place all the year, and likewise trapping.

CHAPTER X

RELIGION (I)

" Religion : a habitual, all-pervading sense of dependence on, reverence for, and responsibility to, a higher power ; . . . any system of faith and worship. . . ."—Nuttall's Standard Dictionary.

THE above definition seems to justify the use of the word " Religion "—rather than " Superstition," or merely " Beliefs "—as applied to the beliefs of the Kaonde and similar tribes. *" Habitual, all-pervading sense of dependence on a higher power "* is a very fair summary of their religion ; and if religion is to be judged by faith, then their religion stands high. The followers of nobler forms of religion may often envy the sincere, complete and unquestioning faith of the natives of Africa whose " higher power " is their family spirits : a faith so real that it almost literally removes mountains ; a faith that makes the most incredible things credible, the most preposterous reasonable.

Surely those who consider these tribes irreligious are wrong, as are those who glibly describe them as immoral ? Their religious beliefs are not ours, any more than is their standard of morals ours : but there is more real adherence, and less lip service, to both with the majority of these Bantu races than there is with most of us. At any rate, it is impossible to understand any tribe like the Kaonde, Lunda, etc., unless one realises what their religion is, and what it means to them, because their religion pervades the whole of their life—and without grasping what it is we cannot understand their lives.

Further, we must approach it with respect. Contempt and derision are out of place. To assert arrogantly to them that their religion is an inferior one (or none at all) closes the door on us, and renders understanding impossible (likewise conversion).

We may feel superior : we have a right to do so ; but we tend to show it too much. We prate of native customs and beliefs being " contrary to *natural* justice and morality," meaning that they are contrary to *our* ideas. We do not always grasp that the natives feel just as superior towards us in many ways. Sometimes one gets an insight into it, however. Recently I heard of a native who had been falsely accused of incest with his mother, remarking, " Why, even a white man would consider that an insult ! " Ponder on that word " even " ! How often do we say, " Why, I should have thought that even a native would have had more sense," and so on.

The proper spirit for approaching the subject of native religion (and through it native life) seems to me to have been indicated in Kipling's lines :

> " For those who kneel beside us
> At altars not Thine Own :
> Who lack the Lights that guide us,
> Lord ! Let their faith atone."

Whilst they lack that Light, let their faith atone for seeming faults, and let it explain much that would otherwise be inexplicable.

WHAT IS THEIR RELIGION ? A BELIEF IN THE SPIRITS OF THE DEPARTED (THEIR FAMILY SPIRITS AND ALL OTHER SPIRITS), AND IN THE REINCARNATION OF THESE SPIRITS IN THE LIVING.

Firstly, let us grasp this salient fact. No native (of these and similar tribes) ever feels free from the spirits. *We* say, " God is everywhere " : *they* say, " The spirits are everywhere." *We* say, " God knoweth all, seeth all " . . .: *they* say the same of the spirits. The spirits are

MOTHER AND CHILD.

The tatoo marks are clearly visible on the woman's arm and body. They have no special tribal signification. The wrap is made of bark cloth.

with the native all his life, and more : from his conception till his death, and continuing thereafter, they are with him. No native does anything without being influenced wittingly or otherwise by spirits. In the majority of cases it is a spirit that causes death directly or indirectly. All life is a fight against adverse spirits, and (therefore) one continual propitiation of good spirits. Nothing of importance can be undertaken without first propitiating the spirits : nothing can be explained without divining for the spirits concerned. The spirits are all-hearing, all-seeing, all-pervading, all-powerful. Nothing but spirits (and in some cases, prescribed payments) can counteract spirits : none but the witch-doctor can show how this is to be effected. Man himself is impotent.

Let us turn from the general to the particular, and note a few representative examples.

The chronic inability to speak the truth, which is so well-known a feature of these races, is sometimes misunderstood. It is not viciousness (frequently the transparency of the lie should make that much patent), but it is a *virtue* taught to all at childhood : the reason being the necessity to deceive the overhearing adverse spirits, and put them " off the track." (Being simple folk it does not appear to them incongruous that such powerful spirits are so easily deceived.) If one grasps that " Thou shalt not speak the truth " is, practically, a commandment, one ceases to wonder at recurrent pointless and obvious lies.

Again, if one realises that it is because the spirits are unpropitious that a village is built on a poor site, when there is a good site adjacent; or that a good village is abandoned entailing much hardship and work, then one does not consider the natives to be such fools as at first appears. One hesitates to call genuine faith folly.

Or, when natives start on a journey, long premeditated, but return before they have reached their destination, it is hasty to conclude that they are like the bandar-log and

have forgotten what they set out to do. Investigation
will show that they have met, say, a live *zere* (form of
grasshopper) on the path, and *dare not* flout the spirits
by continuing after so clear a warning that they should
abandon their project.

So, too, when one sees a man honestly confess to a sin of
which he is innocent, because he has been convicted in a
manner sanctioned by custom, one gets some idea of
native faith.

Above all, when one sees and understands these things,
one begins to understand how and why the witch-doctor
is THE power in the land : since he alone can divine,
interpret, prophesy, show the means of propitiating,
counteracting, circumventing the forces of life. He
alone can help when spirits trouble. He alone can avert
death (or avenge it) by naming a witch or indicating
which of the departed is the cause of trouble.

Then comes the natural conclusion that superstition
(religious credulity run riot) retards all progress ; and
must be circumvented if these races (who are our wards)
are to progress : but to circumvent it one must first
understand it to differentiate between it and the real
religion, and deal with it sympathetically—not try to
cure it by derisory denial, nor (so it seems to me) by
over-emphasising the miraculous in our own religion,
nor by confusing the native mind with dogma (which
is nearly as retarding in its influence as superstition).
Understanding, education, and the spirit of the Sermon
on the Mount, are probably the first steps in removing
the curse of Africa—the witch-doctor ; remembering
that we will never remove (or render harmless) the witch-
doctor until we remove the need for him.

To the native mind there is little that is wonderful
in Jehovah smiting Egypt with plagues ; in Aaron
turning his stick into a snake ; or even in most of the
miracles of Jesus Christ. To practical or material people
like ourselves these things are miraculous, and, therefore,

impressive : the natives can equal them from their own experience,[1] so such things do not impress them with the superiority (or extra-divinity) of our religion : rather do they tend to the idea that there is not much difference after all between the two.

There is an even greater danger than this with regard to many of the miracles in the Bible. To the native mind some of them are of the type only accomplished by wizardry, i.e. they are not an act of God (or of His servants) but are " the work of the devil " ; for while to them their religion—the belief in the family spirits and in reincarnation—is sacred, witchcraft (which may be the relic of an older religion which is dying hard) is an abomination, precisely as it was in Europe. It seems to me that if we emphasise the working of certain miracles by holy men, " servants of God," we risk making our religion seem unclean and thus tend to make the natives harden their hearts and suspect the real essentials in Christianity.

The above is not written provocatively : this book has no such aims ; but it seems necessary to show why an understanding of the chief influence in native life is absolutely necessary for all who live and work amongst natives, and to help that understanding by detailing as much as is possible of native religion ; since, though it may not seem much in our eyes, it is everything to them.

The reader must not expect anything very remarkable or sensational. The religion has no ritual to speak of, no temples, and no priesthood—only the witch-doctor is always in evidence. It is just " a habitual and all-pervading sense of dependence," accompanied by a few simple prayers and rites : just what might be expected from such simple agricultural people living a primitive communal life, and believing implicitly and devoutly in reincarnation.

Further, in this section more than in any other, it must be understood that these notes are very incomplete. It is harder to get details about religion than about anything else from such people. Reticence is natural; and, moreover, there are many things that they cannot—dare not—discuss.

The first element in this religion is

" CHIMVULE "

In a man's lifetime he has his *chimvule* : everything has a *chimvule* : the trees, rocks, huts, everything—it is a shadow.

When a man dies his corpse is buried, but not the shadow. The shadow remains in the village where he lived—his soul, his spirit : it is still called *chimvule* (it is also then called *mufu*).[2]

These shades of the departed are the " higher power " of the natives' religion; it is on them that they have the habitual all-pervading sense of dependence. It is the shades who guard and protect them, the shades who try to hurt them, the shades are those to whom they pray, the shades are those whom they fear and must placate. The shades are that from which they can never escape. It is the shades who control every act and thought.

As there are many kinds of people : relations, friends ; people whom one has befriended ; those whom one has injured, angered or slighted ; open enemies, hidden enemies, hereditary (vendetta) enemies, personal enemies, and so on, so are there many kinds of *vimvule*.

The man who loses his shadow. Sometimes a man, who wants to live for a very long time, decides to " bottle " his shadow (*chimvule*) and takes it—I cannot discover how, but it does not need a witch-doctor's assistance: either the man does it for himself, or asks the help of a *mulunda*—and puts it into an antelope horn. Then he hides it somewhere, e.g. in a hole in the ground, believing that, if his shadow be safe, he cannot die. This is a risky undertaking, however, as, if the horn gets destroyed, lost or stolen, the man has then lost his shadow, and will die within the year.

A man may have his shadow eaten by a form of witch-craft " familiar," called *nkala* (*vide infra* WITCHCRAFT), which kills him.

WA-KISHI

The family spirits (or spirits of departed ancestors). (R.E.B.W. tells me the word *Mupashi* is also used for *mukishi* : e.g. " *Mupashi wami wankwasha* "= my good spirit has helped me. I had heard it, but thought it was a " foreign " word, but I gather now that it is really Chikaonde.)

The Ba-Kaonde pray to their *Wa-kishi* at any time (to pray to= *kupeshya*). They consider that these spirits are at all times accessible to sup-plication ; but there are also special occasions on which it is customary and advisable to pray to them. Such arise when about to proceed on a journey, before going hunting, when setting out to seek work, when ill, and on similar occasions.

A Chipanda

The " altar " at which the praying is done, and offerings made, is a stick, called *chipanda* *wa. wa-kishi*, which is made of the wood of any of the following three trees : *Musole, Kawalawala* or *Muwumbu*.[3] The *chipanda* is stationed outside the verandah of the hut, on the side near the door. It may be a stick, as in sketch, or an inconspicuous branch, as in photograph, or an erection surmounted by horns, etc. At any ordinary prayer a little flour is taken, or some *mpemba* (white clay) which is sprinkled (A) at the base of the *chipanda*, the supplicant praying thus as he sprinkles it :

" Ye spirits, spirits of my departed ancestors, protect me on my journey (or, let my hunting prosper, and so on) and guard my children and keep them safe while I am away."

He then places some of the flour (or *mpemba*) on his face, between the eyes, and at each side of the eyes; and similarly on the faces of his children if he is praying for their protection in his absence.

Another time for prayers to the *Wa-kishi* is preparatory to the reaping of the crops (kaffir corn=*mebele*). A little

Luembo.

of the first fruit of the corn (*mebele ya nsomo*) is taken and ground, after which it is mixed with water and placed on the ground by the *chipanda* of the village headman : what remains is placed at the cross-roads

near the village (*mansang'a*). Then libations follow. Beer is made one night from corn that is not quite ripe (*ntongo*). The next day at sunrise the *luembo* or *luonge* (a kind of gong, part of hereditary insignia) is sounded, and the beer is drunk ceremoniously. Dancing follows and then some *nkula* (powdered red bark) is placed on the right cheek and *mpemba* on the left. This is done to everyone—men, women and children. The *nkula* is especially for the spirits of those who in their lifetime were guilty of homicide. If any worshipper himself has ever killed anyone he

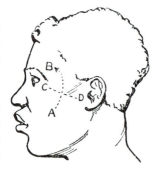

rubs his *nkula* upwards from the right cheekbone to the forehead above the right eye (from A to B), then repeating the process on the left side with the *mpemba*.

If any worshipper has inherited the name of a homicide, or if he has been named by the name of one, he moves the *nkula* and *mpemba* above his cheeks from C to D (near to the ear).

The above is all before the reaping starts. When it starts two or three heads of corn are taken by the cultivators and placed on the *vi-panda :* a private individual will place one on the headman's *chipanda*, one on his own,

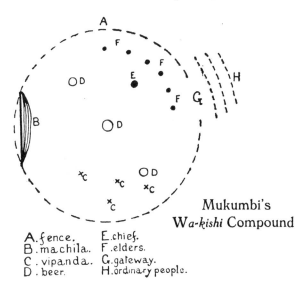

Mukumbi's Wa-*ḳishi* Compound

A.fence.   E.chief.
B.machila.   F.elders.
C.vipanda.   G.gateway.
D.beer.   H.ordinary people.

and one on a friend's. The headman will place one on his own and the others on any other *chipanda*.

After a fight was another time for general prayer to the *Wa-ḳishi*. With the skulls of the slain before them the survivors placed the (red) feathers of the *nduwa* bird in their hair, and offered up prayers for the departed and for themselves. If a man had killed one foe he placed one feather in his hair on the right side of his head : if he had killed two or more he placed a bunch of feathers in his hair on the left side.

Chief Mukumbi Luwinga has a *wa-kishi* compound, in which are the *vi-panda* of his *Wa-kishi*. He pays a ceremonial visit to this once every year at the reaping season ; and he and the elders offer libations of beer to the spirits, and pray to them. When this takes place he takes with him the empty machila (hammock) of his predecessor, and hangs it on the inside of the fence of the compound while the prayers are in progress. The machila is kept at his hut the rest of the year ; but it is not specially sacred and can be used ordinarily on any day except the prayer day.

Chief Kapiji Mpanga Mwandwe has the following ritual. Before the first reaping of the *mebele* (kaffir corn) crop each year (and, of old, before starting on a campaign) he places stakes all round an anthill. Then inside the circle of stakes a row of *vi-panda* made of *muwumbu* wood (one *chipanda* for each person whom he has inherited) are placed by a deputy. The chief must not do this himself. The deputy then prays ; and by each *chipanda* a hole is dug into which beer is poured. Dancing, feasting and drinking last all through the day on which this ceremonial takes place.

Other chiefs have other varieties of ceremonial prayer.

The offerings made to the *Wa-kishi* after a successful elephant hunt are described under Hunting.

Iron working. The Southern Ba-Kaonde do not appear to have been iron workers, preferring to buy their tools from the Mambwera ; but the northern section used to work a good deal both in iron and copper.

Iron workers formed a kind of guild, and the secrets of the craft were handed on from father to son. The worker in iron, having been initiated by his father (deceased) would take a *chipanda* of *muwumbu* wood on the day before starting his work ; and, after placing a circle of flour at the foot of it, would pray to the *mukishi* of his father :

" Oh ! Spirit of my father : who worked iron here of
yore,
Listen to me, and hear my prayer.
To-morrow I, too, will work at the iron.
I pray thee, help me, and guide my work, that it may
prosper."

If the *mukishi* be adverse the ore will turn to water and not
to iron. Such adverse attitude will follow if the prayer
be not offered up properly.

At the smelting operations the workers must avoid
intercourse of any kind with womenfolk. This appears
to be merely a taboo : to break it would be merely
busanda and it is not connected with the spirits.

Among the Alunda iron work is much more intertwined with spirit worship, and every part of the
apparatus is sacred, and being ordained by divine custom
cannot be changed. We tried to introduce a simple
but much more effective bellows among Alunda iron
workers, the special merit of which was that it saved a
great waste of time and energy. Several of these bellows
were made at Mwinilunga by a native (under supervision) from a model made at Kalene Hill Mission, and
Mr. Bruce Miller had hopes that they would be of great
assistance to the smiths. They indeed admitted the
superiority of the new model and its simplicity, but they
would not use it, as the innovation would have
aroused the spirits to anger. In another case a Kalunda
smith who was making a regular income from his smithy
stopped work for a year because the spirit of his deceased
wife was adverse.

These small examples throw some light upon the uphill task that confronts all who try to help the local
Bantu to advance : one continually comes up against the
wall called " Custom," which being considered divine is
(at present) insurmountable.

There is one marked difference between the Lunda and

the Kaonde smelters which may be connected with this difference in sanctity as regards the craft. Those of the Kaonde are of the ordinary cone-shape, and quite plain. The Lunda smelters are of fantastic shapes, generally representing the human figure, with certain members thereof unnecessarily enlarged ; and on the construction of these smelters great pains are taken and great ingenuity exercised.

This is one of the signs that make one think that the Alunda are more ritualistic than the Ba-Kaonde (I understand that the Valuena on the other side of the Ba-Kaonde are still more so) whereas the Ba-Kaonde have more glimmerings of a theistic belief than their western neighbours.

Bena-mikola—the spirits of the place (literally : " of the rivers ") and ghosts of previous inhabitants—known or unknown (*not* family spirits). The Ba-Kaonde pray to the *Bena-mikola* when starting new gardens near their existing village ; and when selecting the site for a new village.

When starting new gardens two small anthills

(*mafwafwa*) are lifted and placed leaning against each other so as to make a kind of arch (A). Under these a little food is placed (B) and the cultivators pray as follows :

" Ye who lived and died here long ago : ye spirits of these streams, be propitious and let these gardens that we are about to make be productive, and bring forth abundantly in due season."

Similarly at the reaping a little offering is made to the *Bena-mikola* on the spot, in addition to the offering made to the *Wa-kishi* at the village.

When choosing a site for a new village great care has to be taken to find that the spirits of the locality are not adverse ; for to fail in this is to invite disaster of some kind or other to the community.

When a likely spot has been seen and has been favourably reported on an inspection takes place. If it seems, outwardly, to be a desirable place a party from the village goes to the site and a shelter is built there to accommodate them. When this has been done two elders of the proposed settlers take a little flour, and go—one upstream, the other downstream—carrying their flour. Each, separately, makes a small conical heap of his flour, at the same time praying in these words :

" Ye who lived by this stream of old : ye who lived and died here long ago, who tilled this soil and drank of this water ; list, and if ye favour our coming here to settle, then leave this heap of flour undisturbed; but if ye favour not this proposed settlement, and want us not, then—on the morrow—when we come to seek your answer let us find that ye have scattered this heap ; and we will abide by your decision."

The following morning the two heaps are inspected, and if either is found scattered—even only a little—the people will seek a site elsewhere (on another stream) for their new village.

The first Rains. When the first rains fall, all work in the gardens ceases. On no account must any work be done, no matter how urgent it may appear to be. The reason given being that if any garden work is done it will " cut off " the rain, and the crops will be spoilt.

This is apparently connected in some way with the spirits, therefore, although there is no direct reference to them, the note of this custom is inserted here.

(Rain-making, or praying for rain, not being connected with the spirits, is inserted in its proper place
under *Lesa*.)

¹ Similarly in the earlier plagues we read : " And the magicians of
Egypt they also did in like manner with their enchantments " (Exodus
vii. 11). " And the magicians of Egypt did so with their enchantments,
and Pharaoh's heart was hardened " (*ibid.* 22). And again (*ibid.* viii. 7).
Snake production is a common ' miracle,' and I know a witch-doctor who
claims to be able to bring a dead man back to life.

² The same root appears in *Lufu* death, *Kufwa* to die, etc.

³ *Musole* is the timber chosen for the *chipanda* of the spirit (*mukishi*)
of a person who has been tried by *balaye* (q.v. under DIVINATION),
because in this form of divination the calabash containing the medicine
is placed, at one part of the proceedings, in the fork of a stick made from
the *musole* tree.

Kawalawala is used for the spirit of a man who has killed elephants,
or other animals, the heads of which adorned his *chipanda* when he was
alive. Similarly for the spirit of one who inherited the dead hunter's
name.

Muwumbu wood is selected for the spirit of a man who had killed
people in warfare and had, in his lifetime, placed the skulls of his slain
enemies on his *chipanda*. (Likewise anyone inheriting the dead warrior's
name.)

Apparently one of these three qualifications always exists, as no other
kind of tree is ever used, nor has any other kind ever been used
according to tradition.

CHAPTER XI

RELIGION (II)

Evil Spirits, Adverse Spirits

(*MITALA OR MIKENAMO*)

Anyitanda in Lunda

JUST as it is natural that one's own parents, who loved one in one's life, should—after death—be good spirits, so it is but reasonable that the shades of one's enemies become *mitala*, and not only the shades of actual enemies, but of all to whom one has done any harm, or to whom one owed any obligation—*if that harm or that obligation had not been requited in full*.

To grasp this fact is of the greatest importance because we then see why it is that natives pay such apparently absurd compensation for accidents, why they will—if they can—pay in full seemingly extortionate demands of *u tuzhi* and so on. They believe that, if they do not, they will make another *mutala* against whom they must for ever be on their guard. The fear of *mitala* is, generally, recognised as a dominating influence in native life : even a new-comer will grasp this in a vague way ; but it is not so generally realised that the fear of creating *mitala* is every whit as dominating : in some ways even more so.

The simplest forms of *mitala*-making hardly need explanation. A dies, and B has to make *u tuzhi* payments, but fails to do so : A's spirit becomes a *mutala* to him. Again, A does an actual injury to B, kills him, or makes him suffer in some way and B dies (not necessarily from the injury). If A has not compensated B for the injury,

141

or paid B's relatives for his death, B's spirit becomes a *mutala* to him. (In any such case the spirit becomes a *mutala* not only to the defaulter or offender, but to his family and heirs, which accounts for the large number of *mitala* that a man has, even if he himself has walked uprightly, has loved his neighbour as himself, and owes not any man.)

Here are less straightforward ways of incurring *mutala*-hood.

A sends B, his brother, to go to hunt for him, or to cut trees for him. If B dies by misadventure, and A fails to pay for his death, B's spirit will become a *mutala*. It matters not how accidental the death—it might be a snake bite—A must pay for the death, or incur a new *mutala*. So, when A and B were out together cutting trees, A had a spear with him and, while engaged in cutting a tree, gave it to B to hold. When the tree was about to fall, B ran to get clear of it, tripped over a root, fell and transfixed himself with the spear—A's spear. If A did not compensate his people—pay for the death—B's spirit would haunt him.

Once more. A and B are brothers, and conjointly receive inheritance fees (*u tuzhi*) from certain people, owing to the death of a relative C. A keeps more than his share. B acquiesces ; but some years later reviles A for his greed. He would at once be told to stop, because if he continued to revile A about C's *u tuzhi*, then C's spirit would become *mutala* and would cause trouble : it might bring sickness to the whole village ; or it might, more particularly, bring trouble to A, an accident (a lion or a snake) when at home or on a journey. In this case B would have caused A's death by reviling him, and so wakening C's spirit and turning it into *mutala*. It may seem illogical, as A was the original offender, by cheating (and if B died without having had the original " doing-down " made good, doubtless B would be *mutala* to A), but B in such a case has created a fresh offence by raking up a grievance that has been allowed to rest, and if he does not desist he will turn C's spirit into *mutala*. When one sees how native quarrels do drag on, one can understand that this is a very salutary belief, and one wishes there were more stringent beliefs on the same lines.

If one tries to envisage an ordinary community, one will see at once the enormous number of potential *mitala* it contains. This gives a faint idea of the number of *mitala* left to each poor individual by previous generations! No wonder the native treads warily to avoid adding unnecessarily to their number; no wonder that he seeks the help of his *wa-kishi* against the existing ones, and that he tries not to enrage any *mutala*. No wonder that the witch-doctor flourishes, for he alone can trace which *mutala* is giving trouble; he alone can lay the ghost.

The following beliefs may well be inserted here, as they deal directly with the rousing to anger of certain spirits, and thereby causing them to be actively adverse.

Chimalwamalwa. (The fear of death, caused by committing incest.) "Thou shalt not sleep with those in a prohibited degree, or thou shalt surely die." This is a primary commandment.

The first man who committed incest died (or was killed) for his sin; thereby establishing a precedent, and proving to future generations that this is "a deadly sin."

So tradition has it.

Incest is not as repugnant as the word itself connotes to us. The prohibited degrees are far more numerous with the Kaonde and similar tribes than with us; in fact, some of the marriages lawful to us would be considered grossly incestuous and immoral by the natives (raising once more the query as to what is *natural* morality). Not only can a native, for instance, not marry his aunt's daughter, but when we write " a man may not marry his mother," this implies to the native that he may not marry, nor have connection with, either his natural *or his inherited mother*, who might be a young second cousin, or the numerous relations whom he calls " mother " even when his mother is alive. The prohibited degree, to trespass on which amounts to incest, goes still further than this ; all within the same totem are within it, even if they are of a different tribe and entirely unrelated. It must be understood, therefore, that incest is a word used in its native sense and not in the English sense. (It is not easy to say to what extent exactly this holds good, as a man incurs death for himself by incest with the comparatively near degrees ; but only incurs barrenness for the woman if she is a distant connection, or an unrelated totem-mate.)

If a man commits incest now he gets *chimalwamalwa* (the fear of death), because he rouses the spirit of the first incest-sinner. This spirit says to him :

" You know that I gave up my life because I committed this sin. Yet you, who have had my awful experience to warn you, go and sin in the same way. Your sin is greater than mine, so you will surely die."

Death, however, can be avoided and the fear of it driven away, by payment. If the sin were committed in ignorance a small payment to the woman is sufficient ; but if it were committed wilfully owing to incestuous lust a bigger payment has to be made to the relatives of the woman. In such case (the greater degree) the offender may also be driven from his village, besides having to pay.

Kuzhula kapuki. This is very similar. Long ago, chronic adulterers, persistent sinners in this way, were killed. An order was then issued in their village, stringently forbidding *all* adultery for fear of angering the spirits of the slain adulterers.

When some people in the village start this immorality again they get the same kind of fear as *chimalwamalwa*,

THE FIRST STAGE—OR OPENING CHORUS—IN THE BWILANDI DANCE.

The dancer wears a kilt made of 20 genet skins and has one vertical and five horizontal chalk marks on his back. There are three drummers and a large chorus.

but called *kuzhula kapuki*. They are identified by the witch-doctor, and then their sin, and the fear, can be removed by payment. (In this divination there are two steps, first to find out which spirits are troubled : this is done by the divination called *kansheku* (*vide* DIVINA-TION). When it is found to be the spirits of the dead adulterers that are angry, the new offenders are divined by means of *balaye*.)

Mitala are generally, like the *wa-kishi* and the living man's shadow, without substance. They are shades, spirits, souls. Restless ones, resenting some wrong done to the person with whom they walked in his lifetime, they wander around and avenge themselves on those who did wrong, and on their relatives and associates.

There are, however, forms of *mitala* that have sub-stance. These take the form of a corpse—the upper half only : being legless as the legs have rotted away, and only the trunk, arms and head remain. This kind of *mutala*, which is much dreaded, creeps about at night, pulling its legless trunk along the ground, and propelling itself with its arms, as a child when first beginning to crawl. It enters the hut of its enemy, and, as he sleeps, pulls some hairs from his forehead and then departs. A fatal sickness comes on the person attacked by the *mutala*. (I cannot find any special name for this form of *mutala*.)

Appeasing the Mitala (Laying the Ghost). (Various references to this will also be found under DIVINATION, especially under sub-headings *Chilola* (i) or *Mang'ongu ; Kansheku* and *Kaneng'eni*, q.v.)

This is one of the principal powers of the *ng'anga* or witch-doctor, and tends more than anything to promote his greatness, and to enhance his value to the community.

When a person is sick, or is suffering from any trouble, he goes, or sends, to the witch-doctor, and calls on him to divine for him, and ascertain the cause of the trouble. If he finds that the spirit (*mufu*) of some dead person is the cause of the trouble, i.e. has become *mutala*, he proceeds to divine what spirit it is. This is generally done by means of the *mang'ongu* test, when the antelope horn guides the enquirers to the grave of the deceased whose *mufu* is malignant.

When located the doctor digs up as much of the corpse as remains ; if it has not already rotted only the bones are removed and the flesh is returned to the grave and burnt. (In some soils it is wonderful how long the flesh remains ; I have had ocular proof of this.) The leg and arm bones are ground into medicine to be placed in the guiding horn. The other bones, similarly treated, are kept in a basket for further use.

The party returns to the village after the exhumation, and the village is swept clean. All old fire and ashes are collected and thrown away, and new fires are kindled. The doctor receives (received) a slave as his fee for this service—nothing less, and he always left the village before dawn on the day following the exhumation. To fail to do so would spoil the whole business. The name of the person whose body has been exhumed is never to be named thereafter, or the whole trouble would recommence, showing that even this drastic treatment of the corpse does not kill the *mufu*. (According to some of my informants.)

Laymen do not appear to understand how it is that as the *chimvule* or *mufu* lives in the village where deceased used to live and not in his grave, it is affected by this treatment of the corpse.

The witch-doctors themselves are not very clear about this. One, for instance, disagrees about the *chimvule* staying in the village, and informs me that it is the Kaonde belief that when a man dies his shadow goes to *Lesa*, and that when a *chimvule* (or *mufu*) causes sickness it has come from *Lesa* in the wind. When the person afflicted dies from this sickness (or while he is still ill) divination by the *ng'anga* follows, after which the relatives carry out some divination of their own to verify the *ng'anga's* " post-mortem " or diagnosis. Satisfied as to which *mufu* has caused the death or sickness they proceed to exhume the corpse in the manner described above. The doctor then gives the relatives medicine to drink and to wash in, which acts as a prophylactic against the *mufu*. This informant of mine *implied*, rather shamefacedly, that the exhumation is irrelevant, and that it is only done to enhance the reputation of himself and colleagues. If it were a simple matter of washing with medicine the people either would dispense with his services or would pay only a small fee, but as they believe the exhumation is essential, and as no ordinary person dare exhume, the doctor gets his big fees.

No witch-doctor is ever likely to emulate Elisha, cf. 2 Kings v, 10 sqq.

"And Elisha sent a messenger unto him, saying, Go and wash in Jordan. . . . But Naaman was wroth, and went away, and said, Behold I thought He will surely come out to me, and stand, and call on the name of the Lord his God. . . . And his servants came near . . . and said, My Father, if the prophet had bid thee do some great thing, wouldest thou not have done it? . . ."

The witch-doctor always bids them " do some great thing.

Other of my professional friends disagree entirely with the above, and the following appears to be the " standard belief " among Kaonde *ng'angas* (remembering, however, that different sections of the Kaonde differ in many things).

After the divination and before the exhumation the doctor washes the invalid (if he is in time to prevent his death, otherwise, the body) with a decoction of leaves. He then takes the leaves from which the brew was made, and, holding them in a bundle, presses them against the chest of the invalid, calling loudly on the spirit to leave him alone; he then draws the bundle of leaves slowly down the body, pressing hard on it the while; thus he extracts the spirit. After this addresses it thus:

"You, spirit, you must leave this person alone, and you must leave this village. Come! I will take you to your own body. Come with me."

He then goes to the grave, and exhumation follows as described. He places a part of a *chitola* tree in the grave, and makes a fire from the *mwanga* and *ndale* trees, with which the remains that are to be reinterred are burnt in the grave. Then the leaves, which contain the corpse's *mufu*, are thrown in, too, and burnt, and all is covered up again. In this way the spirit is killed.

The *ng'angas* say that the spirit is really killed, not merely laid. It can never return. One informant (though modestly asserting that he was no more than a spectator!) says he has "witnessed" this on three separate occasions in different vicinities.

On the journey back from the grave no one is allowed to look back. (Why this precaution, or why the name of the person whose *mufu* caused the trouble is not to be mentioned if the spirit is really killed, I cannot find out.) On their return to the village the old fires are removed and taken to the cross-roads and new fire is kindled by the doctor.

A Lunda Luena doctor tells me that he does not exhume corpses in these cases, but goes straight for the *mufu*. To start with he digs a big and deep pit. In this he places the sick man, who is troubled by the *mufu*. The invalid sits in the pit, holding a cock in his hands and has a pot of medicine by his side. The doctor beats a drum, and calls loudly to the spirit that has caused the sickness to come to him. In this case the spirit is not supposed to be in the sick man's body. When the doctor sees the spirit approach he takes the patient out of the pit, leaving the cock and the medicine pot. The sum-

moned spirit enters the pit to eat the fowl; the doctor
jumps in, with an axe, and kills it. Then he puts the
sick man's clothes and the fire from his hut inside the
pit, and buries all together.

The spirit, when it comes, assumes the form of a
hyena.

If the spirit does not come, then the sickness was not
caused by a *mutala*, but is natural, and the doctor cures
it by medicine. [I should add that my informant has a
great local reputation as a *ng'anga*, over a very wide
area, too. My own opinion of him, however (and I have
had a good deal to do with him, one way and another),
is that he is more of a charlatan—or, maybe, more
clumsy—than many of his colleagues. I give his account
of his own methods for what it is worth. I have since
heard, but cannot verify it, that a very similar procedure
exists in Korea.]

Metempsychosis. (Reincarnation, or transmigration of
souls. No word exactly covers the idea, as will be seen.)

As has been stated already, these tribes believe in reincarnation; in fact, this is the basis of their religion.
The dead are the real rulers of the country, for the souls
of the living come from the dead. There is not so much
continuity among the natives as regeneration. This
accounts for the sanctity of the *wa-kishi*, for the im-
mutability of custom and for the suspicion and actual
fear of innovation. The Ba-Kaonde do not appear to have
anyone akin to the Ba-Ila prophets, who (so Mr. Smith
tells us in his book) occasionally change and modify
custom by their interpretations; the customs of the
tribe appear never to have been changed intentionally.
Excrescences grow—as with all unwritten laws, ideas and
beliefs—but these arise unconsciously, and, though the
origin of and reason for many laws and customs is completely forgotten they are implicitly and devoutly
believed in, and meticulously obeyed, because they are
the customs of the elders reincarnated from generation

to generation. The spirits, or souls, resident in the living, or awaiting a new body in which to reside (it is believed), visit sickness, bad luck or other misfortune, on those who depart from the right path. This is the basis of native religion and of native life, and natives tell me that any new religion or law which enforces new ideas or prohibits old ones will never be wholeheartedly accepted by the majority because of this belief. A few may change, but nearly all will, at most, pretend to do so, for fear of the terrible penalties (especially the death of a child or children) that follow any divergence from the old customs.

After a man dies he is not, strictly speaking, reincarnated in a baby; but his *mukishi* (spirit) enters the baby in the womb, and, being composite, can enter several children—or even animals. It is more accurate to say that the spirit of the new infant emanates from a deceased person; it is not reproduced in full, though apparently each emanation is complete. This reincarnation (for want of a better word) is sexless (i.e. a woman's *mukishi* can be born into a male child, and *vice versa*): it is limited to two generations, and generally goes from grandparent to grandchild, or from uncle or aunt to nephew or niece. The child may have its *mukishi* from either side of the family, but never (except in one case to be mentioned later) from outside it.

The *mukishi* of deceased can also enter animals of any kind: hippopotamus, bush-pig, hyena, etc., and its presence can be ascertained by divination (as with a baby); but there appears to be no taboo against killing nor against eating such reincarnation, even it be the hunter's (or feeder's) near relative or chief.

The Ba-Kaonde do not appear to have any idea of a cycle in the transmigration of the soul. Each time there is an emanation from a deceased person into a baby or into an animal it is conceived as being an emanation independent of all others, thereby differing from other similar beliefs (e.g. in ancient Egypt, Buddhism, etc.).

As regards lions the case is different. Ordinary *wa-kishi* do not enter lions; but if a chief be so disposed he can take certain medicine in his lifetime so that after death he becomes lions (plural) which are called *mikumbe*. After burial, if maggots are seen to emerge from the chief's grave it is known that he has taken this medicine, and each maggot becomes a *mukumbe* lion, who is the chief, directly reincarnated in a multiple form. (This is considered to be a direct reincarnation and not an emanation from the chief's *mukishi*.)

In none of these cases of *wa-kishi* in animals nor of *mikumbe* is it alleged that the animal makes known its personality to people by speech nor in any other way. In all cases of ordinary animals this is only ascertained by divination, and in the case of the lion-chiefs by the actual witnessing of the maggots.

Sometimes on divination at the naming of a child no family *mukishi* can be traced on either side, and then the *ng'anga* finds that the father of the child once killed an animal that had the *mukishi* of *Kananga* (" so-and-so ") in it, and that this *mukishi* is the one from whom the child's soul has emanated. In such case the child is called *Chiwilo*[1], because its clan is changed : it is of another totem, i.e. has an alien *mukishi* (often, even, from an alien tribe).

Another form of reincarnation (or transfiguration, or resurrection) is known as *wanga wa wusangu*.

This is an interesting belief, said to be of Luba origin, and to be firmly believed in by the Kaonde, Sanga, Lunda and other neighbouring tribes.

Sometimes when a man dies and is buried, he rises again (instead of becoming a decomposing corpse and a wandering *mufu* (spirit) ; that is to say, on his resurrection he becomes another human being, complete with *chimvule* (shadow).

Sometimes one knows that a man who has, apparently, died is *wusangu* ("immortal," as a rough rendering). One knows this, because before he "dies" he confides this secret to his wife. After the seeming death she tells the villagers, and to save the poor man trouble he is not buried, but is laid out—above ground—in a *jitu* (grove of swamp timber), whence he can rise again, and start on his new existence without trouble.

One may bury one who is *wusangu* owing to ignorance of the fact; in such case he will rise from the grave. The man who is *wusangu* had more trouble if he were killed in battle in the old days, for then his head would be cut off. Being immortal he would awake, but headless, and in this condition would stagger about blindly, until his headless shoulders knocked against a tree or other obstacle, when a new head would grow thereon, and he would be suitably equipped for starting on his new career.

During his periodical existence on earth the man who is *wusangu* is like any other individual, having nothing to differentiate him from his companions. Presumably, as he knows he is *wusangu*, he has some knowledge of his previous existences; but I have had no opportunity of meeting one, and of hearing from his lips "the finest story in the world"; nor am I likely to do so, as such people keep the secret of their nature closely guarded, till on the point of reincarnation. It is, however, not considered at all rare.

Chanswe is "bad luck," "ill chance," "accident," especially when unaccountable, and when it seems to dog a man. Thus a man who hits his toe on a hidden rock, or one who loses his goods in a seemingly easy crossing of a river is said to have *chanswe*. Another, in referring to such misfortunes, will say, "Oh! it is just his *chanswe*."

Chanswe is attributed to *mitala* only. It is not caused by *Lesa*, nor is it a matter of *bulozhi*. It might be described as "minor manifestations of the *mitala*," not taken very seriously, but probably attributed to their influence simply because nothing is supposed to happen without some directing power. It is supposed that only the spirits of near relatives (on either side of the family) can cause *chanswe*; the spirit of a distant relative or of one not related might, when it was *mutala*, cause serious trouble—death and sickness—but would not cause mere bad luck.

Kushamwa is to be unlucky; *Kushulwa* to be lucky.

---

[1] Derived from *Ku wilwa*, which signifies "to inherit a quality or predisposition." It is also used in other cases, e.g. if a youth becomes an exceptionally good hunter he is supposed to have inherited this skill unexpectedly from someone deceased, and is called his *chiwilo*. (R.E.B.W.)

CHAPTER XII

RELIGION (III)

LESA (" GOD ")

I HAVE deliberately placed this section of the native religion after that dealing with the spirits, since it is (to the natives) much less important. Nevertheless, it must not be overlooked that these natives do believe in a God—the Creator: A God, unseen and living up above, a supreme being. They have —as will be seen later—a distinct idea of a divine creation, resembling though differing from the beliefs of other Bantu races; and not without resemblance to that described in Genesis. It is essentially part of their belief that LIFE is the gift of God: that God created the first man and woman and gave them life: that such life has been handed on from generation to generation; and though their religion is now more centred on the spirits the existence and the power of *Lesa* is an actuality to them. This fact, coupled with the negative fact that they worship neither natural objects (like the sun) nor idols, seems—to me—to place them definitely as a non-pagan race. However, with one exception noted here-under, they pay little attention to *Lesa*.

This God-the-Creator is known as *Lesa*, or *Chipan-gavije*, or *Shyakapanga*. (Three names for one being.) Some of the Kaonde (e.g. Kapijimpanga, but not the southern section) believe that *Lesa* is married, and while he lives above in the sky and shows his power by thunder and lightning—which latter occasionally kills people—

154

his wife *Chandashi* lives in the ground and manifests herself by means of earth tremors (which are common hereabouts). Kapiji tells me that " one knows it is a woman because she makes a lot of fuss and does nothing ! "

Lesa can kill people by other means than lightning : e.g. by sickness, accident and so on. Ordinary deaths, " from natural causes " as we would say, are sometimes, though not often, attributed to him, but epidemics are more often considered his work.

Lesa manifests himself by thunder (*malazhi*[1]), by lightning (*kuwezhya :* no true noun is used) and by the rainbow (*kakongolo*). The only belief or superstition about any of these concerns the rainbow : it is believed that if a man goes where the rainbow reaches the ground he will be bitten by a snake. A comet is called *chinge-likezhya*, but no superstitions appear to attach to it.

Prayer for Rain. *Lesa* is approached and prayed to on one occasion only. This is for rain, and the Kaonde believe that rain is a gift from *Lesa*. There are no " rain-makers " among the Kaonde : rain-making is not an accomplishment of doctor or chief. If the season of *Chiwundo* (about November) advances and no rains fall the people then pray to *Lesa* for rain. This prayer is not offered at all to the *wa-kishi*, only to *Lesa*. Early in the morning a tall white pole (any tree so long as it is straight) is put up on the outskirts of the village and all the people congregate there—men, women and children. They sit in a circle, and the headman sits in the centre near to the pole. The headman then prays as follows :

" *Owewa Lesa, Wonse twi wantu wowe, Witupe mvula !* "
(" Thou God, we are all thy people. Send us rain ! ")

Then the people all clap their hands (*ku-popwera*) and return to the village. The pole stays where it was placed until—owing to the ravages of white ants or other causes—it falls : after which it lies as it fell until it rots. This is particularly interesting as showing a definite, and true, theistic belief; and it may be noted that the sole occasion on which these people turn to *Lesa* rather than to their spirits has reference to the seasonal change which is of more importance to them than anything else. Failure of the rains would mean famine, so in such danger they turn to their Creator, and pray "Save thy people." The fact that there is no rain-making ritual, no calling in a professional, nothing but a simple prayer by an altar which is a *chipanda* on a glorified scale, is also noteworthy. The prayer, too, is offered direct, not through any intermediary, and is proof that the Kaonde believe—in this matter at any rate—that *Lesa* can hear human prayers.

THE STORY OF THE CREATION

The creation took place somewhere to the north-west. No one seems to know the exact locality, but all agree about the direction. The Ba-Kaonde state that men came here from the north-west, so that the first men must have been created there. (From what we know of the general migration in which the Luba races partook this is whence these people came.)

Lesa created two people: Mulonga, who became the first man, and Mwinambuzhi, who became the first woman. At first they were not man and woman but sexless persons, and besides lacking genital organs they also had no anus. The deficiencies in their anatomy caused them discomfort, so Mulonga went to *Lesa* to consult him about it. *Lesa* saw that his work of creation had been imperfect, and took two packets, which he gave to Mulonga, saying: "See, here are two packets, one is for you and one for your companion. Take them with you, and at night take one packet and place it in your crutch. The other give to your companion who must do likewise." Mulonga then returned to earth, but the way was long and he had to sleep on the way. When lying down to sleep he did as directed and placed the packet between his legs. In the morning he found he was a man, and complete in every respect. He picked up the other packet, but happening to smell it, thought from the evil odour that it had gone bad, so he threw it away. On his return to his companion the latter noticed the difference in him, and asked how it had happened. Mulonga told Mwinambuzhi how *Lesa* had changed him, but made no reference to the second packet ; whereupon Mwinambuzhi decided to visit *Lesa* too, to seek a cure. On arrival *Lesa* said, " But I sent a packet for you, too : did not Mulonga give it to you ? " The other answered " No, I saw no packet, nor did he tell me of one : only of his own did he speak." *Lesa* said nothing but gave a fresh packet to Mwinambuzhi, with identical instructions. These were obeyed and Mwinambuzhi awoke the next morning a woman. Then sexual desire awoke in their hearts, and Mulonga had carnal knowledge of Mwin-ambuzhi ; but after this they both felt anxious and frightened, not understanding the knowledge that had come to them. They, therefore, returned to *Lesa* to put their doubts before him. *Lesa* listened, and said to Mulonga, " When last you were here did I not give you two packets, one for yourself, and one for your com-panion ; and did you not throw hers away ? " Mulonga agreed that this was so. *Lesa* then assured them that this knowledge that had come to them was nothing to fear, since he had given it to them ; but he said to Mulonga, " You sinned in throwing away the packet that I gave to you for Mwinambuzhi, so though you have each joined in this act, having each of you the desire to know each other as I intended, still you shall pay Mwinambuzhi a *muketo* (marriage gift) for having known her ; and hereafter, for ever, the male offspring of yours shall pay the female offspring *muketo*, whenever they marry." " And that," say the Ba-Kaonde, " is why man has to pay *muketo*."

Now a little later *Lesa* called *mayimba* (the honey-guide bird), who was a friend of Mulonga and Mwinambuzhi, to him and gave him three gourds, each of which was closed at either end. " Go, take these," he said, " to the man and woman whom I have created, and open them not on the way. When you hand them to the people, say unto them, ' Thus says *Lesa* : Open this one and that one which contain seeds for sowing, so that you may have food to eat; but the third one you shall not open until I come. When I come I will instruct you as to the contents of the third package.' " *Mayimba* took the gourds, but his curiosity as to their contents was great, and he stopped to open them. In the first two he found seeds of corn, beans, and of other food-crops, and having examined them he replaced them, closing the gourds as they had been closed before. He then untied the third gourd, inside which were death (*lufu*), sickness, and all manner of carnivora and death-bringing reptiles. As soon as he opened the gourd these escaped and *Mayimba* could not catch them.

Lesa came and was very angry. He asked *Mayimba* where were the things that had escaped, and *Mayimba* said he knew not. *Lesa* and he went together to search for them, and found the lion in his lair, the snake in his hole and so on, but could not catch them again. *Lesa* said to him, " You have sinned greatly and the responsibility is yours. *Mayimba* was frightened and flew away to the forest and dwelt there, living no longer with man.

When hunger overtook him he would come to his old companions, the man and the woman, and call them to some honey which he had found ; and they, guided by him, would take the honey and leave a little on the ground for him.

Thus it was that death, sickness and fear came to man. *Lesa* realising what had happened said to Mulonga and his wife " *Mayimba* is a great sinner. I told him that on no account was the third gourd to be opened until I came ; but he disobeyed me. Thereby he has brought

Religion 59

you much trouble, sickness, death ; and the risks from lions, leopards, snakes and other evil animals and reptiles. This I cannot help now, for these things have escaped and cannot be caught ; so you must build yourselves huts and shelters to live in for protection from them."

Lesa also realised that the people would want tools, so he gave them a puku (*nsewula : cobus vardoni*) and told them to kill it. (The Ba-Kaonde do not know in what way it was killed.) Then he told them to skin it, which they did with sticks and their finger nails. The skin being taken off they softened it with stones, and then *Lesa* instructed them in the art of making bellows, sewing the skin by means of a stick as needle and strips of bark as thread. *Lesa* then showed them how to make fire by friction, giving them two trees called *kashimba* and *sempwe selekete*, sticks of which they rubbed (by revolving between the hands) on dry *mufuto* wood. The next lesson was in the making of a furnace of clay, inside which they put pieces of ironstone (*mutapo*) to which charcoal (*mashyanga*), made from the *mukoso* tree, was added as a flux—(in smelting copper (*mukuwa*) lime (*mpemba*) was also added, but not with iron). The nozzle, made of bark, of the bellows, was placed through a hole in a small ant-hill into the furnace, and the ore and flux were blown upon until the ore was smelted. The smelted metal (called *chiera* when smelted) was then beaten by a stone hammer (*kunko*) or a stone anvil (simply called *jibwe* = stone). *Lesa* then showed them how to fashion an axe and a hoe : only these two implements. Next he showed them how to make two big hammers of iron, and when they were finished he told them that with their help they could make whatever tools they fancied, as occasion arose. One of the first things they made were spears to protect themselves from the wild animals that *Mayimba* had let loose upon the world.

How totems started (soon after the Creation) is

described in the chapter on TOTEMISM. The origin of different tribes (*milaka*) is a point I have not been able to clear up. Very many elders of the Ba-Kaonde whom I have consulted, and who are willing to help me, say that they have no tradition as to this.

Failure has also met my efforts to find out how *bulozhi* (witchcraft) first came into the world, and who was the author of it. In fact, except for the above notes there is nothing to my knowledge that remains of old tradition of the Creation and early days of man. I might add that even this is nearly lost; for only a few elders remember it—but those who do remember all tell practically the same story.

Oaths. To take an oath (or, possibly, to invoke) *ku-chipa.*

The taking of an oath, giving testimony on oath and so on is common. In serious matters, in promises made sacredly, in answering accusations, it is customary to swear to the truth. Oaths are of three kinds, and—so far as I can ascertain—there is no difference in importance between one kind and another: that is to say there appears to be no degree of sanctity.

    i. A common form is to swear by " God."
       Shyakapanga anjipaye. " May God kill me . . ."
       (*Shyakapanga* is another name for *Lesa.*)
   ii. To swear by the name of a dead ancestor is equally
       common.
       Mwaiya Tata . . . (or *Mwaiya Nkambo, Mwaiya*
       mwishyo, etc.) " By my dead father . . ." etc.
  iii. A variant of No. i.
       Mulolo ununka! " May a snake bite me ! "
       Bokwe unja! " May a lion eat me ! "

There appears to be no known penalty for perjury, but I fancy such oaths are taken seriously, and a wilful perjurer would expect to be killed by *Lesa,* or to incur the hostility

THREE KAONDE MEN CUTTING DOWN A TREE.

This forms an important part of garden work.

KAONDE WOMEN CARRYING FLOUR.

The flour is made from Kaffir corn and is carried in plaited baskets called *vilukwa*.

of the spirit of the dead relative whose name had been taken in vain, or to meet with misfortune from snake or lion as the case might be. To what extent a denial on oath would save a person at his trial I cannot say : I am inclined to think that an oath given in such circumstances would not be taken very seriously.

[1] R.E.B.W. says *malazhi* is lightning (cf. Chinyanja *njazi*) and *kuwezhya* is to lighten, and that *Lesa* is used for thunder.

CHAPTER XIII

ASPECTS OF RELIGION

Lunda Tribe

By J. L. KEITH

FOLLOWED BY SOME SUPPLEMENTARY NOTES BY F. V. BRUCE MILLER

[Author's Note. Mr. Keith has kindly allowed me to include these notes—which are the result of original research by him—in this book. Apart from their intrinsic ethnographical value they seem to me to be a particularly valuable study on the inner meaning and general bearing of native religion ; they give a real insight into native thought and native ideas, and are a testimony to the confidence which Mr. Keith inspired in the natives among whom he lived. I hope that some day he will have the opportunity to expand these and other notes on a singularly interesting tribe, and will publish them in book form. F.H.M.]

*N*ZAMBI. God the creator (in the sense generally understood) is called *Nzambi* by the Alunda : he is inaccessible to and remote from humans, and his influence on human affairs—once the initial creation is over—appears to be considered indirect and negligible. He is obscured by the vast crowd of the tribal spirits who interfere directly in every phase of local life. *Nzambi* is said to be the creator of all things : of vegetable and mineral as well as of animal life; and also of all things spiritual. It is his business to make spirits in the tribal sense, but not in the family sense, except indirectly : " *mudimi windi wa ku lenga akishi.*" *Nzambi* is somewhat of a tribal deity, and the ancestor of the family *akishi* appears to have been made by him. His name is constantly used in oaths, " *Nzambi yami !* " (" My God ! ") etc., both seriously and profanely ; and it is usual to swear that a statement is true by the name of *Nzambi* in legal cases. *Nzambi* is much joked about, is taunted with his stupidity —in making rain when it is not wanted and so on—and also he is said to have amusing relations with certain animals—quarrelling with them, etc. ; but he is never prayed to (*pesha*), not even, as among the Ba-Kaonde, for rain : nor is he considered as the object of a cult. The Alunda are inclined to think themselves the centre of the universe : the sun and the moon as very local phenomena —in legend each has a personality, being enemies and jealous of each other. (The spots on the moon are said to have been made by the sun in a beer quarrel, the latter throwing mud at the moon ; " and how should the moon wash it off, having no hands? ")[1] The stars are said, jokingly, to be the wives of the moon, or even the fires of another world turned upside-down. They say that the sun goes quickly with the wind and that it is easier for it to go down than to come up. The sun falls in the west and runs round behind the atmosphere (*luzwizwi*) so as to be ready to rise at the proper time in the morning. The rains are locally controllable, and a small horn provided by the " doctors " will often blow away any inconvenient storm, but *akishi* (family spirits) can bring rain at certain times, and are prayed to therefor. I can find no belief in occult influences of the sun or moon or stars. The Alunda express great surprise at hearing that the same sun and moon can be seen as far away as where the whites come from. Asked how far away they consider the sun to be from the earth they often say, " About as far as So-and-So's village, but in the morning and evening it must be much farther as the heat is less."

The fable of the origin of the diverse tribes is interesting, and is considered to be an authentic tradition. It is said that the first man was created at the Katu-

kang'onyi (a river in the Belgian Congo not far from
Mwachiamvu's[2] village site); *Nzambi* at this spot began
the work of creation—making all animals, trees, etc.
There can, it is said, be seen a human footmark in the
rock, also the spoor of a dog and of a bush-pig, traces of
man's early hunting activities. For a while all men lived
together at this place and walked in one path (*njila
yimu*) when (some say on the advice of *Nzambi*) the
elders decided to go forth to seek lands where they could
live and multiply. Some went to Barotseland, others to
Achokweland, and so on; but the elders of the Alunda
tribe (or, rather, the Aluunda from whom the Andembu,
Akausa, etc., spring) decided to remain where they were.
Before the others left they planted a *muyombo* tree at
which the original elders' spirits could sit. This tree,
grown to an immense size, is said to exist to-day. Hence
the Alunda say that they are the greatest of tribes, from
which all the others have issued. (The paramount chief
of the Barotse is, for instance, called the *Mwanika
Mwachiamvu*: Nyakutolo, the Aluena chieftainess is
also considered inferior to Mwachiamvu, etc. etc.)

Of the actual creation there are many fables. One
story gives an alleged origin of death.

"*Nzambi ni Kasulungunda*" (God and His Rainbow).
In the twilight of antiquity God slid down to earth on a
rainbow. He found the earth a pleasant spot and He
improved it by the creation of trees, animals, etc. He
then created a man and a woman, and said to them
"*Sumbukeni! semenu anyana.*" ("Marry and have
children"). He put *akishi* (spirits) into their bodies.
They married and had children, and their children had
children. *Nzambi* put only one restriction on the
humans: that none might sleep while the moon walked
the skies; and the penalty for so doing was to be Death.
The old "Adam" was failing in sight, and one night, the
moon being hidden behind some clouds, he failed to
observe it and slept: and sleeping, died. Since then

everyone has died in his turn because none can keep awake while the moon is up.

Wumi (Life). All living things and creatures have *wumi* (life) in them. All *wumi* comes from *Nzambi*, and in man (and some animals) *wumi* is conceived as a shadow (*Mwevulu*) : *mwevulu* is also a shadow in the ordinary sense. This *mwevulu* is separate from, and can exist independently of, the body, which is an envelope for the *mwevulu* or *wumi*. The *mwevulu* after death leaves the body and becomes a *mukishi* (family spirit). The Alunda do not appear to hold that trees and all inanimate objects have an active living spirit in them, according to the usual animistic belief.

Wumi as conceived by the Alunda is very difficult to understand. It is possible to *sweka wumi mu chitumbu* (to hide one's " life " in a medicine) so that one's enemies may not destroy it by witchcraft or other means. Some " doctors " have a recipe for this : the " life " is drawn from the body and placed into a *mbachi* (=shell, usually of a crab) and can be given to a dog or other animal to eat, or can be hidden in a convenient spot : yet *wumi* appears to be essential to an animate body. Perhaps *mwevulu* and *wumi* are separate : the latter depending on the former. The *Chiyomboka* (witch-doctor) can make a false sort of *wumi* (*ku-hora*), but he cannot make *nyevulu*. *Aloji* (witches) can make their evil spirits with a *wumi*, but they cannot make *akishi* or *nyevulu*.

The supernatural world. The supernatural world is believed to be inhabited by three different kinds of beings:

  i. The family *akishi* (spirits, or souls departed).

 ii. The tribal *akishi* (spirits).

iii. The horrors and abominations made by the *aloji* (witches and wizards) which are created by a generally detested misuse of the supernatural elements.

These last are of a different nature from real *akishi* and in certain conditions can be made visible to human eyes. They are materialistic conceptions, whereas the *akishi* are spiritual conceptions. On these supernatural " creatures " is built the fabric of local superstition ; and the superstition at first sight obscures the very religious and moral theory of the family *akishi* on whom the whole tribe depends.

Akishi. 1. The family *akishi*, or souls of the departed.

Nzambi is said to have created the first Alunda with living shadows in them (*Mwevulu :* which may conveniently be called soul) and these souls, when death comes, depart from the human shell, and exist eternally. (Their activity as souls does not appear to last long ; but all informants agree that *akishi* cannot entirely die nor fade away.) Every living man is but an " emanation " from a departed soul : hence all the living, as far as the breath of life in them is concerned, are but emanations from the dead ; and these emanations, when they depart from their shells, also become eternal souls, with the will and power to reincarnate themselves as many times as they think fit. The departed soul (*mukishi*) when it reincarnates itself (*semuka*) does not itself enter the womb, but sends off an emanation of its eternal self ; and itself remains as it was before. The emanation gives life (*wumi*) to the embryo in the womb, and as soon as the pregnant woman feels a movement she can declare that the *mukishi* has entered into her, and she can feel gratitude to some, as yet, unknown *mukishi*, to whose cult she immediately devotes herself lest the spark of life should be withdrawn. In due time the child is born, and the question as to whose spirit it comes from has to be settled. The infant is taken to an elder or to a *chimbuki* (doctor) who divines with a rod and names a deceased relative. From several signs it can be told whether the divination is a correct one or not. (For example, the child has a coin or beads put into the hand, and the name of a *mukishi* is called several times, during which the child is observed. Should it throw down the object and cry it is decided that the divination has been incorrect. Also, should the child be intensely ill after it has been named, another doctor is called in, who may decide that the former *mukishi* was incorrect and suggest another.) Immediately after the successful divination the parents cut a stick of the *muyombo* tree, and shave the head neatly, and plant it in front of the child's hut : thus the worship of the child's *mukishi* begins, and continues throughout the whole of its life. Hence the Alunda tribe consists of the Souls departed, and the Souls living : the latter proceeding from the former. The departed are said to retain their individuality (except as regards sex) : yet the Alunda's conception of them is very spiritual—neither body nor form ; but invisible and impalpable, like the wind (*neyi mpepela*). They are not to be confused with any of the witchcraft ghosts or horrors, nor could they be made visible to anyone by the application of medicines (*yitumbu*). In a limited way they are omnipresent and take a lively interest in the doings of the living. (They are localised but appear in dreams to distant relatives, when they take the form of their bodies in life.) The souls departed are said to reside with their dependents ; and, though they are without form, their presence appears to be localised : that probably is the orthodox opinion, and it is supported by many elders ; though many Alunda would say that the *akishi* are " all over the place." Should a village move, the *akishi* move too : in fact, the living, as in nearly every matter, follow the departed for reasons that will be explained later. Several trees are said to be especially appointed by tradition as the trees to be planted by the devotees (*kombela*) as points of contact— (as far as one can understand the spirits are said to " sit "

Bark remov-ed

TOP OF MUKISHI STICK

(*shakama*) at their sticks. The *muyombo* tree is the most frequent. As the Alunda do not believe that trees can have a spirit in the same way that a living person has, the trees themselves are not worshipped).

The question then arises as to the relations between the living and the *akishi*, and how far the interference of the latter in human affairs can go. The departed souls have a will, and their interference can be felt to such an extent that it is necessary and profitable for every Kalunda to confirm to this will. Hence the family *akishi*, having lived on earth some time, and having had their own ideas on human affairs, are said to impose upon the living the duty of following the tradition of their elders. Law and custom proceed from the elders—i.e. from the *akishi* ; and the action of the *akishi* on the living is more or less dependent on the living's conformity with their will. It is this that gives the moral force to their religion ; and the force is the greater owing to the fact that the *mukishi* displeased is said to have the power of reminding the sinner very forcibly of his omissions. The general attitude of the living is, therefore, one of trying to please, so that there may be no unnecessary trouble. Hence a conformity to tradition is desirable and the wisdom (*mana*) of the departed is carefully followed. This would appear to be the chief basis of all local custom, and the guiding principle of nearly every considered act. Marriage, birth and death customs, the initiation of girls, circumcision : the arts, decencies and industries : the legal code in all its branches, and every other ceremony and custom of local life is more or less directly dependent on the will of the *akishi*. The elaborate code of *nsonyi* (lit : shame) which influences nearly every movement of Lunda life : the general relations between individuals, conversations, eating, greetings, respect towards elders (very jealously guarded by the *akishi*), the outward relations between men and women, sex relations and—most important of all—the degrees within which one may or may not marry, all depend on the *akishi*. (The family spirits visit incest (*kushima*) with death, or at least with the death of all issue, unless elaborate compensations are paid to the outraged parties, living and dead.) Breaches of custom and tradition, also lack of attention and worship are also punished by the *akishi* with sickness, bad luck, bad dreams, depression, sterility, sickness of dear relatives ; and all the minor worries of life : the hunter will miss an easy shot, the pot maker will break a nearly finished pot, the wife will spoil her husband's food, and so on. The Kalunda has no disinterested motive in worshipping, and his prayer is always " Leave us in peace," " Aid us," " Do not spoil this, that or the other." There is a general dependence on this power ; but the Kalunda has the means of a happy life within his power (were it not for *uloji* [witchcraft]). Asked whether the family *akishi* are evil, the answer is, " No, if we listen to their tradition all is well ; they do not hurt us, we Alunda hurt ourselves. ' *Leka uloji anyana a ku vula* ' (' Leave witchcraft and the children will multiply ') says our proverb : the witches and wizards are the enemy, not the *akishi*."

I have heard the Alunda reason thus when told that witchcraft is an imaginary thing, and that God is the Author of all things : " God must then be evil. We say that all evil comes from man—i.e. witches and wizards—but, if the latter do not exist, then whence can come evil ? "

It may be added that, except in the case of incest, the *akishi* do not appear to be very severe.

Kukombela. (To erect an " altar " for worship.) Before nearly every Lunda hut one or more sticks may be seen fixed in the ground (usually of the " sacred " *muyombo* tree). They are usually erected for the family spirits, though sometimes for special spirits (to be mentioned later). Game heads and rags sometimes decorate the top. Frequently the base is made like a human face, at other times a plain circle is the distinctive mark. Each separate stick represents a separate *mukishi*. These sticks are the family altars, and form a convenient point of communication between the living and the dead. The process of erection and the upkeep of these sticks is called *kukombela*.

Kupesha. (To worship and to appease by worship.) The family *akishi* have apparently a pathetic longing to be remembered by the living; and are jealous and offended if any family or personal event takes place without a prayer and an offering being made to them, in exchange for which they are willing to give help—or, at least, to abstain from interference. Before a beer drink a little beer is poured on to the ground by the *muyombo* : before a feast food is offered, etc. etc. Should illness be divined by some *chimbuki* to have been caused by a certain *mukishi* a small offering is made. Should a youth be going far to work he will often touch his particular *mukishi's* shrine with a plate or other object which he will carry with him as a charm ; and while at work will dedicate something, such as a cloth, to the *mukishi* : this will be ceremoniously placed on the *muyombo* on his return, and removed again.

The devotee always has the *chimbuki* (doctor) and the *chiyomboka* (witch-doctor) to turn to on points of difficulty ; or even his elders and chiefs, who can tell him to which spirit to turn, and what particular offering to make.

The reincarnation runs in the family only, both on the maternal and paternal sides—it is said never to be inter-family. It does not appear to jump more than one generation except in very exceptional cases. Grandparents are very often reincarnated in their grandchildren, and uncles and aunts in their nephews and nieces. The following table shows typical reincarnations :

when all the people concerned are dead, there would be
six *akishi*.

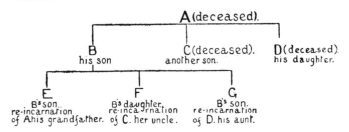

As can be seen from the above an emanation from the
mukishi of a female can enter a male, and *vice versa :*
the *mukishi* being conceived as sexless.

When the *mukishi's* relatives have died off to the second
or third generation it would appear to be held that the old
mukishi loses interest in the affairs of the living. In some
cases, however, when the deceased was in his lifetime
pre-eminent in some way or other, he is longer remembered
after his death than less important persons and may be
pesha'd for generations.

The immense force for conservatism will be noticed :
the inevitable argument against an innovation is that
what was good enough for our elders is good enough
for us : in other words, there is fear lest the family
akishi will be displeased and will withdraw their
support.

Akishi and succession. Should a chief or headman die
and a successor be appointed, that successor, though he
takes the name of his " father," the deceased, is not
necessarily a reincarnation of the deceased chief, but he
assumes a special devotion to the deceased ; and
supposing him to have been correctly elected and
appointed—the deceased chief's *akishi* will take a special
interest in him. For example, the deceased Sailunga is
elaborately *pesha'd* by the present one, but the Sailunga
mukishi has its emanations entering into other relatives,

the result being infants of his name (the name being speedily changed in the usual way).

Reincarnation into animals. Not only have the deceased power to send emanations into their relatives, but certain *akishi* appear to reproduce themselves into animals. This (as with humans) does not mean that the whole *mukishi* is reincarnated in the animal, but only that it sends off an emanation from the soul into the beast. It is frequently suspected by villagers that certain animals by signs (perhaps by continually haunting the village precincts or by talking to hunters) are possessed by *wumi* from their elders. *Ayimbuki* or wise men are consulted, and if the decision be arrived at that the animal is so possessed care must be taken not to kill or hurt it lest the *mukishi* be offended, and visitations on the offenders be made. (The late Paramount chief, Kanongesha, is said to have an emanation from his *mukishi* in a rabbit.) This belief appears to be the origin of the taboo of certain kinds of game among certain members of the tribe.

Mutanda. (An adverse spirit.) Should A have a case against B, and A dies before B has settled the case, then if B neglects to settle it with A's legal successors, A's *mukishi* becomes *mutanda* to B ; and unless B takes further steps to settle the matter it will haunt B and worry him with disease and misfortune. This belief has immense weight in support of morals and law and order. It makes the Kalunda anxious to conform to tradition so as to avoid trouble.

It is also most lucrative to the *ayomboka* (witch-doctors), one of whose great uses is to find out who is the particular *mutanda* who is troubling the client.

This belief accounts for the inheritance of *nyilong'a* (crimes) and is the native legal basis on which all such claims rest. The " virtuous " man will pay just claims against him, to avoid having *anyitanda* against him.

Pesha (by deputy). It is possible to *pesha* one's

mukishi by deputy. Busy men, such as government messengers, and those in employment anywhere, often leave this duty to their old parents in the village. This accounts for many grand erections of *mukishi* sticks outside old people's huts, and the absence of any from the huts of some youths. The old person who undertakes this duty as the absentee's deputy is paid for so doing.

2. The tribal *akishi*. Nearly every activity is said to have a special spirit that concerns itself with it. Hunting, village building and moving, pot-making, fishing, etc., all have special spirits, and these pursuits can be interfered with to such an extent by the spirits that it is necessary for the people to appease them by prescribed observances. Some of these spirits are quite separate from the family spirits, and the Alunda say that they were made by *Nzambi* and will always be a trouble to the tribe. Others appear to be family spirits who are localised and whose names are handed down owing to their activities.

Chihamba is the most remarkable of the purely tribal spirits. It appears to be a kind of infectious disease, which attacks the person or " possesses " it. When one is possessed one is infectious. Thus if a person who is in good health eats a cock when enjoying the hospitality of one who is " possessed " by *Chihamba* he will himself become infected. Again, by eating white beans with one possessed the disease is transmitted. *Chihamba* is described as " like the wind " : it is liable to attack anyone at any time : after being infected or possessed the person gets the shivers right through him and falls ill. *Chihamba* can be easily detected by the village *chimbuki* (doctor), and rarely results in death. There is a prescribed ceremonial for its removal : a dance party is organised and proceeds to the neighbouring bush, the patient being left in his hut in the village. A rough *nkunka* (shelter) is built in the bush by the dancers, some of whom then rush back to the village, seize the patient, carry him on a mat into the *nkunka* and wash him with a lotion of certain medicines dispensed by the *chimbuki*. After much song and music the patient is removed from the mat, which is left in the *nkunka*, and (presumably) *Chihamba* remains too. *Chihamba* would appear to us to be merely a disease, but it is always referred to as a *mukishi*.

Kamwenja is another spirit known throughout the whole tribe. It interferes in domestic life, disturbs the sexual relations of married people, spoils the wife's cooking, and is generally a bane to married life. *Kamwenja* is also reputed to cause people to steal and to be generally vicious. Next to *Chihamba* it is the most active and prevalent of the troubling spirits. Fortunately it is easily appeased by any village doctor who makes a shrine by the troubled hut, the shrine being made of two bent sticks placed cross-ways and surrounded by a chalk line, with certain medicines placed in the centre.

Nkura (or *Nkula*) is a *mukishi* that causes barrenness in women, and prevents the family *akishi* from giving life. Should a woman of bearing age, being married to a man who is obviously not sterile, fail to become pregnant the village *chimbuki* divines that she is possessed by *Nkura*. A small hut is built at the rear of the woman's hut and inside a bowl of medicine is placed. *Nkura* is thus enticed away from the woman's hut to the small hut. *Nkura* is very prevalent and much dreaded, as child-bearing is desired by all married women and barrenness is shameful.

[As stated elsewhere it seems to me that these evil spirits may be connected with witch cult or with some old religion. Further research would be most interesting. Some additional notes made quite independently by F.V.B.M. appear at the end of this chapter ; but there remains a great deal to be investigated. Unfortunately I have no chance of being able further to probe this matter and must leave it to others. F.H.M.]

There are a vast number of other tribal *akishi*, especially for hunting. Near most villages may be seen a small pathway cleared up to the base of an anthill and terminating in a forked stick on which are often hung shreds of cloth or bits of animals' entrails. The sticks are often placed in the centre of the village, and the bark trays used for carrying in the killed game are piled round the base. These are the shrines of the hunting spirits who have different names in nearly every village, and are often more family than tribal. A celebrated hunter dies and his spirit is supposed to have certain influence in the local hunting grounds. In time the hunter is forgotten but his name lives as that of a *mukishi* to be propitiated if bad luck is to be avoided.

The guardian *akishi* of the *luteng'u* (forge) and of other arts arc probably family *akishi*. The real tribal *mukishi* like *Chihamba* appears to have nothing to do with the souls of the departed and to be, rather, the deification of a certain trouble in life and thus to become a perquisite of the village doctors who profess to control them. [Is it not possible that instead of being what Mr. Keith calls " deification of certain troubles " they are—to use our phraseology—rather satellites or attributes of the devil? F.H.M.] They are not personified at all, and no Kalunda can profess to describe what *Chihamba* is like. They are felt, not seen. Graven images are made of (? for) the local hunting spirits, often like a pair of lions, one male and one female (perhaps this has another signification : see chapter on DREAMS. F.H.M.), but these images do not represent the spirit, but are merely prescribed images that are supposed to give pleasure to the spirit, on which the offerings of blood and intestines are placed. When diseases are attributed to some local spirit a clay image of a snake is made, but the Alunda do not believe that the spirit itself has this form. In no case do the Alunda worship idols.

NOTE ON WORDS WITH THE STEM—*Kishi*

There are three words with different meanings that have this stem.

	Sing.	Plur.	Meaning.
i.	*Mukishi*	*Akishi*	a spirit.
ii.	*Mukishi*	*Nyikishi*	a drawing or image.
iii.	*Ikishi*	*Makishi*	a dancing man.

A face or image made at a shrine would be called *Mukishi* (ii). The dancing men at funerals (*makishi a kadangu*) and at circumcision camps (*makishi a mukanda*) (*vide* Chapter III) are dressed up to worship the *akishi* of the departed.

The *akishi* of the *m'bong'i* are also not really *akishi* but *makishi*. They are distinctly interesting. At important deaths before the successor is elected, on a moonlight night a drum is taken into the forest and a dance is started. Men on high stilts quite naked, and whitened from head to foot with chalk, emerge from between the trees and flit about in a ghostly way among the boughs " like spirits of the dead." Many of the more superstitious and children flee in terror to the village in spite of the fact that the ceremony is acknowledged to be a fraud to give pleasure to the departed. The *m'bong'i* are very rarely held now, but one was held at the death of sub-chief Kakura in 1921. [The continuance of symbolic acts, etc., after the people have ceased to believe in the reality of the representations, is common to many religions. F.H.M.]

A FURTHER NOTE ON *Chimbuki* AND *Chiyomboka* OR *Katepa* (the doctors) AND *Uloji* (witchcraft), AND *Chitumbu* (medicines)

In every village there are elders who are skilled in the cult of the spirits and can locate spiritual troubles by divining with a rod (*ng'ombu*) or other means. They are

THE CHILOLA TEST FOR DETECTING A TROUBLESOME SPIRIT.

Two villagers grip a horn (of a sable antelope) filled with *Milondo* medicine, which moves and guides them.

DIVINING BY NGOMBU.

The audience are giving the correct responses.

often called *ayimbuki* or doctors (pl. of *chimbuki*). They
are frequently skilled herbalists, they put a patient
through a course of washings with medicines as an anti-
dote to *Chihamba*, sell charms against all spirit evils,
name the family *akishi* of children, and give advice
regarding worship. The spirits if treated properly are
very tractable.

It is witchcraft that poisons the tribal life. Lunda
life is indeed a struggle against witchcraft, and the
chiyomboka (witch-doctor) is their only help in the
struggle. The *chiyomboka* often develops out of the
chimbuki, but he has superior powers of divination.
Debased and unnatural persons are said to get hold of
chitumbu (spells or witchcraft medicine), i.e. make
themselves living creatures (=familiars. F.H.M.) who
nourish themselves and their masters by ghoulish means
and keep their masters from death and disease. Some
fearing death from witchcraft acquire *chitumbu* to protect themselves, others to kill undesirable relatives or
enemies. Chiefs and headmen possess *chitumbu* so as to be
feared or so as to be powerful. Everyone is, therefore, in
fear of death from *chitumbu*, and the majority of elderly
persons are suspected of being (or actually believed to be)
in possession of these horrors, and many would even
appear to believe that they do possess them. The pos-
sessors, male or female, are called *aloji* (sing. *muloji*),
i.e. witches or wizards, and most deaths and most ills,
from a miscarriage to an epileptic fit, are attributed to
uloji. The *chiyomboka* is said to be able, by his occult
powers and divination, to settle the suspicions of witchcraft on the guilty one and have him or her punished,
and he is therefore considered necessary to the welfare
of the community. In Lunda eyes the *muloji* is the
people's curse, and the *chiyomboka* the protector ; and
they cannot believe that we have their interests at heart
when the *chiyomboka* gets punished and the *muloji* goes
free. Witchcraft is a very present terror to the whole

tribe, and it seems intolerable to them that their fellows should be able to murder them with impunity : the *chiyomboka* being, in their eyes, the only remedy that they have.

The above completes Mr. Keith's notes as supplied to me, and except for a very few interpolated comments I give them as written. Much more will be found about witchcraft in the following chapters, but I think that the following pages extracted from Mr. F. V. Bruce Miller's notes should be recorded. They were obtained quite independently of Mr. Keith's and of my own. I omit all that are identical with Mr. Keith's :

Chihamba. When a person is sick for some time lots are cast, and while this is being done the name of *Chihamba* is frequently mentioned, and he is requested to leave the invalid and allow him to recover. If *Chihamba* does not go the patient dies. If the patient recovers but becomes ill again the root of a tree (*musambazhita*) is taken, cut up and put into water with some of the bark of the same tree. The invalid is washed in the concoction which is supposed to cure him. The root is called *ikamba ja Chihamba*. The object of casting lots in the first place is, apparently, to find out if it is *Chihamba* that is responsible for the illness or something else.

Nkula. If a man is impotent or a woman barren the spirit *nkula* is said to be the cause. There is a special doctor who deals with this spirit. The person concerned builds a grass hut at the back of his house, and the doctor takes a special kind of root (unknown to anyone but himself) and makes medicine which is used to wash with. He or she (the patient) mixes red clay with oil and makes a mark with it across the forehead. No fresh meat must be eaten after doing this, and no one else must use the fire of the patient; this practice is supposed to cure the impotency. After a child is born the same doctor gives medicine to the parent who was formerly impotent or barren, and he or she can then eat meat and resume former mode of life.

Ubwango. When a woman bears twins the spirit " Ubwango " must be propitiated or the twins will die. The doctor presiding over this spirit gives medicine to the parents who then walk about naked and receive small presents from the villagers. The doctor takes " mpemba " and makes white rings round the eyes and marks on the chest of everyone present ; the doctor also names the twins—the first is called " *Mbuyu* " and the second " *Kapya,*" irrespective of sex. These names are changed when twins grow up.

Karombo, or *Ntambo.* The hunting spirit. If a man who is a good hunter suddenly has a run of bad luck and wounds or misses game without killing he has lots cast, and if the man who presides over the lots attributes the failure to the influence of this spirit, the hunter goes to the " Karombo " doctor. The doctor and he then proceed to an anthill in the vicinity, and they make clay into a heap and hoe a little path up to the side of the ant heap. A pot is placed on the heap of clay inside which is put a certain medicine. The doctor makes the hunter wash in this concoction, after doing which he returns to the hunt. If he kills game he returns and paints the pot with the blood of the slain animal. In this manner is the spirit appeased and ill luck warded off.

Kamwadji, is the spirit which gives sexual powers to a man. If any individual loses his powers in this respect the doctor of the spirit takes two pieces of stick and places them on the ground parallel to each other and places a pot containing medicine on the ground between them. The patient sits on a mat between the sticks and washes in the medicine. While doing so he must try and be cheerful and laugh all the time. If the spirit is sufficiently appeased by this the supplicant will find that sexual connection with his wife after the foregoing ceremony will provide him with inordinate pleasure.

From the above practices it will be seen that the spirits are not meant to be worshipped but only to be appeased—and are only responsible for ill fortune and never have an influence for good.

[It fell to me, just before I left the Kasempa district, to review a case from Mr. Miller's court in which occurred the following sentence :

" To be a herbalist without bringing in witchcraft seems to me to be quite beyond the local native."

I queried this, chiefly so as to get further information, and in return I received a memorandum from Mr. Miller, from which the following is an extract. It throws interesting light on the profession (s) of doctor and witch-doctor. F.H.M.]

" I believe this (the sentence quoted above) to be a fact. The Alunda will *tell* one that a person can die of *musong'o ho* (illness only), but when any person is ill the villagers begin to wonder what spirit has been neglected. They therefore do their best to propitiate one or more of the malevolent spirits—little attention being ever paid to the benevolent. The patient's condition not improving, a *chimbuki* is called in. On his arrival, and after sundry incantations, some medicine is given to the patient. If the patient improves the *chimbuki* is paid and goes on his (or her) way. Should the patient get worse it is obvious that the *chimbuki* must consider his reputation, for with a few unexpected deaths his practice would dwindle, and to save himself he accuses some unfortunate person of harbouring one or more of the many evil spirits (i.e. familiars, F.H.M.) with which the Alunda are supposed to be well provided. Therefore, although in theory a person *can* die of *musong'o ho*, in practice it does not happen, the *chimbuki* covering his failure (as a doctor) by entering the domain which should really belong to the *katepa*." (In parenthesis I may add that among the neighbouring Ba-Kaonde I have known of cases in which death has been attributed to natural causes : " just illness " ; and though they are admittedly rare, they are not unknown. F.H.M.)

" The *chimbuki, mbuki* or *ng'ang'a* is primarily a herbalist : when he gets a difficult case he will get medicines from the bush with which he will anoint (*sonza*) his eyes ; which anointing enables him to see things of the spirit world : such as to find out who has *malomba* or *andumba*, which need to be killed before his medicines can take effect. A very advanced *chimbuki* (who would more often be called a *mbuki*) is said to do nothing but hold himself in readiness to answer calls for killing *malomba*. (*Andumba* and *malomba* are explained in the chapters on witchcraft.)

The *katepa* is the witch-doctor proper and works on a bigger scale by drumming, dancing and divining. He discovers who is the witch in the village, and when he has found one calls in the *mbuki* to kill the evil spirit (if it be an *ilomba*). When the *ilomba* dies the owner dies at the same time (as explained elsewhere). The *chiamboka*, whom you spell *chiyomboka*, is apparently a new designation. I heard it for the first time in the—— case (January, 1921), and Mrs. —— informs me that she heard it for the first time in August, 1921. Headman Yanga Yanga informed me this morning that the word has been imported from the Valuena, with which others agree. As far as I can gather it means one who discovers *andumba* only, and one who owns them. If well paid he will remove the *andumba* from their owner, and with them the stigma of witchcraft. He is also a herbalist."

[In a subsequent letter Mr. Miller informed me that he had been told that the Alunda appeared to have introduced the *chiamboka* idea with a view to attempting to deal with these witchcraft familiars by driving them out and not killing their owners, so as to protect themselves from evil and yet keep within the law, but I know too little about this yet to express an opinion. The whole subject bristles with difficulties but is extremely interesting. F.H.M.]

[1] The Wakwa in Tanganyika territory have a similar belief. Cf. *Through the Heart of Africa*, p. 39. " They believe that the sun had at one time a battle with the moon, in which the latter was badly worsted, the signs of the conflict being still visible upon its face." (F.H.M.)

[2] I write this as Mr. Keith spells it ; but from other sources I gather a more correct spelling is *Katokang'onyi*. *Kato*=the bush or woodlands. *Ka*=of. *Ng'onyi* chieftainship, the country of chieftainship. (F.H.M.)

[3] Mr. Keith spells this Mwachiamfwa, but for consistency I have changed it. (F.H.M.)

CHAPTER XIV

WITCHCRAFT (I)

(*BULOZHI*)

INTRODUCTORY

(Throughout this and the following two chapters the word "witch"
is used for "wizard" or "witch.")

I ONCE described witchcraft as the poisonous
creeper that spreads over Africa and impedes all
progress. To a certain extent this is realised by
many students ; but, so far, it seems to me that
witchcraft is really very little understood. When a
subject is as important and looms as large across the
outlook as does witchcraft and the profession of the witch-
doctor, it really merits very close investigation—investigation that should be undertaken after one has cleared
one's mind of prejudice.

Witchcraft is a part of demonology : that branch of
religion which deals with evil spirits and demons ; and
it is probably a relic of the oldest religion in the world.
In every religion the presence of spirits is recognised
together with their antagonism to the beneficent powers.
When one reaches the stage at which the beneficent
agents—divine or semi-natural—are prominent, but at
the same time man feels it necessary constantly to be on
the watch to propitiate evils spirits, then the witch-
doctor, whose powers are handed on in a kind of guild,
flourishes. This represents a well known and definable
stage in the evolution of religion, *and it is the stage which
most of the Bantu religions in this part of the world have
reached to-day.*

African natives skipped a stage in their evolution by passing direct from the Stone to the Iron Age. We are at present helping them (wisely or not) to skip a good many ages : socially, ethically and economically. We are also, by introducing Christianity in its twentieth-century shape, attempting the same thing in religion. We are apt to overlook the fact that Christianity, even in its simple original form, was not considered a suitable religion for Abraham, Isaac and Jacob, or the advent of Christ on earth would not have been so long deferred. I believe that this may account in part for our rather unequal progress in civilising, elevating or converting the natives ; and the following features appear to be worthy of notice as an introduction to the study of local witchcraft beliefs which must be understood if they are to be eradicated. I have added this chapter to the original scheme because there appears to be no side of native life that is less understood than witchcraft : therefore, anything which throws a little light on it must be of value to the student. In all that follows I have, however, no wish to " lay down the law " : my knowledge is far too limited, and these notes represent no more than fragmentary evidence pieced together under difficult conditions, together with the conclusions drawn therefrom.

Like most primitive races the Bantu peoples do not confuse witchcraft with religion : with *their* religion, that is. Their religion may not be a high one, though it is one that has been grading up for a long time,[1] and it is intelligible. Witchcraft is not. We know little about it and they themselves know less. I have never succeeded in finding even a fair tradition as to its origin : which, in a negative way, seems to favour the belief that it is a relic of an earlier age . . . precisely as it was in Europe. It may be even the very same religion that existed in Europe in prehistoric days. Professor Sir Arthur Keith states (quoted in *The Times*, April 27th, 1922) that he considers the Broken Hill skull is akin to those of Europeans

A GROUP OF LUNDA CHIEFS.

In the centre is Musokantanda XIII seated on a lion skin, his head is covered by a calico skull cap.

in the Ice Age. There is nothing inherently impossible in the idea that one race and one religion existed in Europe and Africa at some prehistoric date. Skipping a " period " it would be interesting (in the search for a link) to ascertain if there is any anthropological connection between the two primitive types of Lapps and Pygmies.

These Bantu religions of to-day have in them some demonology since they recognise not only good spirits but bad (or, more correctly, adverse) spirits. In this way they border on witchcraft ; and it is at times hard to sift the one from the other ; but they are, nevertheless, entirely distinct from it. To the natives their religion is sacred : a part of life, which is a gift from God the creator. On this is built the belief in metempsychosis or reincarnation : the belief that the dead are in the living and that the breath of life has been handed down from one ancestor. This applies to the family spirits, those that are favourable or beneficent, and those that are hostile or maleficent. The help of the former is invoked while the latter have to be guarded against and propitiated ; but all are sacred since they are the reincarnated spirits of the dead. (It is possible that some general or tribal spirits are connected with the old witch cult ; but not —I feel sure—the family spirits.)

Witchcraft is, on the contrary, universally considered an abomination, and those who practise it (the wizards and witches, *not* the witch-doctors) are evil and in league with evil. They merit death. This belief is a healthy one : that is to say, since the natives believe in the existence of witchcraft—and they do—it is a healthy sign that they abhor it and those who practise it.

Let us first deal with this belief—a big obstacle with many. The same difficulty has arisen in Europe (including England) : it is not new. The following is an extract from *The Witch Cult in Western Europe* by Margaret Alice Murray (Clarendon Press, 1921), to which book I am greatly indebted for providing me with many links since I started these chapters ; and from which I have borrowed freely. The book and its bibliography are invaluable to the student of this subject.

" It is interesting to note the class of mind among those contemporary writers who believed in the reality of the facts confessed at the trials (of witches) as compared with those who disbelieved. It will be seen that the most brilliant minds, the keenest intellects, the greatest investigators, were among the believers. Bodin, Lord Bacon, Raleigh, Boyle, Cudworth, Selden, Henry More, Sir Thomas Browne, Matthew Hale, Sir George Mackenzie and many others, most of whom had heard the evidence at first hand. The sceptics were Weyer, pupil of the occultist Cornelius Agrippa ; Reginald Scott, a Kentish country squire ; Filmer, whose name was a by-word for political bigotry ; Wagstaffe, who went mad from drink; and Webster, a fanatical preacher (see James Crossley's Introduction of Potts' *Discoverie of witch-craft*, Chetham Society, pp. v–xii). The sceptics, with the exception of Weyer, appear to have had little or no first-hand evidence ; their only weapon was an appeal to common sense and sentiment combined ; their only method was a flat denial of every statement which appeared to point to supernatural powers." [Precisely, I am afraid, the attitude of most Europeans to African witchcraft to-day.] " They could not disprove the statements : they could not explain them without opposing the religious beliefs of their time, and so weakening their cause by exposing themselves to the serious charge of atheism ; therefore they denied evidence which in the case of any other accusation would have been accepted as proof."

No less an authority than Lord Coke actually defined a witch : " A witch is a person who hath conference with the Devil, to consult with him or do some act." And he held that even if a witch used her skill for good and not for evil, provided it were proved that she had obtained her knowledge from the Devil, she had broken the law and must die. Sir Matthew Hale (1664) declared that the reality of witcheraft was " unquestionable."

Again, familiars were recognised by law in England, and the feeding, suckling and rewarding of them was a felony. (Bishop Francis Hutchinson's *Historical Essay*, p. 77.)

There is a list of no less than 511 witches who were tried in England and Scotland alone in the seventeenth century, when witchcraft suppression was at its highest. Turning to the Continent of Europe for a few examples we find that one Judge (Remy) boasted that he had put 800 witches to the torture in 16 years; the Bishop of Wurtemburg that he had burned 900 *in one year ;* and at Geneva 500 *were burned in three months !* A witch was legally executed in Western Europe as late as 1782, only 140 years ago. (Date given on authority of Lowie *Primitive Society*, p. 406.)

The Protestants were as emphatic in their belief in the detestation of witchcraft as was the Church of Rome. Luther expressed his belief in the Devil (being visible, etc.) many times. Calvin when remodelling the laws of Geneva left those against witchcraft intact. John Knox declared that witches should be put to death. Cranmer charged his clergy to seek out " any who used charms, sorcery, enchantments, witchcraft . . ." Even as late as 1768 John Wesley wrote : " It is true likewise that the English in general, and indeed most of the men of learning in Europe, have given up all accounts of witches and apparitions as mere old wives' fables. I am sorry for it, and I willingly take this opportunity of entering my solemn protest against this violent compliment which so many that believe in the Bible pay to those who do not believe it."

I think that, with these facts before us, we may be chary of laughing at the Bantu belief in witchcraft. We even have the maypole and other relics of the witch cult in England to-day to testify to the reality of a similar belief amongst our ancestors.

Having dealt with the belief let us next examine some records. The most minute record existing of a primitive people is that of the Israelites. There is little doubt that they believed in witchcraft and witches, and abhorred them. The witch of Endor is a much quoted case, but I will confine myself to three quotations :

Deut. xviii. 10–12.	" a witch . . . a consulter with familiar spirits, a wizard . . . are an abomination unto the Lord."
Lev. xx. 27	" a man also or woman that hath a familiar spirit, or that is a wizard, shall surely be put to death."
Ex. xxii. 18.	" Thou shalt not suffer a witch to live."

If these quotations are unfamiliar to the reader they will give him cause for reflection ; and all who are studying the wilder Bantu will find much that is useful in comparative ethnography in the early books of the Bible, especially in Leviticus.[2]

The gospels, too, distinctly recognise that disease was the result of " possession " by demons, and the early Church carried on Christ's method of expelling them. Exorcists long formed an active minor order, and the name still remains in the Roman Catholic Church. Late examples of the belief in witchcraft may be found in Burton and Sir Thomas Browne. The belief in vampires is chiefly found in Slavonic lands, but many references to succubi and incubi may be found everywhere. The idea of bewitching a pregnant woman so as to give her child harelip forms a prominent feature in Knut Hamsun's *modern* story of the Baltic—*The Growth of the Soil.*

" The continuity of the ancient religion is proved by the references to it in the classical authors, the ecclesiatical laws, and other legal and historical records." (*The Witch-cult in Western Europe, sup. cit.*) But here it will suffice to quote three examples :

Laws of Athelstan, 924–940.

" We have ordained respecting witchcrafts, and lyblacs, and morthdeads . . ." etc.

Laws of Cnut, 1017–1035.

·" We earnestly forbid any heathenism : heathenism is that men worship idols . . . or love witchcraft, or provoke morth-work in any wise."

Bull of Pope Innocent VIII, 1484.

" It has come to our ears that numbers of both sexes do not avoid to have intercourse with demons, Incubi and Succubi ; and that by their sorceries, and by their incantations, charms and conjurations, they suffocate, extinguish and cause to perish the births of women . . . making and procuring that men and women, flocks and herds and other animals shall suffer and be tormented both from within and without, so that men beget not, nor women conceive ; and they impede the conjugal action of men and women."

The connecting points which run through this pre-amble are the very real belief in witchcraft by all kinds of peoples and in all kinds of creed ; and the general belief that it emanates from the Evil One : that its votaries are in league with that one, and that they are an abomination. In Europe there is any amount of proof of the witch-cult being devil worship, e.g. :

" The Diuell comaundeth them that they shall acknowledge him for their god, call vpõ him, pray to him, and trust in him—Then doe all repeate the othe which they haue geuen vnto him ; in acknowledging him to be their God." (Dannæus E.1, ch. iv.)

So Madame Bourignon (1661) " will allow no other god but him." So also Isobel Gowdie " Ve get all this power from the Divell, and when ve seek it from him, ve call him ' Owr Lord,' " etc. etc.

I have not found any Bantu who have what one might call an indigenous devil, but all seem to agree that witchcraft is the work of an evil power, and that therefore those who practise it (the witches) are an abomination.

Witchcraft must be divided into operative witchcraft and ritual witchcraft. Under the former are classed all charms and spells whether for good or evil. Such charms are common to every nation and country and are practised by priests and people of every religion. They are part of the common heritage of the human race ; and while interesting and worthy of study and record are of no practical value in the study of any particular cult. It may be noted, however, that it inevitably happens that a new race or a new religion always has great faith in the potency of the evil powers of its predecessors and often adopts or adapts its charms so as " to be on the safe side." Thus many charms originally applied to witchcraft will be found to be used in the new religion.

Ritual witchcraft embraces the religious beliefs and ritual of the people who are called witches. Witchcraft appears to have been the ancient religion of Western Europe ; and, as has been pointed out above, it may have been the ancient religion of Africa. In Europe it was probably the religion of a race of dwarfs, or " little people," in Africa it may have been the religion of a race of pygmies : the present Pygmies or their predecessors.

It has been, unfortunately, beyond me to find out much about ritual in the witch-cult of the Ba-Kaonde and their neighbours. For various reasons this is so. Firstly, witchcraft is " prohibited " by us, and is hated and feared by the natives, so that those who practise it do not advertise the fact and are naturally reticent. Once one has their confidence one can obtain a good deal of information as to the *modus operandi* of the witch-doctors, who consider their profession a meritorious one ; but the witches, being proscribed, will not talk. As will be shown later, on conviction by native means, they do not deny their witchcraft, any more than convicted witches did in Europe (most of the data in the next chapter but one is based on the admissions by convicted witches as to how they accomplished their ends), but in cases of trial by Europeans, knowing our generally expressed disbelief in the cult, they strenuously deny their powers, plead causeless persecution and claim our protection. This brings me to the second cause of failure in investigation : the fact that witchcraft is not only " proscribed " but (somewhat illogically) is also " denied " by us—as a race —so that we are looked upon, in this matter, either as senseless in that we deny the obvious and demonstrable, or as scoffers. In spite of these disadvantages reference can be made to one or two points—leaving a tremendous amount for further investigation that might prove of unique anthropological value if we could only free our minds of prejudice and study the whole question scientifically.

All witch-cult has always been connected with fertility —especially of humans and animals. It was originally a fertility cult, but seems gradually to have become degraded into a method of blasting fertility ; and this, I think, is as true of Africa as of elsewhere. The witches who had once been the means of bringing prosperity to the people by driving out evil influences, in process of time were looked upon as being the evil influences themselves, and were held in horror accordingly. Thus, Jonet Clark (Edinburgh, 1590) was tried " for giving and taking away power from sundry men's genital members " (Pitcairn's *Criminal Trials*, I, pt. ii., 206) and Bessie Roy for " causing women's milk to dry up " (*id.* 207). A very large number of midwives practised witchcraft and claimed to be able to cause or prevent pregnancy, to cause or prevent easy delivery, to cast the labour pains on an animal or human being and in every way to have power over the generative organs of both sexes. In fact, in the sixteenth and seventeenth centuries " the better the midwife the better the witch " (Murray). The same is literally true to-day in many parts of Central Africa ; and the midwives are not only much resorted to for abortificants, but are greatly feared and respected.

Henri Boguet (*Discours des sorciers*, Lyons, 1608, p. 211) says of witches, " Ils font cacher & retirer les parties viriles, et puis les font ressortir quand il leur plait. Ils empeschent aussi antost les nerfs & estant la roideur du membre ; et tantost la procreation en destournant ou bouchant les conduits de la semence, pour empescher qu'elle ne descende aux vases de la generation." Kaonde girls have practically the same fear of their parts being " closed " (*vide supra* Ch. V), a fear which is very genuine, but I can find no proof that such is attributable to witchcraft, though it is likely that such is its origin. It is also probable that the Alunda tribal *akishi* " *kamwenja*," which interferes in domestic life, disturbs the sexual relations of married people and " *nkura* " (or " *nkula* "), which causes barrenness in women and prevents the family *akishi* from giving life, are both relics of an older cult connected with witchcraft : at any rate, they are greatly dreaded by the Alunda of to-day. I think there is little doubt that the Alunda are lower down in the religion scale than the Ba-Kaonde, and I believe the Valuena are still lower. Investigation among them might carry one further. There is no doubt that miscarriage is a misfortune generally attributed to witchcraft ; but on other points I have not sufficient knowledge to sift the powers of the spirits from those of the witches.

From a general point of view there is not much more to say—particulars will be found in the following chapters, with notes on the similarity to the witch-cult in Europe—but it might be mentioned that the trials of suspected witches bear a resemblance that is more real than superficial to those of which we have record in Britain and in Europe. The methods of divination are described further on, but it may be recorded here that there is a formality attending them and an atmosphere of determination which is strongly reminiscent of the ecclesiastical courts conducting such cases in Europe.

In the case of Joan of Arc, which is not only the first great trial of strength in Europe between the old and the new religions, but is one that is easily studied since the documents are accessible, the judges were ecclesiastics, and their questions show that they were well aware of an underlying organisation of which they stood in some dread (as did the king, Charles VII). In native trials the judges are the witch-doctors, the " priests " of the newer religion, who are equally determined in their attitude. " We have caught her now," said the Bishop of Beauvais at Joan's trial, which is a literal translation of words often used to my knowledge at native trials : " We have caught you, now: you witch," being practically the native formula used as a verdict of guilty.

" And she was burned without even the formality of handing her over to the secular authorities " is the record in Joan's trial. Precisely the African procedure.

Continuing with this trial : " On the fatal Tuesday when she learned her doom, flesh and spirit quailed at the prospect of the agony to come, and she cried out. . . . Yet within twenty-four hours she went to the stake with courage unquenched. . . . Like John Fian nearly two centuries later, her spirit had sunk at first and again like Fian she endured to the end." (Murray.) At African witch-trials the witch when condemned falls on her knees and appeals for mercy : offers herself as a slave, and so on ; but towards the end she admits her witchcraft, giving full details thereof and ceases to supplicate. It may be only because she realises that her case is hopeless, or it may be " that the witches are so devoted to his (the devil's) service that neither torture nor death can affright them, & they go to martyrdom & to death for love of him as gaily as to a festival of pleasure and public rejoicing " (de Lancre). I know not, but I do know that generally the witch in Africa confesses her witchcraft, and hides nothing, and then faces death bravely.

It seems to me that, whatever the origin of witchcraft, the natives here to-day are in approximately the same relative position towards it as was Christendom some 250 years ago ; and—considering what backward races they are in other ways—this speaks rather well for them and for their religion. In the following chapters which, except for the footnotes on European resemblances, were compiled some time before this, will be found such details of witchcraft as I have been able to accumulate among this group of tribes. I neither believe nor disbelieve them. All I know is that not only do the bewitched and their friends (the majority) believe in them, but that frequently, at any rate, the " witches " (the minority) also believe in them. Consequently when the whole of the governed have a belief, that belief is worthy of study by the governors.

1 The somewhat common use of the epithet " degraded " to these religions appears to the writer entirely inapplicable.

2 See also especially Numbers v. 11–31 for a comparison with *mwavi*.

CHAPTER XV

WITCHCRAFT (II)

General Aspect—Locally

" It was an excellent thing to destroy wizards, Buldeo thought. . . .
" But, said the charcoal burners, what would happen if the English
heard of it ? The English . . . were a perfectly mad people, who would
not let honest farmers kill witches in peace.
" Why, said Buldeo, the headman of the village would report that
Messua and her husband had died of a snake bite. . . ."

KIPLING, *The Second Jungle Book.*

AS in India, so in Africa. The Native Commissioner, visiting a village and checking the
census is told that an old woman Na Kananga[1]
" has died of a snake bite," or that the old
greybeard Shanjia Kananga " died of fever last rains."
At other times the headman will come in himself to
report that some aged dame went out collecting firewood
and did not return . . . possibly a lion killed her . . . one
had been heard roaring about that time.

And behind all this lies the ever-present tragedy of
village life in Africa. Accusation, divination, trial and
execution for witchcraft.

One day Na Kananga hears the first rumour ; a crony
of hers falls out with her : tongues are loosened ; and,
mixed up with a stream of lewd and filthy abuse, the
word " *mulozhi* " (witch) is heard. She resents it : her
antagonist justifies her use of it. . . . The quarrel past,
it is forgotten, but another day someone repeats it. Then
a neighbour's baby dies : Na Kananga is " looked at
sideways." Perhaps the crops are poor, or the fowls die

of disease : then pneumonia comes among the villagers, and Na Kananga is not a victim. Rumours give place to consultation, suspicious incidents in her past are raked up. The witch-doctor is called in and . . . she " died of a snake bite."

In the above sketch of a common occurrence I have drawn the picture from one side—from the side of an innocent old hag, done to death. There is the other side. The people believe with a genuine belief that they have been bewitched, and so far as I know the evidence is not sufficient for us to state as a fact that they have not been ; and they have no other means of protecting themselves than by finding the witch and killing her. It really is extraordinary, considering the importance of witchcraft and its side-issues, that it is so little understood, and the following seem to be some of the more usual misunderstandings.

Firstly, it is often asserted (even by those who deny the existence of witchcraft !) that witchcraft is a common practice. I do not know : it may be, but I doubt it. Suspicion and accusations of witchcraft are common, so is witch-finding : so common indeed are they that they represent the normal state of affairs ; and it is almost impossible to think what native life would be like if they could be banished. Nevertheless, though natives would deny it—an irrelevant fact, since they are prejudiced—the practice of witchcraft is, probably, not common.

Secondly, many think that the witch-doctor (*ng'anga*) is a witch (*mulozhi*). Even Sir Harry Johnston in his great work, *The Comparative Study of Bantu Languages*, gives *ng'anga* and *mulozhi* as alternative translations of " witch."

I have tried scores of witchcraft cases. I have read the records of scores more (having to review the cases of lower courts every month) ; I have talked for hours with witch-doctors and with " laymen," and never once have I heard a *ng'anga* called *mulozhi*. Never have I heard of a witch-doctor divining a colleague as a witch. The witch-doctor does not practise witchcraft. He dabbles in the occult, he mystifies, but he does not—in his professional capacity—bewitch (he is very often a charming old village headman, with more intelligence than his peers, by which one may often know him). He is no more a witch than a chemist is a poisoner. A chemist may be a poisoner, and a *ng'anga* may be a witch : that is all.

All, that is, unless one includes indirect attributes to the word. We say that if a chemist provides a man with arsenic knowing that he is going to kill some person or persons with it, he is a principal in the murder, or an accessory before the fact. So, in our law, if a *ng'anga* provides Kananga with a *mulombe* (which can only be used to remove undesirables, and which is the only means of bewitching that may be obtained from a *ng'anga* . . . and of this even I am not sure) he is equally guilty with his client. The native does not think so. The doctor has supplied his client (patient, if you will) with something he needed, as the ironsmith might provide him with a hoe. It is a trifle illogical when we consider how far a native carries vicarious responsibility in other ways (e.g. A, using B's boat, is drowned. B is responsible for A's death —an idea which would spread consternation among our riverside watermen !) This distinction may be simply illogical ; or it may be but another example of the complete divergence, absolute reversal, of ideas between black and white ; or, again, it may be due to the fact that a native, *compos mentis*, will never dare to accuse a *ng'anga* of anything. (A native cornered, one brooding for long over some injustice, or one who is fuddled, may do so, but never when normal.)

Therefore, let it be recognised that a witch-doctor or witch-finder is perfectly distinct from a witch.

A third fallacy is that we, the governing race, stop witchcraft. We may flatter ourselves officially that we do, but we do not. We have a " Witchcraft suppression proclamation," but it does not suppress *witchcraft*. The natives even say that we support it and protect the witches, because the thing against which we have legislated, and for which we prosecute, is witchcraft-accusation, witch-finding and witch-killing. One of the chief complaints against our rule is that (in native eyes) we punish the conscientious man who discovers a witch ; the "friend of mankind"—the witch-doctor ; the bereaved who have naturally avenged the death of a relative, and the executioners, while we let the abhorred and dangerous witch go at large. This is largely due to the pervading misconception, or lax definition, of witch-craft. On the supposition that witchcraft does not exist, the belief in it will need years of education and elevation (to all intents and purposes not yet started) to eradicate. If it does exist then we should co-operate with the natives in suppressing it, which while tempering their barbarity would get them on our side. Meanwhile, as a first step, I would suggest that since we have started at the wrong end, our penal laws on this subject need revision, and need coupling with them the provision of witch colonies, where " convicted " witches (native convictions) can live, *whether we believe in the existence of witchcraft or not.* They, the " witches," would welcome such colonies, and we would then appear to the natives less criminally in support of the Evil One than we do at present. It is a pity that we cannot remember more consistently how backward are these people, and how recently " we " believed the same ourselves when we had centuries of Christianity behind us, and when our evolution was incomparably more advanced than that of the Bantu to-day.

The terms used here are easy to define.

A witch is a person who, by subtle means, spells, or the possession of familiars and other unnatural things, bewitches (or is alleged to bewitch) a person or a community or anything : causes death, illness or other misfortune.

Witchcraft is the possession or exercise of these powers : the act of bewitching people or things.

The witch-doctor is the person who divines, finds, convicts and sentences the witch. He may sometimes provide the means for bewitching, but in most, if not all, cases the means are obtained elsewhere. It is not his rôle, but he may in a few cases do it as a chemist may provide a poisoner with poison. On the other hand the witch-doctor enables conviction to result as the chemist often by his analysis secures the conviction of a poisoner. Eliminating for the moment the possibility that the witch-doctor is working with religious zeal against the evils of an older religion, this duty (which I have compared to that of an analytical chemist at a poison trial) is his chief rôle so far as witchcraft is concerned.

The witch-doctor, let me repeat, does not exist to provide witches with the wherewithal to bewitch. If ever he does it is but rarely, and witches and witchcraft would flourish without him, which is, after all, the real test of his position in this matter. His real work is that of diviner, and we should not lose sight of the fact that he divines more frequently to trace and exorcise a troubling spirit than to trace and condemn a living person. He is also a priest, on the reincarnation side of the religion, for he has to divine from which spirit a baby's soul has emanated. He is a provider of charms of all kinds. He can, too, be called a consulting physician, and general practitioner and a dispensing chemist.

Nevertheless, his importance as a witch-finder or witch-diviner can hardly be overrated ; and, with the warning as to his other powers contained in the last paragraph, it is with that aspect that we are most concerned in this chapter. But for him the belief in witchcraft *might* decrease. To a great extent the *ng'anga* flourishes because of this belief : it is, at any rate, one of the justifications for his profession. He is, as was the Inquisition, a sinister institution, and he needs suppressing

or checking; but he is nevertheless, in the present condition of things, *indispensable*. The only way to obliterate
him (as witch-finder) is to remove the need for him :
i.e. (if there be no witchcraft) to educate the belief in
witches out of the people. Education, medical assistance
and protective legislation will, in time, render him no
longer indispensable. Penal provisions by themselves do
but render him more cunning, more secretive and—
because of the risk—more expensive. (And, since we
have demonitised the high currency of the country—
slaves—it is very hard indeed to pay the high fees exacted
in smaller currency—goods.)

I fear that penal laws, alone, will never prevail. They
are most useful and necessary adjuncts to government,
but that is all. To attempt to eradicate the belief in
witchcraft—and, therefore, the essential witch-doctor—
by law alone is futile. Christianity and many other
examples exist to prove that a belief thrives most when
it is proscribed. Until we make some effort to elevate
" the man in the village " we will never make headway
against this belief. So it comes about that, at present,
the witch-doctor is the greatest power in the land. He is
equal to, and a part of, the all-pervading, unseen power
·called " Custom."

It seems strange at first that, considering the universal
preoccupation of the natives in witchcraft—i.e. the way
in which they attribute so much to it—that there is
relatively little to record about it. Really it is not
strange. Partly, of course, because no white man can be
initiated into all the details, but chiefly because in some
cases at any rate all that exists is the belief in witchcraft
rather than actual witchcraft. The extent to which the
cult actually exists cannot be defined. In the following
pages an effort is made to describe what powers are
believed to exist and to be used, both by the layman who
has the means and the will to bewitch and by the professional who provides the means, and himself—at times

ADMINISTERING THE MWAVI (i) TEST.

An old man is being tried for witchcraft. He is sitting on a rough bench (*chitala*)
with his feet off the ground, on a stool. A man called the *chiwala* is administering the
mwavi to him in a calabash. Round the neck of the accused are strung the heads of fowls
already " tried by mwavi."

KAONDE MEN SMOKING.

The two front men have *fwishyo* pipes, those behind them *kapoji* pipes.

—uses his occult or pseudo-occult knowledge for his own ends.

As stated above, the witch-doctor belongs to a guild: his powers or knowledge are hereditary and involve long training : when trained, he is an adept at sleight of hand, a good hypnotist and ventriloquist. He is also an encyclopedia of knowledge and knows the local " Who's Who " by heart. He is at times *clairvoyant ;* and, by practice, skilled in reading men's hearts. He needs all his training and all his skill if he is opposed to a far older guild (also hereditary) ; whereas if these " doctors " are only fighting an imaginary enemy which they have created, or at any rate keep alive, their skill in doing so provokes admiration. One might add, in this connection, that much of the paraphernalia employed by the *ng'anga* does not appear occult to the ordinary native—only incomprehensible. A calabash filled with oil that is supposed to talk, for instance, appears to him very much as the cardiograph, or X-rays, or even the stethoscope, does to the average patient at home.

For some time I have had a suspicion, and reasonable ground for the suspicion, that there may be a class of professional and hereditary witches behind the scenes : men (and women) who habitually provide the means to bewitch, or impart the necessary knowledge to the lay-man to enable him to carry out his desires. They may just conceivably be in league with the *ng'anga*, but I do not, myself, believe that they are. If such exist they would be the people on whom to concentrate ; but they would be very hard to find : one might even find an intermediate class of " touts." At home, even, in a matter like cocaine-selling—for instance—the actual vendors or hawkers are easy to apprehend : one can even find the " retailer," but the wholesale merchant or *entrepreneur*, the man at the back of it all, keeps himself secure behind a wall of secrecy. In all the " under-world " at home the brainy initiators, and other useful people like the receivers, are but rarely given away. I have often been on the tracks of such " master-witches " but have never found any direct evidence, and I gather that the confessions of convicted witches as to the source of their supply or knowledge only relates to other " casual witches " or to what may be called agents. It is, however, extraordinary how often one finds that in cases of witchcraft the witch went " to some man who he thought was likely to know about such things," or " went to so-and-so because he had heard that he could provide him with what he sought," or " consulted a certain person because he was the obvious person to consult." A would-be bewitcher does not ask these things at random, and so pile up evidence against himself : he does not go first to one, then to another ; but, just as a native woman who seeks the means to procure abortion goes straight to the right woman, so (apparently) does the man, or woman, who seeks some particular form of bewitching medicine go straight to the purveyor, or to his agent. I fear that one would need to be a " naturalised native " to find this out, at the present day anyhow. I submit, however, that it is possible, even probable, that besides people who might be called incidental or casual witches, namely, those who obtain and use the means of witchcraft against their enemies there are also what may be described as master-witches who are instructed in witchcraft from childhood and are as much an hereditary guild as are the witch-doctors. If it be an old religion they are the real guardians of it. One wonders if they make a bargain with their clients for their souls—their *vimvule ?* In such case, then, the witch-doctors would appear to be the hierarchy of the newer religion, one of whose principal objects in life is to wage incessant war on the old cult and its votaries. If so they supply a remarkable parallel to the clergy in western Europe in the sixteenth to eighteenth centuries. They may be trying to keep in with both religions (as happened at times in Europe), or they may be particularly zealous against witchcraft (may bolster up the belief) solely for their own glorification. In any case, before condemning the whole order of witch-doctors it would seem that more evidence is required as to the existence or non-existence of the witches.

The next chapter, it is hoped, will be of material help in this investigation.

---

[1] "*Kananga*" means, roughly, "so-and-so," and is convenient in such examples as this. *Na-Kananga*="Old mother so-and-so," etc.

CHAPTER XVI

WITCHCRAFT (III)

DESCRIPTION OF VARIOUS METHODS

THE form of witchcraft which is most often encountered is undoubtedly *Tuyewera* : the second most common is *Mulombe*. These two words are always on the tips of native tongues in any quarrel, in any suspicion. I obtained details of the latter in 1917, but for some reason that is hidden from me I was not able to find out about the former until 1921 : the reticence by people who certainly knew about *tuyewera* was very marked. However, at last I got an authoritative account—since carefully checked—which is as follows :

Tuyewera are sprites, of human shape, about three feet high with protruding bellies and with the body facing the wrong way in relation to the head and legs. They are invisible to all who have not certain medicine : the " owners," of course, always have this medicine and can see them and converse with them.

A is a friend or blood-brother (*mulunda*) of B's. A has some *tuyewera*, B has not. One day A asks B :

A. " I say, my *mulunda*, are you a clever man ? "

B. " I'm sorry to say I'm not."

A. " Have you much wealth ? Are you well supplied with all you need ? "

B. " No, worse luck. I'm but a poor man."

A. " Well, you're young ; if only you had a little more enterprise you could soon get rich."

B. " I'd like to have things, and be well off like you ; but I don't know how. I never seem to have anything."

A. " Would you like to know ? "

B. " Yes. How ? Not . . . er . . . work ? "

A. " No, silly. I can show you an easy way to get things."

B. " Splendid. You're a real friend. Please tell me."

A then tells B about his *tuyewera*, and because of the *bulunda* between them he gives him two of them, a male and a female, saying : A. " They are quite harmless things, you know : won't hurt anyone or kill anyone : you needn't be scared of them. Just treat them nicely and they'll go and steal for you :[1] get you guns, dogs, food, whatever you will ; and its quite safe with them, you will never be found out. Have *tuyewera*, that's the way to be happy and have all you want."

B takes the *tuyewera* eagerly. They are kept in the bush, and no one can see them. They visit their owner in his hut at night. They help B as A had promised ; and soon he becomes a man of substance.

One day the *tuyewera* say to B :

" Look here, B, we're only two, and you know we have been accustomed to living in a big community. We were quite a crowd when we were with A. Now we are lonely, being only two."

" What can I do ? " asks B puzzled. " I don't know how to get any more. I expect you'll get used to it all right."

The *tuyewera* take the matter into their own hands. They get a bit of grass that has a hollow stalk (called *mumpenende* or *muntente*) and with this they approach a man, C, when he is asleep in his hut. Placing one end of the *mumpenende* in their mouths they put the other end into the mouth of the sleeping C, and then proceed to suck out his breath : quickly closing each end with their fingers and then sealing the end with wax (wax from a kind of ground bee called *kamwangi*). After having had his breath taken in this way C gets ill and dies.

After C's burial the *tuyewera* go to the grave, and blow back C's breath into him, thus reviving him. They then wash him with warm water and pull out the arms (folded at burial) and make them supple once more. Once C can move his limbs he becomes, not a human being as he was before, but another *kayewera*. Thus they are three.

B has no knowledge of this, but one day he sees three instead of two *tuyewera*[2] and asks :

" Hello ! Who's the new comer ? Whence comes he ? "

" We told you we could not stay only two," answer the *tuyewera*, and then they tell B what they have done.

B, horrified and frightened, says :

" Well, you must not do it again."

" Oh ! mustn't we ? " answer the *tuyewera*. " You'll forbid us to, will you ? Very well, if you won't let us acquire companions in this way, we will kill *you*."

So it goes on.

Suspicions are aroused. Divination follows, and B is discovered to be an owner of *tuyewera*. He is killed. (A will also be killed if B incriminates him as he is likely to do, and provided that he can be got at . . . not for supplying B with *tuyewera*, but for owning them himself.)

Tuyewera also cause death by accidents, as well as by sucking breath. They can, for instance, cause a tree to fall on a man. They are also sometimes responsible for suicide, by prompting the person to kill himself.

A man can inherit *tuyewera* unconsciously. Thus X succeeds Y, who was a *tuyewera* owner. The *tuyewera*, who cannot live on their own, transfer to X.[3]

The Method of Killing the Guilty Witch. This applies to all forms of witchcraft, except *mulombe* (and, of course, after *mwavi* (i) in which death proves the guilt). After the divination and conviction the *mulozhi* is tied up and a kind of inquisition follows to find out why he killed so-and-so, and also what manner of witchcraft was used. In the case above B would answer that he did kill people by *tuyewera*, which he had obtained from A, and so on. In other cases he will say he hated C for adultery with his wife, or was jealous of his prosperity, so he killed him ; and that he accomplished this by *wanga wa nkatulo*. I am credibly informed that no case is known where a witch has denied the charge[4] provided the divination has been properly carried out. After the inquisition the *mulozhi* is speared to death and his body is burned.[5]

Mulombe. The *mulombe* is also called *mulolo.* An archaic name is *sung'unyi*, though this is rarely used now. It is a snake with a man's head, made by certain *ng'anga's*, that kills the people indicated to it by its owner. Unlike the *tuyewera* it is acquired deliberately and not innocently or involuntarily. Therefore, the killing by *mulombe* is worse than the killing by *tuyewera ;* but as the punishment for the lesser offence is death, equally with that for the greater, this is unimportant.

A man wants to acquire a *mulombe* because he desires to get rid of an enemy in a secret manner ; he, therefore, goes to a *ng'anga*[6] who has the reputation of being able to make one ; and when the bargain has been made, he is directed by the *ng'anga* to procure five duiker horns. Supplied with these he is escorted into the bush by his mentor, who collects certain medicines, which he places on a piece of bark and mixes with water. He then puts the five duiker horns on the ground near the concoction ; after which he proceeds to pick some spiky grass (*luwamba*) and plaits it—the plait being about 15 to 18 inches long and from $\frac{1}{2}$ to 1 inch wide. At one end of the plait he places the five duiker horns. Parings are then taken from the client's finger nails and placed inside the horns. Incisions are next made on the client's forehead and chest, blood from which is added to the medicine. Some of the mixed medicine

is then given to the client to drink. After this the plaited
luwamba is laid on the ground, the duiker horns being
at the end away from the *ng'anga* and towards the
client. Another plait of *luwamba* is then made, and
dipped into the remaining medicine, and the medicine
is sprinkled in this way by the second plait upon the
first, which is lying flat. At the first sprinkling the
prone plait changes into a white substance (the colour of
white ashes). At the second sprinkling it becomes a
snake. At the third sprinkling the snake assumes the
head and shoulders, in miniature, of the client. Soon
the shoulders fade ; the rest, except the head, remaining
like a snake. This snake has also in miniature any ornaments that the client may be wearing at the time, such
as a shell, beads, etc. This is the *mulombe*. It rears
itself on its tail and thus addresses the client who has
sought for and obtained it.

Mulombe. " You know me and recognise me ? "

Client. " Yes, I do."

Mulombe. " You see that your face and mine are
similar, and that my ornaments are also similar to those
you wear ? "

Client. " Yes."

Ng'anga. " Yes, that is the *mulombe* you asked me
for : take it and tend it carefully. You can keep it
where you will—in the reeds at the riverside is the usual
place—but tend it continuously. It will always be with
you now, and so long as you treat it well, so long will you
live. You will not die until all your relations are dead,
so care for it as well as you can. Fare you well."

They then separate. Before long the *mulombe* says
to its owner, " I want a person to eat his life." The
owner then names his enemy, and tells the *mulombe* to
go and kill him. After the kill the *mulombe* comes back,
very happy, and crawls all over its owner, licking him
as he crawls.[7] This makes the body very clean and also
makes the owner fat and sleek. It is not long, however,

A Bearer (Kaonde) Sitting at the Door of a Hut after a Funeral.

From his forelock hangs a bead, and on his face are smudges of meal. (The bandage on his leg is owing to tropical ulcers and is not connected with the funeral ceremony).

before the *mulombe* gets " hungry " again—hungry for
killing, as he does not actually eat the victims, only
" eats their lives." The man then indicates another
victim. If he refuses at any time to name one he becomes
ill, and cannot be cured until he has given way to the
importunities of the *mulombe*.[8] As long as the beast is
satisfied the man will wax fat, and will go on living.

However, after many deaths have occurred suspicion
is naturally aroused, and a *ng'anga* is called in to divine.
This he does by *ng'ombu*, *chisoko* or other forms of
divination. He also divines the hiding-place of the
mulombe. Not a hint of this is given to the owner, who,
unsuspecting, stays happily at home. Then the diviner
chooses five strong men and guides them to the *mulombe's*
lair, by the river. Arrived there he takes some medicine,
already prepared, and sprinkles the ground around the
lair. Rumblings ensue : the water rises till it reaches
the thighs of the men. Then fish come out in large
numbers, then crabs, and, finally, the *mulombe* itself.
Angered, it rears itself up ; but is quickly shot with a
poisoned arrow that has been brought ; and falls
writhing to the ground. Simultaneously the owner, at
his home, feels as if he had been shot by an arrow, and
falls writhing. The *mulombe* soon dies ; and so does
his owner. The deaths in the village then cease.

The *ndumba* of the Alunda is practically the same as the
kayewera ; and the *ilomba* the same as the *mulombe*.

There are one or two marked differences between the
two. It is stated that while men may, and very often do,
own *ndumba*, these sprites are more often owned by
women, but the *ilomba* is owned only by men and never
by women.

Again, the *ilomba* " eats a man's life," but he does not
eat human flesh, whereas the *ndumba* is considered to be
very fond of human bodies as a diet ; and when a
ndumba has sucked the breath out of a man and he is
buried, it goes to exhume him, not only to turn him into

a *ndumba*, but also to eat the body : vivid pictures being given of the ghoulish feasts held by *ndumba* at their exhumations.

The powers of the *ndumba* as thieves on behalf of their owners are considered such that some natives say, for instance, that had we the medicine to see them we would see crowds of *ndumba* at each Government station, whose presence there is for the purpose of stealing food from the Government grain store for their owners. As for their prevalence it is said that could we but see them we would be astonished, when entering a village and being greeted by the people, to see the crowds of *ndumba* squatting behind each person as they sit to welcome us ! [9]

Nkala (a crab). I am indebted to a colleague (V.R.A.) for putting me on the track of another interesting " familiar " believed in by the Alunda. For a long time I failed to find any corroboration as to this— alleged to be a crab some 4 foot long that kills people by eating their shadows—and I began to despair of verifying it. Fortunately I have found a *ng'anga* who claims a great reputation as a slayer of these *nkala*, and I give herewith his account.

He says that a *nkala* is owned in much the same way as a *mulombe* (*ilomba*), and that it causes death by eating shadows. It lives in the river, very much as the *mulombe* does, and needs an expert *ng'anga* to destroy it. His own method, which he assures me has been frequently proved effective, is as follows : he prepares medicines largely made of other *nkala*, and puts some of this preparation in one duiker horn, which is filled to the brim and carefully sealed with wax (*ndunda* in Lunda, *bupula* in Kaonde), another duiker horn has only a little placed in it, and is not sealed. Accompanied by a party a road or path is scuffled to the river bank, and the accompanying friends, with the sealed horn, hide in the grass or bushes. The *ng'anga* then whistles on the partially filled horn (as one does on an empty cartridge case), and uses this as a call for the *nkala*. Answering the call the *nkala* appears : it is about four feet from head to head—for it has a head at either end—and is nearly as broad as it is long. Each head resembles the head of a hippo, having the same lumps on it by the eyes. When it is eating a person's shadow it eats with both heads simultaneously. As soon as it appears the hidden people arise and shoot it. When it is dead the *ng'anga* removes from the dead monster both " noses," the big claws and some of the other claws, from which he makes powerful medicine : the said medicine being chiefly used as part of the ingredients for filling the horns when engaged in killing another *nkala*.

The following further methods of bewitching are all well known ; and each one has been described (and admitted) by at least one convicted witch as the method used by him (or her).

Wanga wa nkatulo. A is jealous of B, or wants his goods, or is angry with him ; so he watches to see where B micturates, and when alone he proceeds to gather up some of the impregnated earth (which is called *nkatulo*), and mixes it with some medicine. This medicine he has obtained from another *mulozhi*, or from some expert in such subjects, at the time that he (A) took to witchcraft.

One night he visits B, when that individual is asleep. He enters B's hut, not by opening the door, but by passing under it ; and passes some of the medicine mixed with *nkatulo* all round B's neck. Then the head comes off, the body remaining asleep where it lies. A takes B's head outside and tosses it up and down like a ball. (If A has an accomplice the two of them throw the head from one to the other.) If the head drops A knows that he will succeed in his witchcraft. Then he replaces the head on B's shoulders ; and the next day B falls ill, and dies.

Divination by *mwavi* i and ii shows A's guilt. Death follows if guilty, and the body is burned.

Another way (name not known). A has had poor luck as a hunter, and seeks hunting medicine. He approaches another hunter, who is reputed to be clever at such things; and from him he receives certain medicine, but is warned that it is such that when, by its help, he kills an animal he will be sending a man to his death simultaneously. Therefore A is warned that he had better get some of the impregnated earth (*nkatulo*) of an enemy, rather than risk killing a friend. The *nkatulo* procured, it is mixed with the medicine and some of it is placed with the gunpowder. Firing with this doped gunpowder he kills a beast, but at the same time his enemy dies.

The coincidence arouses suspicion and a *ng'anga* is called in : he divines by the *chilemba* divination. A is convicted and killed, and his body burned.

Wanga wa wunshengwe. A has an enemy B, whom he wants to bewitch. When B is away he makes little incisions round the lower part of his belly, into which he rubs certain medicine. He then sleeps with B's wife, and is enabled by contact to pass this medicine (*kukaya wanga*) to her.

B returns, and cohabits with his wife. He becomes bewitched from the contact and dies. People note that B was strong on his return home, yet died suddenly. They ask his widow if she committed adultery in his absence. She admits it, and names A as her partner. The people accuse A, and examine him, finding the incisions on his belly. He is killed for his witchcraft; and the widow becomes taboo.

Another wanga wa wunshengwe. A's enemy is B. A wants to bewitch B. He asks a person C, who has a reputation in witchcraft to help him. C takes him into his (C's) hut and provides him with a certain medicine to mix with B's *nkatulo*. At dawn before B wakes, A sprinkles some of the mixture on B's doorway. When

B leaves his hut and passes on or over the medicine he
feels a pain in his back, and when he goes to relieve
himself he finds that his scrotum is swollen. He
gets very ill, and if he cannot find a *ng'anga* to cure
him the testicles will return to the body and he will
die.

After his death divination by *mwavi* i and ii follows,
and if A is found guilty he dies from the test, and his
body is burned.

Wuta wa kumalele, or *Katuluzhi*. (Stated to be
originally Lunda, but adopted by some Kaonde.) A
has an enemy B; and approaches C, who he has reason
to believe can help him. C sends him to a tree (name
not divulged) to dig its root, and also to a grave. He
has to walk round the grave and collect certain leaves
from its vicinity. The roots and leaves when dry are
pounded and mixed with gunpowder. A loads his gun
with the mixture.

At sunrise he takes his gun, and mentions B by name,
saying: "B, come between me and the sun!" He
then aims at the newly risen sun and fires. At the
shot B gets ill and quickly dies. A *ng'anga* is called in
to divine the cause of B's death (*mwavi* i and ii). A is
convicted and dies.

Wanga wa musantu. A has an enemy B. So he
approaches C, a likely man, to ask his help, saying he
seeks medicine (*wanga*) to cause elephantiasis (*musantu*).
C tells A to get the root and the leaves of a tree (name
not divulged) and a chameleon, which he has to kill.
The root is cut into two pieces: both pieces, with the
leaves and the dead chameleon, are placed in a bundle
of grass and taken to the cross-roads, near the village
where B lives. Here A digs a hole in which he buries the
bundle; over the hole he makes a fire and sits by it
warming himself. He makes a few incisions on his belly,
and rubs in some of the ashes from this fire. Then he
names B, putting a curse on him.

"You, B, whom I hate, because . . . (giving cause of hatred). You will pass this way, yes, you will pass close by this fire, and that which it covers. When you do so, let my *wanga* get to you, so that you will sicken and die."

B passes, and soon develops elephantiasis in the leg ; and probably will die of it. Others can pass the spot with impunity : only the named man who has been cursed will be affected.

(The following powers of bewitching are stated to belong solely to *ng'angas*, and to be practised only by them. I have not personally met a doctor that admits or claims the powers, nor have I met anyone who attributes them to a *Kaonde* doctor. If the reader bears in mind that I am a magistrate, he will understand that this may be only natural. The powers may or may not be " held " by Kaonde doctors. On the other hand, the people who hold such powers may not be *ng'angas* at all.)

Uhori (the power of invisibility). This was told me by M., a *ng'anga*. He said that the power is not one which he himself possesses, but that he knows one colleague (Lunda-Ndembu tribe) who has it. My informant states that he himself witnessed it, after having first been given medicine to drink by his colleague. The doctor puts some special medicine inside a reedbuck horn, and then places the reedbuck horn inside a roan antelope's horn. This renders himself and the horns and the clothes he wears invisible. This done he can go where he likes, unseen. For instance, when he wants a person—say, as his slave—he goes, unseen, to where that person is. Arrived there he places his hand on the person, and jabs the point of the roan horn into the ground by him, so that it sticks there—upright. The horns then assume the shape and attributes of the person, who simultaneously becomes invisible like his captor. The doctor can thus remove him easily.

Both invisible they proceed to a big pit which the doctor has previously dug. This pit is timbered and roofed like an underground hut (it is called " *ihung'u* "). In this " dungeon " the invisible captive is placed.

Meantime the substitute man, though it looks like the real man, behaves like him and talks like him, is very weak: he soon gets ill and dies. The doctor—still invisible—has been watching for this, and is present at the mourning and at the burial. When the burial party leaves the grave he puts medicine on it : the grave opens and he thus recovers his horns and medicine. He takes them back and makes a bed for them from guns which he has broken for the purpose. When made, the horns are laid thereon to rest till they are wanted again. His prisoner is now visible again, and is sold as a slave. (He will never be missed, as the people all think he is dead and buried.) Kapiji Mpanga Mandwe (Kaonde chief) says he had a brother-in-law stolen in this way.

Ntuta yuma (creating an invisible assistant). A *ng'anga* tells me that he has a colleague among the Choka people who can do this.

The doctor models a man out of wood and makes a clay pot about half the height of the image. Round the rim of the pot is a string with a fringe of loose ends. The wooden effigy is placed inside the pot, and tied in securely with the ends of string. Round its neck and waist are beads, from its neck hangs a *mpande* shell. The doctor then builds a hut, thatched entirely with the flat cutting grass called *luwamba*. Inside the hut he makes a platform (*chitala*), and on this he puts the pot containing the effigy. Then he places two bits of mica in the effigy's face for eyes. These preparations completed he approaches the wooden man and drops one drop of medicine into each of its eyes and one drop into its mouth, which results in his model becoming a man . . . but an invisible man.

This man is called *Nzhila ya bunda*, and the doctor

sends him out to steal, or " to acquire goods," for him.
Guns, cattle, anything is feasible. He goes to the villages
and just takes what he wants, removing them to the hut
wherein he was created. The doctor takes them thence
and puts them in his own hut.

No one sees the thief nor is conscious of the theft,
because the thief replaces everything he takes with a
bit of stick, or bark, or something which turns into the
double of the stolen goods. When I asked my informant
if it would not be much less trouble for the *nzhila ya
bunda* to have his factory at home, he said that it might
be ; but it would not do, since the substitute goods
which he made were no good and perished very quickly.
He instanced that if the *nzhila ya bunda* were to take
my coat for his master, and to substitute a bit of bark,
the bark would appear to me to be just like my coat,
but that it would wear out in no time, being just bark !

Uhori wa nyalumaya. The following note is supplied
by J.L.K.

Nyalumaya is a *chitumbu* (medicine) in the form
of a stick—a human head in miniature made from
human flesh with human hair on the " head." These
sticks are owned by the most celebrated Andembu headmen, and are let out on hire in the following circumstances. If Kananga wants to raise money, or get rid
of an enemy without "murder," he hires a *nyalumaya*,
and lures the prospective victim to the bush (the visit
of a passing gang of slave traders was the occasion
usually chosen). Kananga places the *nyalumaya* secretly
at cross-roads which the victim will pass. On passing
he is caught and bound and dosed with medicine obtained from a doctor, which gives him *kavulamuchima*
(complete forgetfulness), and should he want to run
away he cannot do so, because thus dosed he does not
know where to go. As soon as the victim is removed
Kananga goes to the *nyalumaya* and says a formula over
it, so that the stick takes the outward form of the

victim and makes straight for the village. The *nyalu-maya* goes direct to the victim's hut, greets the victim's wife and cries out that it is ill. It sits down and dies the same day, for—it is said—the *uhori* cannot last after the sun is down. Of course, everyone thinks that the victim is dead and " it " is buried. " It " does not remain long in the ground before it shrinks to the original *nyalumaya* stick. The owner, or *kananga*, who had hired it, then goes to the grave and removes it.

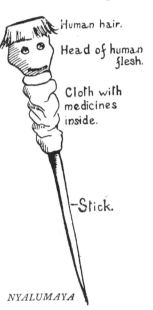

Human hair.

Head of human flesh.

Cloth with medicines inside.

-Stick.

NYALUMAYA

The above is from an account of an actual happening in 1921. Kananga had apparently been spied upon and was seen to go to the grave to remove the *nyalumaya*. The relatives heard that a party of Aluena slavers were camped a little behind and this confirmed their suspicions. Kananga was sued for compensation.

"A man who was arrested among the Ishinde natives," added J.L.K., " had a *nyalumaya* in his possession which I saw. It was a gruesome object, the figure on the top being made of lumps of human flesh sewn together to resemble a head (*vide* sketch). The usual carved stick appears to be modelled on the *nyalumaya*."

It is said that if the dying *nyalumaya* is cut water and blood pours out and the body shrinks to the *nyalumaya*. A clever *chimbuki* attending the alleged dying man might suspect what had happened and would order an incision to be made.

Uhori wa meji. This is another form of *uhori*. As in the last, i.e. when someone wants to get rid of another, a bathing party is suggested, and the victim is detached from the party by some means or other. His absence is unnoticed for some time, and then the plotter (or one of the plotters if there be more than one) cries out : " Look ! a crocodile has taken him."· Near the far bank an arm is then seen waving out of the water. The victim is really bound up by a gang of slavers and the arm is a " medicine " made by a skilled man from human flesh, tied to a log and floating downstream. It has " medicine " in it which makes it wave about for a while and then disappear. This trick, for it is no more, is said to have been used on the Zambezi, Lunga and Kabompo Rivers, for it needs a big river.

The above is as recorded by J.L.K. I went into the matter further myself and a *ng'anga* tells me that his brother Mbamvu was taken in a somewhat similar manner in the Lufwizhi River (tributary to Zambezi) in Angola ; and that a *chiyomboka* called Kasembe " put him wise " as to what it was. With medicine provided by Kasembe, some of which he put in his eyes and some of which he threw into the river, my informant found that Mbamvu was caught by a man called Uludi, who was clothed in a suit of bark (complete with sleeves) so as to resemble a crocodile. This Uludi was swimming under water holding on to Mbamvu. Helped by the medicine my informant realised the deception, rescued his brother and caught Uludi. He took Uludi to the Portuguese " boma " at Kavungu, and he says Uludi was sentenced to five years' imprisonment for this. In this case it will be noted that a man was caught by a pretended crocodile. In the former description there was really neither crocodile nor man : only the pretended arm above water. This " dressing up " was a common practice among witches in Europe in the Middle Ages.

NOTE

The following examples have been selected as showing resemblances between European witchcraft and African witchcraft, especially as regards *tuyewera* and *mulombe*. The italics are mine.

" Witches are likewise reported to have each a spirit or imp attending on, or assigned to them." (*Pleasant Treatise of Witches*.)

Cf. Elizabeth Clarke (1645) : " These imps did mischief wherever they went ; *and that when this examinant did not send & imploy them abroad to do mischief, she had not her health, but that when they were imployed, she was healthfull and well, and that these imps did usually suck* those teats which were concealed about the privie parts of her body."

Susan Cock saith (1645) that her mother Margery Stoakes, then on her deathbed " desired her privately to give entertainment to two of her imps, *and withal told this examinant that they would do her good.* And this examinant saith, that *the same night her mother dyed the said two imps came to her accordingly and sucked on her body.*"

Anne Desborough (1645) whose familiar was a mouse: " About five dayes after the same mouse appeared to her againe, *bringing with it another mouse.* . . . Then the mouse that first appeared said We must suck of your body . . . told her that when she dyed, they must have her soule, to all of which she yielded." (Davenport's *Witches of Huntingdon.*)

Domestic familiars in Europe were always obtained (*a*) by gift from a fellow-witch or (*b*), by inheritance. The resemblance to African witchcraft is striking : " An Essex witch (in 1588) had three familiars one like a cat which she called Lightfoote. This Lightfoote she said one Mother Barlie solde her about sixteene years ago . . . & told her *the cat would do her good seruice : if she would she might send her of her errand."* (Giffard's *Dialogue of Witches.*) Again Anne Weste gave Elizabeth Clarke in 1645 " a thing like a little kitlyn *which would fetch her home victualls for her ; and that it would doe her no hurt."* (Howell's *State Trials*, IV, 834, 836.) Again the Huntingdonshire witch, Francis Moore, received a black puppy from Margaret Simson of Great Catworth and from " one goodwife Weed a white cat, the goodwife telling her that if she would deny God . . . then whomsoever she cursed and *sent that cat unto, they should dye shortly after."*

The profession of the witch-religion being hereditary in Europe the familiars often descended from mother to daughter, e.g. Elizabeth Francis (1556) had one thus " in the lykenesse of a whyte spotted catte." In 1582, Ales Hunt received similarly " two spirits " and her sister got " also two sprites like toades." Alse Gooderidge (1597) got a familiar like a " partie-colored dog red and white from her mother," and so on.

" The Laplanders bequeathe their Demons as part of their inheritance, which is the reason that one family excels another in this magical art " (Scheffer, quoting Tornaeus).

Any student can find other resemblances, but the above seem to suffice to show that there is more than a probability of some connection, if not of a common origin, between witchcraft in the two continents.

---

1 See note at end on the Essex witch's familiar Lightfoote and on Elisabeth Clarke, whose familiar would " fetch her victualls and doe her no hurt."

2 See note at end on Anne Desborough, " the same mouse appeared to her again, bringing with it another mouse."

3 See notes at end on Elizabeth Francis, Ales Hunt, Alse Gooderidge, etc.

4 Similar cases abound in Europe. Witches nearly always died unrepentant, e.g. one of Madame de Bourignon's girls at Lille (1661), aged 22, said, " I will not be other than I am." Rebecca West and Rose

Hallybread " died very stubborn . . . without . . . any terror of conscience for their abominable witchcraft." Major Weir " renounced all hope of Heaven." So Agnes Browne and her daughter, Elinor Shaw, Mary Phillips and others " as they liv'd the Devil's true Factors, so they resolutely dyed in his Service."

[5] So in Europe witches were burned. In Europe and in Africa burning was entirely confined to witches. In the chapter on Hunting it will be seen that a lion that was suspected of being a wizard was completely burnt.

[6] I may be in error in attributing this to the *ng'anga* (witch-doctor). The *ilomba* of the Alunda is not obtained from a *ng'anga*, and I think I am probably wrong about the almost identical *mulombe ;* and that this is very likely obtained from a " master-witch." If this be so it further clears the reputation of the *ng'anga*.

Being now away from the Kaonde country I cannot be sure on this point and leave the description as originally written.

[7] See notes above. Elizabeth Clarke and Anne Desborough.

[8] See notes above. Elizabeth Clarke.

[9] There is a remarkable resemblance to *tuyewera* to be found in a Cornish legend of pixies who rewarded their friends by stealing for them. No one could see them, but one day

" a pixy brought a woman a baby elf to nurse and gave her some ointment to rub on its eyes,"

but told the woman not to put it on her own eyes. She disobeyed and

" as she passed through the streets of Penzance saw hundreds of pixies stealing things out of all the shops."

She called her sister's attention to them, but the latter—not having the medicine could not see them. The pixies, being discovered, blew on the woman's eyes and made her blind. (" *The Little Pixies of Land's End.*) It will be noted that like *tuyewera* the pixies' occupation was theft and that they could be seen only if certain medicine were rubbed on the eyes.

CHAPTER XVII

DIVINATION

DIVINATION enters as much as anything into the lives of the Kaonde. It comprises their method of trial (roughly, at times, both grand and petty jury) and also approximates to the work of a consulting physician, and of a general practitioner. Divination is used (*a*), to discover a living person who is causing trouble, and (*b*), to discover the spirit of a dead person who is causing trouble. Further, it is indispensable at birth to enable the parents to ascertain of which relative the new born baby is a reincarnation. There are many methods of divination.

A. Mwavi (i). Poison tests. The *mwavi* tests (i and ii) will be found to be much more elaborate than is often supposed. There is nothing of drum-head court martial, nor even of summary jurisdiction about them.

The first *mwavi* test (called " i " here) is the " direct " test : administering the poison to a person accused of witchcraft (either accused of practising witchcraft personally, by charms, etc. ; or by such spirits as *tuyewera* q.v.). The poison is administered internally, mixed with beer ; and death ensues if accused be ' guilty, vomiting if innocent. The person who is being tried has to sit on a scaffold (*chitala*) with his feet on a pole, so that no part of him touches the ground. Someone (anyone) administers the *mwavi* (the person administering it is called the *chiwala*). If the accused vomits his relations fight with the *chiwala* or *viwala ;* but if

accused dies his relatives run away, taking the corpse
with them and burning it. (The burnt bones are ground,
and part is put on the face, round the eyes : the rest
being used as *chizhimba* (powerful medicine), and the witch
(or wizard's) children are enslaved (called "*matako*").

B. Mwavi (ii). Generally before "*mwavi* (i)" is
administered there is a preliminary test, called here
"*mwavi* (ii)." This is the application of the same
poison test to fowls. This is usually the first step in
divination for witchcraft (Note: *mwavi* (i and ii) is only
used in charges of witchcraft, not for other crimes). A
person suspects witchcraft, but does not know whom to
accuse. With three or four companions, he catches a
fowl and ties it up, saying to it : "If there is a witch
hereabouts we will kill you." The next day they carry the
fowl to the bush, and with some water (from a different
stream from that at which the villagers draw their
drinking water) they fill a calabash, and cover it with
grass. They also take some broken pieces of pot (called
vi-inga) and a stone (any kind). The *mwavi* is placed on
a *chi-inga* and mixed with some of the water : a funnel
and a cylinder are then made of the leaves of the *mulum-
bwelumbwe* tree : the cylinder is placed in the fowl's
mouth and the medicine (mixed *mwavi*) is put into it
from the funnel. The person administering the *mwavi*
places his fingers on the fowl's eyes to stop it seeing.
They then say to the fowl : "If there is a witch, die !"
If it does not die a second, and further doses, are administered, until it does die. [This preliminary in other
words seems to be a mere formality, as the persons
arranging it always go on till the fowl does die : i.e.
until it is proved (*sic*) that there is a witch in the neighbourhood.]

After this preliminary every man and woman in the
village has to try a fowl similarly, but only once—until it
happens that the fowl of a person dies under the test.
This incriminates that individual.

To make sure then, the person so incriminated goes on with the test, administering it to a second, third (up to fifth and sixth) fowl, so as to make sure that there is a true bill against him (or her). Even this is not enough, for after the series of fowl-trials, *mwavi* (mixed with meat soup) is given to a dog. If the dog dies, too, so-and-so is " committed for trial as a witch " (grand jury at least : a true bill).

Then the chief (or headman) is informed of all that has taken place.

After this the accused has " *mwavi* (i) " administered to him (her) as described above : and at the trial the decapitated heads of the fowls are strung on a string (or placed in a bag) round his (her) neck, and the dog's head is placed near by, on the ground.—(For the boiling water ' *mwavi* ' test, *vide infra* " *mwavi* (iii).")

MPINGO

C. Ng'ombu. This test is done by a witch-doctor. He takes a small calabash cup (*chipeshi*) generally ornamented with beads sown round the lip, or sometimes with a skin [such as a genet (*nshimba*) skin] attached to it : in this calabash are placed some small pieces of pierced wood (*mpingo*) and occasionally pieces of human bone from the leg. (Note. This is the only way in which bones are used by the Ba-Kaonde for divination : " bone-throwing " not being practised locally.) The calabash containing the *mpingo* is held in the left hand : in the right hand the doctor holds a rattle. He moves round shaking the *mpingo* about (or, making many incantations, answered in set words by the people gathered together for the trial, names them one by one). When opposite the guilty person (or when naming him), the *mpingo* stands on end in the *chipeshi* instead of lying down.

D. Chilola (i) (also called *mang'ongu*.) Two men take hold of a big horn (e.g. the horn of sable antelope) and grip it.

THE CHISOKO OR BASKET-TEST FOR DIVINING A WITCH.

The witch-doctor raising the convicted witch from the ground by means of the "Magic Basket." On the right foreground is seated the village headman, and near him the drummers.

The horn is quiescent when they are near any innocent person, but when they approach the guilty one the horn makes their hands go up and down violently (pump-handle fashion) over the guilty person's head. The two men doing this are chosen from the throng, and the witch-doctor himself, who provides the horn and fills it with medicine (called *Milondo*), is not one of them: he stands by shaking his rattle and chanting.

This method is also used to find the spirit of a dead man who is causing death or sickness. It will lead the people holding the horn to the right grave, even many miles away (described to me as having done this for as much as 16 miles). Having had the grave whence works the disturbing spirit indicated, the corpse is exhumed and some (or all) of the bones, and any beads or other ornaments worn by it, are taken, broken up and crushed and put in horns to be used for divination work. Then a fire is made in the dug-up grave. (This bone medicine, called *Chizhimba*, is mixed with commoner medicines and is not used by itself.)

E. Chilola (ii). ("Water-gazing.") This is a form of divination and method of gaining information (somewhat akin to crystal gazing) which is also called "*Chilola*."

In a pool in a river—in the open, not in a *jitu* nor under trees—some medicine (*wanga*) is placed, and the person seeking information or guidance peers into the pool. Herein he sees the hitherto unrevealed past, or the secrets of the future.

[Among the neighbouring Alunda the water is put in a pot with the medicine in it, which turns the water black. It is largely used for the interpretation of dreams : in the case of dreams—or merely of suspicions—it enables the person to discover what it is that is troubling him ; e.g. if it is an enemy's *mulombe* that is the trouble, he will see the *mulombe* pictured (or reflected) in the water.]

F. Kalabi. In this method the doctor takes a very small calabash (smaller than that used in *ng'ombu*) filled with castor oil and medicines. In the evening he asks questions of the calabash and the calabash answers the questions (orally).

G. *Balaye.* If a woman be barren, or if her children die, the husband gives some beads to the witch-doctor who places them under his head at night, and dreams. Then he goes to the woman's hut and boils some water with medicine, placing it first in a calabash in the fork of a *musole* tree, rubbing the concoction over her and saying :

" So-and-so died (the name has been revealed to him in the dream) because of your adultery (or some other sin), and his spirit is still troubled, because you are continuing this evil thing. The troubled spirit, seeking the rest it cannot find, is making you barren (or killing your children). If you stop sinning the spirit will get the rest it seeks, and its curse will be removed from you."

While this is going on the husband sits on a mat by the side of his wife. After this the doctor takes some of the husband's nail-parings and some hair from his forehead, and places them in a reedbuck horn (" *chitanda* ") and hands it to the woman, to wear on her thigh, as a woman carries a baby ; saying as he does so : " If you cease from your adultery (or other sin) you will soon become pregnant." After this none can enter the hut (except by paying a fee of a few beads) until the woman is confined.

This form of divination is also used in certain adultery cases (*vide Kuzhula kapuki*).

H. *Chisoko.* The basket test. This (so I am informed) not a Kaonde method of divination, but Luba. However, the Kaonde being but a branch of the Luba family, and as I have known it practised by a Kaonde witch-doctor (Kayumba) in a Kaonde village (Kazembuzembu) among Kaonde natives, it comes, fairly, within a list of Kaonde methods.

The witch-doctor undertakes this test at night. The people having been summoned, sit round him, and he dances, singing his incantations. He has with him a basket, in which are placed medicines. After much singing, he takes the basket and places it on the head of a member of the audience (resting on the head, not reversed and placed over it). The basket still contains the medicines : the doctor then says : " If you are innocent, the basket will come off," and pulling the basket from the head of the person being tried (who is still sitting) it comes away easily. When the guilty person is reached the basket sticks to his (her) head, so that when the doctor tries to pull it off it will not come away, but, instead, pulls him (her) up from the ground. Walking backwards—facing the person who is being tried—the doctor thus raises him (her) and pulls him (her) all over the space where the trial is being held.

This trial is used for serious cases of witchcraft such as owning and using *tuyewera* or *mulombe*, and the punishment is death (by beating to death and burning ; or by burning to death).

I. Kansheku. A form of divination used only to find out when spirits of departed are giving trouble : not used for living offenders. The witch-doctor takes an axe, lays it on the ground and mentions the names of deceased people whose spirits may be causing the trouble. As he mentions their names he moves the axe backwards and forwards on the ground. It moves freely till the troubling spirit is named : then it sticks to the ground. This method is also used to find out who is reincarnated in a child. (*Vide supra* " Naming the child.") This is also used in *Kuzhula kapuki* (q.v.).

J. Kaneng'eni. As with *Kansheku*, this method is used for divining spirits. The doctor takes a stick (A) in his left hand, from the end of which hangs a string (B), as with a fishing rod, and at the other end of the string is attached a small stick (C)—or a duiker horn—the point of which (D) rests on the ground. With his right hand the doctor taps an axe, or a log, with a small stick held in that hand ; and as he does this with the right hand the stick (C) revolves on its own point. The doctor names certain spirits, and the stick (C) revolves very slowly until the troubling spirit is named at which it begins to revolve with great rapidity. This is well done, and even a careful watcher cannot *see* the doctor speeding up the revolutions.

K. Mutung'u (i). Individual. A kind of scapegoat (in Lunda called " *Mutung'ho* "). If a man is very ill and the " doctor " is called in, he gets some medicine en route, and arrives with it. On arrival he goes outside the sick

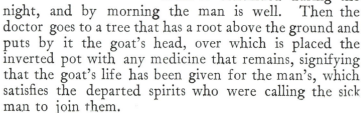

KANENG'ENI

man's hut and mixes his medicine with water, and puts it in a pot on the fire.

The people then get a billy goat and cut its throat, putting the blood in the pot with the other concoction. The sick man is then brought from his hut, a bunch of leaves from the *mkombokombo* tree is added to the mixture, some of which is then sprinkled on him. The dying man revives : this treatment is continued during the night, and by morning the man is well. Then the doctor goes to a tree that has a root above the ground and puts by it the goat's head, over which is placed the inverted pot with any medicine that remains, signifying that the goat's life has been given for the man's, which satisfies the departed spirits who were calling the sick man to join them.

L. Mutung'u (ii). (General.) To clear a village of sickness or guilt. The goats are killed as before, and the blood added to the medicine. Then the *mkombokombo* leaves are added and all the people in the village are sprinkled with the concoction. After this the village is swept clean ; all fires are extinguished ; the ashes, charred or unburnt sticks and all, are thrown away on a *mansang'a* (place where the paths branch : " cross-roads "—called *hamakano* in Lunda). The liver and bowels of the goat are put with the ashes and embers, and all are burnt there. In both these cases the doctor gets the goat as his perquisite, to eat. In *Mutung'u* (ii) he also gets the head.

M. Mwavi (iii). " *Mwavi wa wombwe* " (the boiling water test). This is only used for minor accusations, such as adultery, stealing : never for more serious crimes like witchcraft. The boiling water is prepared, either for the accused, or by accused. The accused then places first the right hand and then the left right into the pot of boiling water. If there are no blisters discernible the day following the test the accused is pronounced innocent; but if blisters appear he (she) is guilty. The Kaonde deny that oil or any other preparation is ever applied to the hands to protect them. If an acquittal ensues the relatives of the accused do the *mikunda* (shrill trilling) to him (her), and compensation has to be paid by the accusers. But if a conviction results the convicted person has to pay for the offence. No similar test with hot ashes or any other form of the same appears to be known.

N. Chilemba. The doctor gets a calabash and fills it either with oil or *mpemba* and places in it a small medicine stick (*kakitsi ka wanga*), which calabash he puts on the ground. He names people, and at the name of the guilty person the medicine stick stands up. In this test the doctor does not touch the calabash during the divination, so that it is more effective than *ng'ombu* test.

O. Masanzo (the hunting test). This consists of going out to shoot, personally or by deputy, and deciding the point at issue by the sex of the first animal killed.

i. It is used at Succession. The heir goes out, or a friend of his, to prove that he in no way caused the death of the man whom he aspires to succeed. If he shoots a female he establishes his innocence. It would, seemingly, appear easy to make this a certainty ; but the Ba-Kaonde believe that the spirits are always too strong for a guilty heir, and that they make him shoot a male.

ii. At Death. If a male animal is killed it indicates that the spirit of some deceased man has killed the person who has just died. If a female be killed it indicates the spirit of a dead woman is to blame.

iii. At Marriage. After marrying, the husband g∩es hunting. If his first kill is a female the omen is propitious : his married life will be happy—and *vice versa*. This is called *kweseka mujilo*.

Some tests recorded amongst neighbouring tribes, e.g. in Smith and Dale's *The Ila-Speaking Peoples*, for instance, divining by means of a pot balanced on an axe, or on a piece of bark rope, are not considered to be really divination, but only " *Chela* " : playing at it, " rag divination " . . . done for a joke.

CHAPTER XVIII

CHARMS AND TALISMANS

I T stands to reason that, with people holding such
strong beliefs in the supernatural, charms, talis-
mans and amulets are common. So common are
they indeed that a complete list could never be
compiled. Nor do I think that anything would be gained
by giving a lengthy list. There are numerous varieties
of each kind that have little special significance, and it
will serve to enumerate a few of the principal kinds.

A. PERSONAL

i. *Kabwanga kamubiji*. The most general prophylactic.
This is worn always—not on special occasions—and is
supposed, positively, to give strength ; and, negatively,
to ward off illness. It is made from *chizhimba* (powerful
medicine concocted from ground human bones), obtained
from the *ng'anga*, which is placed in any small antelope
horn (such as that of the duiker) or in the round seed-
pod called *kakuya*, and is worn round the neck.

(It may be noted that in most cases the *wanga*
(medicine), or some constituent part of it, has to be
obtained from the *ng'anga*, which gives another example
of his indispensability, and of the lucrative nature of his
profession : for the more powerful the *wanga*, the
greater the cost.)

ii. *Mukana*. This is used to protect the wearer from
the machinations of an individual enemy. It is made of
chizhimba of human bones (obtained from *ng'anga*), bits
of tortoise shell and woman's *mwere* (pad) which has been

worn during menstruation. This is placed in the skin of a monitor (*nsamba*) and is worn as an amulet on the biceps.

iii. *Jinyaku.* The purpose of this is to make a journey safe and prosperous, and to ensure that the object of the journey is successfully accomplished. The medicine used is the powdered bark of the *kapwi* tree (or the *mupulampako* tree) and the hair of an albino child, placed in the skin of a small squirrel, a brown variety with a striped tail called *luyeye*, which is made into a little pouch. Before starting on a journey the person looks along the route that he is to follow, takes a little of the powder and rubs it on his face, starting from the tip of his nose and moving his finger right up the forehead : then, in a semi-circular way, moves a finger with some of the powder from each cheek-bone round the outside of the eye to meet the centre mark.

B. INSIDE HUT

i. *Wanga wa nzuwo* (the medicine of the hut). This is to ward off evil spirits (*mitala*), witchcraft "familiars" such as *tuyewera*, and actual witches (*walozhi*). It is compounded of the bark of the *pupwe* tree, powdered, the bones (crushed) of a *kayewera* (which can only be obtained from a *ng'anga*, who kills *tuyewera*), or, alternatively, the bones of a man-eating lion, or the bones of a witch that has been burnt. The mixture is placed in the horn of a duiker or of a bush-buck, and is placed at the head of the bed. It is supposed that if a *mutala*, *kayewera*, *mulozhi*, etc., enters the hut the horn will attack him (her or it) and stab him, from which wound after leaving the hut the evil thing, or person, will die, and the owner be saved from his machinations. Sometimes the horn will awaken the sleeper, who will arise and go out of his hut. On the threshold he will find a witch (in its strict female sense on this occasion), who will be completely nude. He will ask her what she is

AN *IKISHI* DANCING MAN, CONNECTED WITH CIRCUMCISION RITES (LUNDA).

He wears a painted mask surmounted by many different coloured features. His skirt and leg ornament are made of raphia.

KAONDE WOMEN CARRYING TWINS ROUND A VILLAGE.

The woman in the centre of the foreground has two baskets on her head in which to **put the offerings** made on such occasions.

doing. She will reply, " Nothing. I was just being here." She stays there *and cannot go away*. After a bit she implores, " Ah ! let me go." The man replies, " I am not stopping you." She says, " Oh, but you are," and she cannot move till she gives him a daughter in marriage or some other great compensation for the evil she had planned. But the aroused sleeper must be most careful all the time not to move a step : he must stand quite still, or the spell will leave the witch and she will take some of the earth on which he had stood (like *nkatulo*) to use against him for having surprised and shamed her.

ii. *Jinyaku 2*. Also used to ward off *tuyewera*. The roots of the *jitate* tree, powdered, are mixed with some *kayewera* bones (to be obtained from a *ng'anga* who has killed one), and placed in the skin of the *luyeye* (squirrel as above), which is hung in the doorway of hut. Before going to sleep the owner sprinkles a little of the powder round the hut outside, which will keep off the unwelcome visitors. The skin bag is then replaced on the lintel.

C. Gardens

i. *Kukaya wanga* (anti-thieves). Some leaves of the *kalulu* tree are tied in a bundle, and hung on a stick in the gardens. (Note.—This is not used in gardens near to the village, for fear of hurting children who might take some produce innocently. It is used in distant *vitemene*, in gardens maintained at the site of a deserted village, and in the chance gardens that are sometimes made in the bush, e.g. when pumpkins are sown where a big tree has fallen and its branches being burnt a good patch has been fertilised thereby.) A thief who goes to steal in a garden protected by this charm will get sores or boils (chiefly at the top of jaw-bone, or on eye : or swollen lips, bad gums and teeth : or an affliction of the nose). From these he will die. If at the commencement of the sickness the thief goes to the man whom he has robbed, and confesses his sin and compensates him for the injury, the owner can give him medicine to save him from death.

The spirit of the thief, after his death, does not become *mutala* to the man who put up the charm. The people just refer to deceased as " *munguluwe wafwa ku chitamba* " (the bushpig that died of the food he ate).

The same medicine is used to protect beehives.

ii. *Wanga wa kajo* (medicine of food). For abundance. The cultivator takes some powdered *mulunda* wood, little bits of wild rubber, cut very small, and mixes them in a basket with the seed that is to be sown. Then grasping a hoe in the right hand and an axe in the left (in each case the blades only, not the hafts), the contents of the basket are well mixed, both hands working simultaneously. The sowing then begins with the doctored seed. When the basket is nearly empty care is taken to leave a little seed and it is replenished, the fresh supply being mixed with the remains of the old so that the power of the medicine is passed to it. So on until all the garden is sown except a little patch which has been left in the centre. In this patch the remaining seed is sown, and four small pegs (two of the *mulunda* and two of the *chikole* tree) are hammered into the ground together.

At the reaping time some *mulunda* leaves are taken to the place where the pegs are, and are burnt, so that the smoke from the fire is wafted about the garden. This will ensure abundant crops.

iii. *Muchi wa kushika* (anti-bushpig). The bushpig is one of the chief enemies of all local cultivators, so that it is natural that a special charm is used against this enemy. Parts of a tree called *jikasa ja nkalamo* are mixed with old bushpig droppings and placed in a small earthenware pot. The owner of the cultivation takes it and carries it as he walks round his field : then he buries the medicine in a hole, covering it with the inverted pot. When a woman comes to get food from the field, she first removes the pot, uncovering the medicine, and covers it up again, when, with the food, she returns to the village.

The medicine is, originally, mixed with a little water, and on his circumambulation the owner sprinkles a little here and there about the field to spread the charm. The solid part is what is put in the hole and covered with the pot.

D. HUNTING

i. *Wanga wa nama* (simply " medicine of meat "), or *Kantu wanga*. This is to enable the hunter to shoot straight. Two small pierced sticks (*mapingo*) are tied to the gun until the hunter gets a kill : then he takes the eye of the beast that he has shot and the skin of the eyelid, puts the eye and the *mapingo* together wrapped in the eyelid, and ties all together on to the butt of the gun.

E. CONFINEMENT

i. *Muchi wajimi.* Two sticks (*mapingo*) made of *mulemba lemba* wood are tied on the breast and two on the back of the woman before her confinement, so as to make her travail easy.

TWO LUNDA VARIANTS

The following two Lunda charms are not, so far as I know, in use among the Kaonde :—

A small piece of wood, less than an inch in length, attached to a string which is tied round the ankle makes the wearer immune from snake bites.

The top of a small antheap (*ifwafwa*) stuck into the fork of a tree is a boon to travellers, as it prevents the sun from setting too quickly when one is on a long journey.

F. Accidents by River

There are, among the Kaonde, no spells against floods, or rapids, etc. ; but they have one charm against a danger of river crossing, which brought to light a most interesting belief. This charm is called—

Muchi wa kongamato. In certain rivers at the fords or ferries there is a danger of being attacked by the *kongamato* (" ? overwhelmer of boats "), which lives downstream of the ford, and has the power of stopping the waters from flowing away, thus causing a sudden rise in the water level, and overwhelming the passenger. To circumvent this part of the root of the *mulendi* tree is ground by the traveller and mixed with water, the paste being put into a bark cup. Part of the root is cut into strips and tied in a bundle, which is carried when in the canoe, or when crossing the dangerous ford on foot. When the *kongamato* comes the bundle is dipped in the medicine and the water is sprinkled therewith, which keeps off the *kongamato* and his flood.

The investigation of these charms, and the description of this particular charm, led unexpectedly to the most interesting description of the *kongamato*, which is of sufficient importance to deserve a small chapter to itself.

CHAPTER XIX

THE KONGAMATO

The Pterodactyl

AFTER hearing about the charm which is used against the *kongamato*, and the powers attributed to it, I asked "What is the *kongamato?*" The answer was, "A bird." "What kind of bird?" "Oh, well it isn't a bird really: it is more like a lizard with membranous wings like a bat." I write this down verbatim because I was not in the least thinking of, nor seeking for, information as to any prehistoric animals or reptiles. It came on me quite unexpectedly.

Rhodesia and the neighbourhood has rather a bad reputation for brontosaurus yarns : there was one about 1909 from Lake Bangweulu, another 1919, from Katanga. The former I discredited,[1] as I knew the area well, and I discredited it chiefly on two grounds : (*a*) that the local natives whom I knew intimately had never heard of such an animal, and had not even a tradition about one ; (*b*) that in any inhabited area no such animal could exist without its spoor at least being seen. The second reason also discredited the 1919 report.

In this case it seems that the rumour is free from both objections. The reptile is known to the natives, and it is possible that its spoor would not be seen.

Further enquiries disclosed the "facts" that the wing-spread was from 4 to 7 feet across, that the general colour was red. It was believed to have no feathers but only skin on its body, and was believed to have

237

teeth in its beak : these last two points no one could be sure of, as no one ever saw a *kongamato* close and lived to tell the tale. I sent for two books which I had at my house, containing pictures of pterodactyls, and every native present immediately and unhesitatingly picked it out and identified it as a *kongamato*. Among the natives who did so was a headman (Kanyinga) from the Jiundu country, where the *kongamato* is supposed to be active, and who is a rather wild and quite unsophisticated native.

The natives assert that this flying reptile still exists, and whether this be so or no it seems to me that there is presumptive evidence that it has existed within memory of man, within comparatively recent days. Whether it is scientifically possible that a reptile that existed in the mesozoic age could exist in the climatic conditions of to-day I have not the necessary knowledge to decide ; but it must be remembered that the hippopotamus, which was contemporary with the giant sloth, still lives here ; as does the crocodile, which was on the world when the first tree came into existence.

The evidence for the pterodactyl is that the natives can describe it so accurately, unprompted, and that they all agree about it. There is negative support also in the fact that they said they could not identify any other of the prehistoric monsters which I showed them.

The evidence against it lies in the fact that no bribe will induce one to take me to see one, nor to get one to produce a dead one, nor even a bit of one. They say that (*a*) very few people see a *kongamato* and live ; (*b*) it is invulnerable, will eat any missile thrown at it, and that it is immortal, so that no remains are ever found.

The natives do not consider it to be an unnatural thing like a *mulombe*, only a very awful thing, like a man-eating lion or rogue elephant, *but infinitely worse*. Some say it is seen, some say its presence is only felt, but all know what it is like.

The latest known (?) case of its activities is stated to have been in 1911, when two men and two women were killed by a *kongamato* in the Mutanda River near to Lufumatunga village. Sceptics point out that when the said people were killed the river was naturally in flood, and that there were no witnesses as to the manner of death. I think this may be taken as evidence in the belief of the powers of the *kongamato* and no more. I admit I have no faith in these powers ; but I do believe that some such reptile exists or has existed recently ; and the sight of such an unusual and fearsome thing would naturally give rise to a belief in supernatural powers.

Chief Kapiji Mpanga Mwandwe tells me that when the late Mr. George Grey was here in 1897 he (the chief) understood from the traveller's followers that Mr. Grey had shot a *kongamato* at some previous date, near to Fort Jameson (N.E. Rhodesia). I fancy Kapiji got hold of the wrong end of the story, for I never heard that Mr. Grey did so, and I am sure that, if he had, he would have recorded the fact.[2]

The following further attributes of the *kongamato* have been sent me by C.H.H. since I left the country ; and although they are—like those already mentioned— probably due to the fertile imagination of some frightened traveller, they may as well be recorded. Sometimes when a man is in a boat the boat slows down and then becomes stationary in spite of the paddler's efforts. Then he knows that a *kongamato* has caught hold of it underneath. This gives some attributes of amphibiousness to the *kongamato* which seem extra mythical ; and one cannot help wondering what happens to the unfortunate paddler !

From the same source I hear that when a *kongamato* eats a person, he eats no more than the two little toes, the two little fingers, the lobes of the ears and the nostrils. I cannot say, however, if anyone claims to have ever found the remains of one slain and mutilated in this fashion.

I have mentioned the Jiundu swamp as one of the reputed haunts of the *kongamato*, and I must say that the place itself is the very kind of place in which such a reptile might exist, if it is possible anywhere. Some fifty square miles of swamp, formed by an inland delta, as shown in the accompanying sketch map : the Jiundu River spreading out into innumerable channels, and— after receiving several tributaries, reuniting further down into a single stream of crystal-clear water. Much, however, that flows into the swamp does not come out, but vanishes below ground, as many rivers and streams do in these parts. The whole of the swamp is covered with dense vegetation : big trees that grow to a great height, tangled undergrowth with matted creepers and beautiful ferns. The soil is moist loam and decaying vegetation, the main channels and lesser rivulets being reminiscent of the peat hags on a highland moor. It is a reproduction on a big scale of the groves of swamp timber that one sees by most streams (*jitu*) but which I, personally, have not met with in such size except by the Semliki mouth in western Uganda. The whole of the country is of a limestone formation, and outside the swamps, even between the stretches of timber, outcrops are plentiful. In one place just to the west of the area there is a big hole resembling a crater. Nowhere else on high, well-drained ground have I seen such a morass : nor could one conjure up a more perfect picture of a haunted forest.

If there be a *kongamato* this is indeed an ideal home for it.

This swamp has an historical as well as this zoological and possibly mythical interest, for until recently it was the asylum of hundreds of outlaws. Murderers, thieves, mere tax-defaulters, all kinds of criminals and law-breakers, sought refuge in its fastnesses. There in great discomfort they lived, secure from the Government and

A Native Lathe.

A Kaonde native turning ivory on his lathe. The turning is done by means of a bow
held in the right hand, while the cutting is done by an iron tool held in the left hand.

A Fish Trap.

Kaonde man mending the form of fish trap called *chiwinji*.

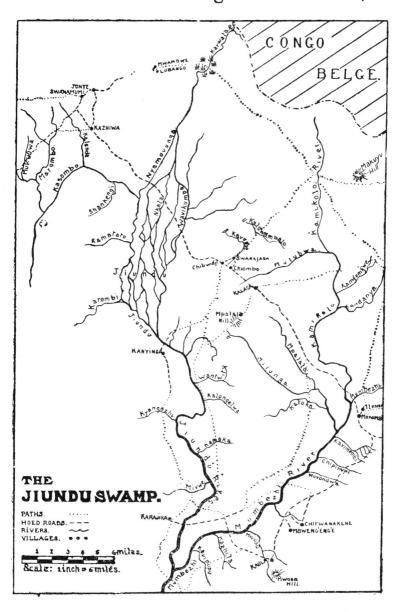

CONGO BELGE.

**THE
JIUNDU SWAMP.**

PATHS. . . . . . .
HOED ROADS. - - -
RIVERS. ~~~
VILLAGES. ● ● ●

Scale: 1 inch = 6 miles.

its servants. Efforts were made to get at them, but with no success. A uniformed man—or any possible enemy—approaching within sight was shot at by unseen outlaws hiding in the jungle. Six years ago these swamps were peopled thus. To-day the outlaws have all left and live in decent villages alongside their former refuge. They have cut a road through the swamp bridging the numerous streams and corduroying the wettest patches, by which one can now pass in comfort—except in the rains. The days of the outlaw colony and of our engagements there are a thing of the past. Last year, besides my own family, others with women and children passed through the swamp, and two English girls went through without any escort.

The human inhabitants are no longer there. Has the winged reptile got this swamp-forest all to himself; or is he, too, but a story that is told?

---

[1] *Vide Geographical Journal*, Oct., 1911 (p. 393).

[2] Since this was written I have had the opportunity of asking Mr. Charles Grey and he says that he never heard his brother mention this.

CHAPTER XX

OMENS AND DREAMS

I. Omens

SO far as I was able to ascertain there is no word in Chikaonde signifying omen: only words for bad omen and good omen.

(A) *Good Omens.* The word for a good omen is either *mupashi* or *musamba.* [R.E.B.W. translates *mupashi* as a benevolent spirit, a synonym for *mukishi,* in which sense it is used in Chiwemba; (*vide* note at beginning of Chap. X); and he translates *musamba* as " one met on the path," anyone or anything met, good or bad (cf. *kusambakana,* to meet). If he is right then *musamba* would appear to mean (in this connection) " omen " (good or bad), but I have had no chance of verifying this and leave my note as it stood.]

The following are considered good omens :

i. To kill a squirrel in one's camp when on an expedition.

ii. To find a variety of honey, called *chilunde,* near to one's camp.

iii. The form of divination called *kweseka mujilo* (*vide supra* Chap. XVII) is really an omen. If the husband kills a female animal first after his marriage, it is a good omen and portends a happy marriage (*vice versa,* if his first kill be a male).

(B) *Bad Omens* are much more numerous ! Such an omen is known as *chivumbi* or *chamalwa* or *mupamba,* the

243

different words being used for different kinds. These are some of the best known :

i. Seeing a dead hare on, or near, one's path.
ii. Seeing a live *zere* on the path (a kind of grass-hopper, or possibly a non-gregarious red-winged locust).
iii. Seeing a snake called *niguwo ya wafu* in the hot, dry months. If seen in the rains or in the cold weather it is no omen at all.
iv. Pregnancy before *chisungu*.
v. Hearing the owl (*fwifwi*) near a village. If the owl merely perches on a hut it is not regarded evilly, but if while there it should hoot it is a portent that the owner of the hut or some relative of his will die.
vi. Seeing a chameleon (*longolo*) that has dug itself into the ground, leaving only its tail visible.
vii. Seeing a leopard eating its kill in a tree.
viii. Wounding a beast in the foreleg and losing it.
ix. Seeing the plantain-eater (*nduwa*) fly across one's path from either side when on a journey, will cause the traveller to abandon his journey and return home for fear of disaster.
x. Seeing anything unnatural, or the reverse of natural, such as a frog eating a snake. No. iii is an example of this, as the *niguwo ya wafu* is supposed to keep underground at that season. So, in a way, the *lutala* and *chisheta* children (*vide supra* Chap. III) may be considered ill-omened.

The following are notes on bad omens among the Alunda (F.V.B.M.). If a man starts on a journey and sees a duiker, chameleon, or a snake like a stick cross the path in front of him he will at once turn back; also when he sleeps and dreams that he has already arrived at his destination, dreams that he is being beaten, or enslaved, or dreams of death—in all such cases will he abandon his journey and return. If a person carries fowls and one of them crows while being carried it is a bad omen, as it is if a cock crows in the middle of the night. An owl hooting at night near a village is also a forerunner of evil. If a man is chasing a hare and the latter turns its head and looks at him the pursuer's fate is sealed. Also, finding a dead hare in the bush is a bad sign. Buzzing in the ears is unfortunate and generally foretells misfortune.

II. Dreams

(A dream is *chiloto*, pl. *vi-* : to dream is *kulota*.)

Dreams are closely connected with omens, and every dream has some signification. The Kaonde idea seems to be that dreams are spontaneous premonitions, and they do not believe that they are messages or warnings from the *wa-kishi* (spirits) nor from any other " power."

It is impossible to enumerate every dream ; but the majority seem to be connected with two things : (*a*), those foretelling good luck and bad luck generally, especially long life or impending death; and (*b*), those foretelling luck in hunting. To these I have added a third class (*c*), in which I have put various dreams ; but those that do not fall within the two first classes are rare.

Class A

If one dreams that one is climbing a tree, or is on the top of a hill, it is good : one has long to live. Similarly, if one dreams that one is flying like a bird.

To dream that one is clothed in white forebodes well ; but to dream that one is wearing dark or any coloured cloth forebodes ill.

If a man dreams that he is walking east it is good, but if he dreams he is going west it is bad, since it signifies that the spirits of the departed are calling him to join them. A northward or southward journey in a dream is relatively bad. (East is *Musela*; west, *Muzhika*; north is called *Kaweta Kawieke* and south *Kaweta Kabulenge*. *Kaweta* appears to mean meridian, *Kawieke* refers to the country of the *Bayeke* who live to the north; and *Kabulenge* to the country of the *Balenge* who live to the south.)

To dream of wealth means poverty for the dreamer, and *vice versa*.

To dream that one has killed an elephant or has found tusks in the bush means good luck in store.

Dreaming that one is in a canoe means good fortune, but if one dreams that one is crossing a bridge it means bad luck.

When one is absent from home and dreams that he is at home it signifies that he will never go to his home again. If one dreams that he is in some other place he is sure of returning to his home in safety.

To dream that one is in the company of a deceased relative foretells the death of another relative.

To dream of kaffir corn or of mealies is good; but to dream of the small red millet (*luku*) or of pumpkins is bad. The reason for this is that the meal made of *luku* is used in embalming. Embalming is sometimes resorted to in the case of chiefs, and the whole body is smeared with a mash made of scalded *luku* meal: *Kuchina kuwola* ("to ward off decomposition") is the expression. Pumpkins are a bad thing to dream of because pumpkin seeds are scattered at a funeral.

A dream of dancing and drum-beating is bad, or a dream of people gathered together to drink beer. Any of these means there is going to be a funeral.

If one dreams that one is washing himself it is good, but if he dreams that he is being washed it foretells early death—corpses are washed.

To dream that one is hoeing *matumba* or *milala* (the raised beds used for cultivation of sweet potatoes) is bad: it portends digging a grave, i.e. the death of someone.

To dream that one is swimming is good ; but if in the dream one appears to be sinking, or even taking a dive, it signifies that a *mulombe* (q.v.) is eating one's life. Dreaming of any kind of snake also signifies death from a *mulombe*.

To dream of dogs, hunting dogs, leopards, baboons, cheetahs or the ordinary wild cat (*felis kafir*) foretells death by *tuyewera* (q.v.).

Class B

The following all foretell good luck in hunting in the immediate future.

Dreaming of blood : e.g. of people fighting and being wounded so that they bleed, or of a man cutting himself and bleeding.

To dream that one is killed by a lion means great success in the chase. (In this case the dreamer goes to a *ng'anga* who interprets the dream as propitious : after which the dreamer clears a little path up the side of an anthill and models a small lion and lioness, which he places in a miniature hut at the end of the path. When he has killed anything he takes the heart from the beast and cooks it by this small hut, so that his good luck may continue.)

The following miscellaneous collection of dreams all have the same propitious meaning as regards the chase.

Dreaming that one is committing incest, dreaming that one is defecating, dreaming of a birth and dreaming of tobacco. I can find no sort of explanation for the way in which these dreams are thus interpreted.

Class C

If one dreams that he is falling from a height and wakes before reaching the bottom it is a good sign, but the Ba-Kaonde believe that if one reaches the bottom he dies at once. (This appears to be a perfectly indigenous belief, and not of European origin.)

If a man dreams that he is cohabiting with his own wife it is a sign that she is committing adultery. If the dream is dreamed in the daytime it means that she is sinning at nights ; but if the man dreams thus in the night it means that his wife's infidelity is a daytime occurrence.

THE JIUNDU SWAMP.

A kind of inland delta, until recently the home of outlaws, and possibly it was in recent years the haunt of the Pterodactyl.

CHAPTER XXI

TOTEMS

(A TOTEM=*MUKOKA*: PL. *MIKOKA*)

IN one's first acquaintance with tribes such as the
Ba-Kaonde one is apt to feel very much interested
in totems: one hears constant references to them,
and it seems as if they must play a large part in
native life. There follows a period when one seems to
find no real meaning in totemism at all, and begins to
doubt if " totem " is the right translation of *mukoka* ;
whether such a translation does not, indeed, invest the
mikoka with a false importance.

It is generally accepted that totemism is connected
with exogamy (marrying outside the family), and on
these grounds the *mukoka* must be called a totem. The
whole essence of the *mikoka* is exogamous. Except for
this one feature, however, it cannot be said that totemism
is of much importance to the Ba-Kaonde (and other
similar tribes) nor of much interest ethnographically.

It is said that Mulonga and Mwinambuzhi (" Adam "
and " Eve ") had very many children, who chose names
for themselves, and choose those of familiar objects
around them. Thus one called him (her-) self *chulu*
(anthill), another *mbowa* (mushroom), another *mulonga*
(water), a fourth *kasaka* (kaffir corn), and so on. [Paren-
thetically it may be noted that many words used as the
eponyms of the totems are, in all tribes, often archaic ;
and form—frequently—connecting links between tribes.
For instance, *kasaka* (as above) is not used nowadays in
Chikaonde for kaffir corn, *mebele* being the word. But

masaka (sing. *isaka*) is the Chiwemba for the same grain. The Wawemba call the duiker *mpombo*, but as an eponym they use the word *kashya*, which is the modern name in Chikaonde for the same antelope; *mulonga* is used in Chiwemba for a stream (or running water), but is only used now in Chikaonde as a totem—with this same meaning, and so on.]

These children of Mulonga and Mwinambuzhi in their turn had children, and the name of the children of the first couple remained as the family (or totem) name : the descendants of Kasaka, for instance, being known as Benakasaka. Thus it became a rule that one of the Benakasaka could not marry another of the Benakasaka, nor one of the Benachulu another of the same totem. There are no beliefs, practices nor taboos connected with the eponym, for in the first case it was but a chance-chosen name, and had no direct reference to its origin. Thus a member of the Benambuzhi will not hesitate to eat goat flesh : one of the Ben-angi fears the leopard as does one of another totem, and will kill it readily if he gets the chance. No one worships, prays to, or offers sacrifices to the eponym of his totem.

Long ago, among the Ba-Kaonde, a man would forgive certain sins if committed by one of his totem—especially adultery and larceny of crops (never in the case of assault). This does not hold good nowadays.

Hospitality is still shown to a stranger of one's totem : a hut to sleep in, food (even a fowl) and so on. If one does not do this it brings shame (*mbumvu*). A common way of finding one's totem mate is as follows :—

Stranger in village. " Here is some (money or goods) : please sell me some food, for I am hungry."
Villagers produce some food.
Stranger. " That is poor measure for my money. It may be, perhaps, that it is one of your own totem whom you are cheating."

A Villager. " What is your totem ? "

Stranger. " So-and-so."

2nd Villager (sitting at some distance). "What's that? What did you say your totem was ? "

Stranger. " So-and-so."

2nd Villager. " Whence come you, and where were you born ? "

Stranger. " I am of the —— tribe, and was born in the village of So-and-so, under the great chief X."

2nd Villager. "And you are of the ——? " (naming totem).

Stranger. " Yes, indeed."

2nd Villager. " Then come and be my guest, for you are my relation."

To kill a fellow totem man is no more and no less a crime than to kill any other.

In war a man would not spare his totem mate on the other side, even if he knew his totem.

Curiously enough this totemism which, though so unimportant, is so widely spread amongst this and the adjoining Bantu tribes is not found among the neighbouring Alunda. The Ba-Kaonde say of this lack of totemism, " A Kalunda can marry his niece," implying (rightly or wrongly) much less strict rules as to exogamy among their Western neighbours.

The most interesting feature of totemism lies in a jest. This was first brought to my notice by a colleague (R.E.B.W.), whose notes on the subject I transcribe :—

Bunungwe (inter-totem jesting). Apparently it is considered facetious when a member of one totem encounters a member of another totem—in cases in which the association of the two totems is sufficiently antagonistic—for the member of the " dominating " totem to chaff his companion ; or, generally, for witticisms to be exchanged. For example, one of the goat totem meets one of the leopard totem. The goat is the natural prey

of the leopard, therefore this is an occasion for a joke.
The leopard man may say, " Ha ! You of the goats, we
eat you." Or the other might start it by saying, " You
of the leopards, take care you don't eat me ! " Similarly
the *Benang'onyi* can tease the *Balembu*, on the grounds
that they (or at least one of their tribe, the honey guide)
devours the honey and young bees. Pleasantries of this
nature are considered extremely funny, and, when
bandied between two people, are often taken up by the
whole community who, in a perfectly good-natured way,
continue for a long time to chaff the one who happened
to be the butt of the joke. After a time he is supposed
to have stood the chaffing long enough and will bring,
either to the people who started the joke against him,
or to the member of the opposite totem who was the
original cause of it, some little present—such as beads,
honey, beer, meat, etc.—so that they may drop the joke
against him, saying, " Receive this little thing, and leave
me now in peace." (The man teased is called *Munungwe
wami* = My tease, or my victim.)

This custom was recently set up as a defence by the
co-respondent in a divorce case in order to explain his
present to the respondent of beads and a bangle, which
her husband had discovered, and which had led to his
suspicions being aroused. The co-respondent admitted
the gift, but declared that it was *bunungwe*, he being of
the bees and the lady of the birds. This was, however,
discounted by the fact that the gift had been made in
private, whereas a *bunungwe* is a public joke to be known
and enjoyed by all, and the gift must be made in public
too.

The following are some of the pairs :—

> *Benanzovu* (elephants) are *banungwe* with the *Bena-
> chulu* (anthill). (Because the elephant stands on
> the anthill.)
> *Benachowa* (mushroom) are *banungwe* with the *Bena-*

chulu. (Because the mushroom grows on the ant-
hill.)
Benachowa are *banungwe* with the *Benaluo* (monkeys).
(Because monkeys eat mushrooms.)
Benangi (leopard) are *banungwe* with the *Benambuzhi*
(goat).
Benang'onyi (birds) are *banungwe* with the *Balembu*
(bees).
Basamba (snakes) are *banungwe* with the *Balonga*
(water).
Batembuzhi (lions) are *banungwe* with the *Benambuzhi.*
Benang'onyi are *banungwe* with the *Benakasaka* (kaffir
corn). And so on.

Lubomboshi. This is another Kaonde custom connected in some way with totems. On a day when the
rain is falling gently a man may go into the hut of anyone
belonging to the same totem as his grandfather (in the
case of a woman into the hut of someone belonging to
the totem of her grandmother's father). He stands at
the threshold and says, " *Lubomboshi !* " while wiping
the water off his face with his hand.

The person demanding *lubomboshi* does not leave the
hut until some present be given him, no matter how
small. The presents are usually in the form of meat,
beads, bracelets, and so on; but sometimes a woman
is given him to sleep with. (In such case the woman,
being a gift for the time being, can demand no present.)
Sometimes even a gun is given. The recipient may
have to give the present, or some part of it if it be
divisible, or some other gift to someone else to whom he
is *benankambo ;* and thus gifts circulate in the village.

When once someone has started this " game," which
it obviously is, it is taken up by the whole community
with much zest ; and all and sundry begin to hunt for
some of their *benankambo.* To demand *lubomboshi* is
known as *ku-bombora.* Like *bunungwe* this seems to have

no religious significance, and to be of no serious import whatever : it might be described as a parlour game for a wet day.

Muzenze (a Lunda custom). As has been recorded above the Alunda have no totems, but they have a custom approximating to the treatment of a visitor of one's totem and to *bunungwe*, which is worth recording ; and though (obviously) it can have no actual connection with the subject of this chapter it may conveniently be inserted here.

The custom of *muzenze* (so I am informed by J.L.K.) is as follows : Should a Kandembu of Kanongesha's country cross into the country of Sailunga's Alunda— be it on a journey or on a visit—he considers all the Alunda to be *azenze nindi*, and the Alunda would refer to him as *muzenze netu* (also *vice versa*) ; and a form of joking known as *ku-zenzeka* is carried on. The stranger can banter and chaff his *azenze* as much as he likes.

The status of a visiting *muzenze* is " legally " recognised, and he holds a privileged position : the view apparently being taken that a stranger away from home is in a defenceless position (the Alunda and Andembu being totemless a stranger cannot seek help or hospitality from a fellow totem man), whereas those who live in the land are many and can look after themselves. Hence a *muzenze* (or *azenze*, such as a gang of carriers passing through) can do anything they like from committing adultery to mere revilings without incurring any pains and penalties. [That is the theory ; but there is a certain sporting " unwritten law " that reduces the *zenzeka* in practice to chaffing on the one side, and hospitality (hut, food to eat and a mat to sleep on) on the other. Very much as with a co-totem visitor where totems exist.] It is a disgraceful breach of hospitality to ill-treat a visiting *muzenze*. (Again similar to ill-treatment or neglect of a visitor of one's totem.)

The *zenzeka* custom causes much harmless merri-

ment : outrageous things being said with impunity, e.g.
by the visiting *azenze* to the women of the village
through which they are passing, such sallies being
accompanied by roars of laughter. These jokes will be
carried on in each village, one of the favourite forms
being to chaff the women about their husbands in the
presence of the latter, which though amusing between
azenze is a crime between others : the fact that this
licence is a privilege presumably gives it its spice.

Muzenze is often pleaded in native cases, e.g. as a
defence for naming another as a witch, " Oh ! she is
my *muzenze* " (i.e. it was not seriously spoken). The
custom is still very much in force, but the plea of being
a *muzenze* does not appear to be as strong as it once
was now that there is so much travelling. It is merely
a custom of hospitality, and while not troublesome in
the days when visitors were rare, might tend to become
a burden if taken too liberally nowadays. Chiefly practised between the Alunda and Andembu and between
sections of each, it also extends at times to visiting
Kaonde and Luena natives.

CHAPTER XXII

HUNTING

THE Ba-Kaonde are great hunters, but can hardly be described as sportsmen. Muzzle-loading guns are the chief currency in their country since slavery was abolished ; and nearly every native owns one gun or more, though it is not every native who hunts actively. That is to say, though all may hunt spasmodically it is but a certain number who do so regularly. Moreover, they are not, in my opinion, good hunters as a race : neither good shots nor clever in spooring and bushcraft, that is, in comparison with some other tribes.

Gunpowder is freely obtained from the Belgian Congo, and every native has all he wants. Some is also obtained from Portuguese Angola, though I have been given to understand that the powder is imported into that territory from the Congo.

Since most of the chase is a matter of shooting with guns at close range it is prosaic and calls for no comment. In the best game districts a good hunter may get from three or four head a week upwards. I remember one chief who sought good " medicine " for his gun because he had been getting *only* about five head a week ! Once when a local trader started buying skins and hides to send South, at a time when prices ruled high, the natives brought them in by hundreds. Game is plentiful in most parts, and the list at the end of this chapter is, I think, fairly complete.

In some parts the bow and arrow are still used, and

there are some excellent archers. A man who had been arrested for shooting at a messenger was given a target at which to aim and performed very poorly. I then placed a messenger's fez cap in a bush at 50 yards from the archer, thinking that this might seem more realistic to him, and with his first shot he transfixed it.

The old way of hunting and harpooning hippo (still

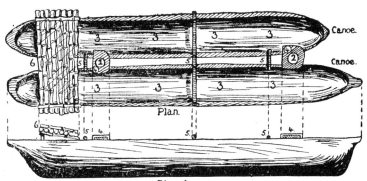

Canoe.
Canoe.

Plan.

Elevation.

(1). Harpooner.
(2). Chief Paddler & Steersman.
(3). Spearmen & Paddlers.
(4). Stool (Chipona), Straddling both canoes.
(5). Sticks (of mutumpo wood) joining canoes.
(6). Bamboo platform (chiwanga, chawa mfulu ; or chine change.

DIAGRAM. 1. 2 canoes joined (viangi).

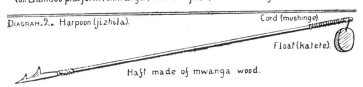

DIAGRAM. 2. Harpoon (jizhila).

Cord (mushinge)

Float (kalete).

Haft made of mwanga wood.

practised occasionally) is interesting, and especially so as it is now becoming a thing of the past. September was the time of year for this event. Two canoes are joined together (*viangi*), as shown in the accompanying diagram. When the crew is on board they go to likely pools. Finding a hippo they harpoon him (the harpoon is called *jizhila*). Occasionally the harpooner is able to get hold of the cord at the end of the harpoon, but more often he has to let go : it is then followed by means of a float (*katete*). The float is subsequently picked up and fastened to the bamboo platform (*chiwanga cha wa mvubu*) : the hippo feeling the barbs in the harpoon pulls the *viangi* along. According to the severity of the wound the hunters may be able to pull themselves in towards the beast or the latter may turn on them. In this case the pressure on the bamboo platform causes the *viangi* to rise at the stern, but it does not capsize. As the hippo gets near he is speared again and again until he is killed.

The old method of hunting elephants, called *wa nzovu wa pa misangi*, was with spears. The hunters would note the elephant paths, and, preceding the herd, would mount a tree with an overhanging branch. Other members of the party would go to herd the elephants in the desired direction. The waiting hunters were armed with spears of an extra large and heavy make. When the elephants came under the tree the leader was allowed to pass, but at the second elephant the hunter hurled his spear, aiming at the base of the neck—so with the next, and at a third if he were lucky : even up to five on an occasion so I am informed.

The natives tell me that if the leader were killed the others would all turn about immediately, and I know from experience that elephants when going in single file and being thus disturbed do not deploy, but " about turn " and retreat on their tracks.

The spears have *wanga* (" luck-medicine," not poison) on them, and also the hunter has medicine rubbed into an incision on his right hand. This is to enable him to kill with one shot. Another medicine called *muchi wa vingonga* (so called because it is put into the empty shell of a hard-shelled beetle, *chingonga*, which I have examined but have not been able to identify), is placed at the back of the hunter's neck, and some of it in his mouth to prevent the elephant seeing (? smelling) him.

On cutting out the tusks all young men are sent away : the elders chew leaves of the *ndale* tree, and spit out what they have chewed as the tusks are removed. No chanting apparently is done. (I have never hunted the elephant in Kaonde country so cannot describe this with any certainty.)

Nowadays the procedure is different, for guns are used to the exclusion of the heavy spears. A shelter is first made near the haunt of elephants, and the youths of the party are left in this shelter. The elders sally forth with their guns to hunt. All guns are loaded, the powder usually being provided by one man. Once the elephants are located a beast is selected and all fire at the same animal, and keep on firing until he is dead. This is much less effective than the old method, in fact it frequently happens that the

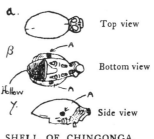

α. Top view

β. Bottom view

γ. Side view

SHELL OF CHINGONGA.
(Life size)

The holes (A) are made by a man.
Colour uniformly black.
Consistence hard.

hunters have to return home to fetch more powder and then pick up the spoor of the poor beast again.

The elephant belongs to the man who supplied the powder. At the death he stands on the top of the carcase while the others sing a song. After the song he climbs down and cuts off the tail. Then the tusks are removed. This done the youths are summoned from the shelter and all camp together to cut up the meat, and dry it. The heart and cheeks are kept to be cooked at the *chipanda* for the *wa-kishi*. On returning to the village with the spoil, beer and porridge are prepared. Three stout wooden stakes are driven into the ground : some medicine leaves are put into a big pot and the meat on top. Red earth is rubbed round the rim, and water, fetched by a child, in a calabash which must be closed with leaves before being removed from the river. This water is carried to the village and poured into the pot. The pot is then lifted by the hunters only : each one holding it with his left hand, and with his gun (grasped in right hand) pressing against it, singing the following song :

" *Ka-teyu teyu tewile mutwe wami.*"

Thus they carry it and place it on the three stakes, and fire—made of *mufungo* wood only—is placed underneath.

Beer drinking and dancing follow until sunset, when the meat is taken out by the hunters, still carrying their guns, and the soup from the meat is poured into holes dug, for the *wa-kishi*, with this invocation : "Help us again in the future as ye have done this time." A small piece of meat and some porridge on the stirring stick are then put on the *chipanda*, and a man (known as *kampenga*) eats this on behalf of the *wa-kishi*, standing up the while.

COOKING POT.

Supported on three stakes
driven into the ground.

Then the others eat the rest of the meat except for a few scraps which are returned to the hunter by the other feasters, saying :

" Hunter ! (*Chiwinda !*) we have returned your meat to you." Then all wash in the pot in which the *wa-kishi's* meat was cooked, after which all go away except the *chiwinda*, who upsets any water left in the pot by the *chipanda*. The whole of this is a thank-offering to the *wa-kishi* for the successful hunt.

If an elephant be killed by the agency of medicine (if success be attributed to such assistance), the man who gave it, and his wife, sit each on a tusk from the slain beast, one on each side of the *chipanda*, and the elephant's tail hairs are fixed on the back of the woman's head.

The following is

and is related practically verbatim as it was reported at the time. The story was so graphic that Mr. T. R. Williams, to whom it was first reported, wrote it down immediately and has kindly allowed me to use it. I can myself remember that the facts are as stated.

"Peace be with you," I say. "Peace, *Bwana*," they reply, and enter. Chindaro, a headman hailing from 60 miles to the south-east is the leader of the party.

"Are the Chindaros strong?" is my formal enquiry.

"Yes, we are strong," replied Chindaro—the royal plural is *de rigueur*. "We abide in peace, and my people, too. But my chief, Kalilele, has sent me with words to the *Bwana*, for they have beheld disaster itself: their people are finished entirely: lions have eaten them all: they are utterly undone."

"How do you say this? How do you know?" I asked.

"The Kalilele people had only slept two nights after the event when we arrived, and Kalilele told me to bring his words to you. He would come himself but the lions are still among his people, they walk in his very verandah, and he said he must stay to comfort his people."

"And what are the chief's words?"

"These are the words of Kalilele, the chief: Sayama, who is the son of headman Chintambila, went out to fence the garden of his mother-in-law, because the pigs were eating the maize. He had not returned home the next morning so Kapobe, his younger brother, went to look for him. He took his gun with him and went to the garden. He had just found the fence where Sayama had begun it when he noticed the track of something dragged. A little way further on he found Sayama's axe. 'I am dead,' he exclaimed. 'A lion has eaten my brother.'

At that self-same moment a lion sprang at him. He dodged and ran hither and thither—the lion pursuing him. But his heart was in turmoil, so that he fired his gun in fear, and missed the lion. So the lion caught him and killed him before he got beyond the edge of the fence, for the lion said to himself : ' If I kill Kapobe I will have him to eat when Sayama is finished ; but if I do not kill him he will surely go back and call all the villagers to come out against me.' So it was that the lion killed Kapobe, and then returned to the place where Sayama's remains were lying in the grass—half eaten.

   " Now it is but a short distance from the village to the garden of Sayama's mother-in-law ; and when at mid-day Kapobe had not returned from his quest the people were saying : ' Now two men have gone out and have not come back : something has happened.' Chintambila said to Kalala, a boy of some sixteen years : ' Go and see what it is that Sayama and Kapobe have found ; and if it be honey bring me a little, for it is not good that they should eat it all alone.' But the boy answered and said : ' How if it should be a were-hyena ? ' but old Chin-tambila replied : ' Little boys should not call the name of a were-hyena : they are the concern of us elders.' ' Well, give me your gun to walk with,' said Kalala. ' All right, boy, take my gun from the rafter of my hut,' said the headman. It was not loaded, but boys like to walk with guns. So Kalala set out for the garden.

   " He was approaching it when he saw the lion raise his head from the grass a long way ahead of him. ' I am dead,' he said in his heart. ' A lion has eaten Kapobe and Sayama.' He did not turn and run, but backed away stealthily, and when he thought he had backed far enough, he broke into a run and so came screaming to the village : ' We are dead ! We are dead ! A lion has eaten Sayama and Kapobe ! ' Chintambila quickly took word to Chief Kalilele close by ; and Kalilele called up all his men from the villages near to him, even old men came, beyond counting. Those who had guns brought them, and those without brought bows and all had spears. Kalilele marshalled them and gave out gunpowder from his own stock to such as had none ; and all went together to the place where Kalala had seen the lion. This was just after noon. But the lion knew that, as Kalala had seen him far away and had escaped from him, he would now have a war-party out against him, and so he had left the bodies. The searchers found Sayama's head and arm and one leg, and Kapobe had not been eaten at all. They followed the spoor of the lion to Lusala village. One man, Mupata, thought that he saw the lion hiding in the grass and let off his gun, but it was just nothing. Then the sun was getting low and they said ' The night is close, and we are far from home. There is a lion who is walking and he has already killed two of us,' so they gave up the pursuit and returned to Kalilele's.

" And the lion came too. As they were nearing home in the dusk they heard him grunting, ' Hahu ! Hahu ! hu-hu-hu ! ' They reviled him obscenely, but still he came with them, following them but keeping out of sight in the bush. When they got home Kalilele said : ' See you, the lion is now angry, for he knows that we are against him : he will excel himself to-night : call together all the aged, and the widows who have not got strong huts, and let us shut them up in the grain-store that the *Bwana* made us build for his grain last year : it was built of hard wood, and there they will be safe ; but their huts the lion would tear down.'

" So they assembled the widows and other feeble ones, who—having no strength—had not got strong huts of their own : or had old huts only, rotten and eaten by white ants ; these they secured together in the *Bwana's* grain store, which is between Kalilele's and Chintam-bila's villages, very close to both. And the door they blocked up with logs ; . . . and all the time the lion was grunting, ' Hahu ! Hahu ! Hu-hu-hu ! '

" All doors were made fast before the night was black. Kalilele himself was the last to shut his door, except headman Chintambila, who was with him. Kalilele accompanied Chifuka half-way to his village, after which they separated, each running to his own village as fast as he could for it was now late.

" As soon as the night was black the lion began to groan and roar and to walk in the roads. People in the huts heard him walk right through Kalilele's village : they heard his feet : pa pa pa pa ; and the same in all the villages. In the middle of the night the lion saw the fire inside the *Bwana's* grain store, wherein the widows were herded, for its walls are of naked tree stems : not mudded, and the fire shone between them. ' Now I will eat them all ! ' he said, and hurled himself at the walls, and tore at the grass upon the roof, so that the widows set up a great wailing, crying out, ' We are dead ! We are dead ! ' The people in their huts in the village called back : ' Yes, indeed you are if you do not hold the door.' But the lion did not come to the door because of the logs that were piled up there; he kept on assaulting the walls, until— toward morning—he tired. Then blowing with his nose through the chinks, he stalked through the village of Kalilele and went away.

" As soon as it was light Kalilele the chief called together all the war-party that had gone forth the day before, all with their guns and bows and spears that they had sharpened overnight, and made strong in their shafts. Truly the lion was dead already—we were like War Transport carriers for number ! The lion's spoor led straight from Kalilele's to the spot where he had found the bodies of Sayama and Kapobe, which the relatives of the slain had buried while we had been following the lion. We saw where the lion had searched for his food and found it not, turning over the grass this way and that. The spoor led away on towards the stream where Chifuka's people draw water. There in a clump of grass

WANGA WA NZUWO.

This shows a native (Kaonde) bed in a hut, and at the foot of the nearest leg of the bed is a horn containing the charm to protect the sleeper from witchcraft.

MODELS IN CLAY OF A LION AND LIONESS.

Made by a dreamer who has dreamt that he is killed by a lion : a dream portending great success in hunting.

in the open ground near the stream the spoor disappeared. Some men went round on this side and some on that, and found no spoor leaving the clump of grass, so we knew that the lion was inside. Mbetela was excited and careless ; and as we were surrounding the spot he called out : ' I see him ! He is not in the high grass, he is hiding in the short grass outside it.' But the lion saw who it was that was calling out about him ; and even as Mbetela was cocking his gun he sprang out upon him. We all saw it, but the lion was so quick that we could do nothing. I was as close to Mbetela as the *Bwana* is now to me, even as I speak these words. Mbetela cowered down, and verily his spirits saved him : for they hid his head and his body —all except his buttocks, which the lion saw and tore open so that there was as it were a hip pocket—your whole arm could go inside it—down the back of his thigh. Many of us had started to spear the lion, being too close to use our guns, and he took fright and bounded away before we had done him much hurt. He ran across the stream and into the bush beyond, going slowly, and looking round at us when he had left us behind. We all ran after him, but when we found him standing facing us from inside the edge of the bush we stopped. He was fifty yards from us ; and, seeing us all after him, he was very fierce. He rose and came at us. Many men scrambled up trees, but Changa could not get to a tree in time, so he said : ' All right, you lion : let us fight here in the open ! ' Then he fired off his gun into the belly of the lion as it sprang upon him. What a lion ! Not a lion at all but a wizard himself ! The lion hit Changa with one blow of his paw and broke his head clean open. His brains splashed twenty yards. Now Changa's younger brother was hiding behind a tree. Seeing Changa killed he rushed out crying : ' You have killed my brother—why should I then fear you ? ' He rushed up to the lion before it had time to turn and shot it in the neck. This time the lion knew that he was indeed finished with the country. He fell on his side : then staggered away, with blood streaming sho-o-o-o-o from his mouth. We all ran at him, and everybody shot him : he climbed the side of an antheap with my spear and several others sticking into him. Then he fell on his back and rolled over—dead.

" Kalilele said : ' Do not spoil the skin further with spears, we will sell it to the *Bwana*.' So we tied up the lion on a pole and carried it to Kalilele's village. There were three machilas : the lion and Changa and Mbetela —Mbetela was nearly dead. So we came back to the village with them ; and we laid the lion out in the middle of the village : the very father of all lions—his head was as big as that safe in the corner—and some went to bury Changa's body. Kalilele told others to skin the lion, but the women from all the villages had collected and they would not listen to Kalilele ; they took hoes and axes and pestles and they chopped and pounded the lion to pieces : dancing the while and reviling him obscenely for killing their men. And that night they fetched wood and piled it up above the lion, and burnt him to the accompaniment of song and dance. We all danced, even Kalilele, though he is a chief. Yes, we sang and danced all night ; none slept. And in the morning the lion was finished.

" That was how we were eaten up by the lion, and how we destroyed him. We slept two nights and behold ! the lion has returned. He has been seen on the road near to Chifuka's village.

" What ?

" Oh ! Yes. His wife : a mother of lions. She was seen early in the morning. She has come to afflict us for killing himself. So Kalilele has sent me with his words to the *Bwana* : he says the *Bwana* will possibly give him some gunpowder as all his is finished and there is none . . ."

I fear that the remaining paragraphs about the chase must seem trivial and that the chapter ends in bathos ; but the following remain to be recorded :

Trapping is a method of hunting extensively practised, especially for the smaller *felidæ* and similar animals like the civet. The trap, called *mfimbo*, is the most common. It is formed of vertical logs with a narrow doorway over which is a heavy log. The trap is baited, and the animal on taking the bait releases the heavy log which falls on it and kills it instantaneously.

With short barrel muzzle-loaders and slugs the Ba-Kaonde are quite successful in getting guinea-fowl, pigeons, etc. Some of them are remarkably expert in this form of sport.

The three principal methods of catching fish are :

i. Spearing fish in flood pools that are drying up. This takes place usually in September and October. A single pointed spear is used, not double as with some tribes.

ii. Fish traps (generic word *muvuwa*) : one kind, the *yamba*, is used in November. Two other varieties (*a*) *chiwinji*, or *wa ngwashi* (large) and (*b*) *musalala* (small), are used in April.

iii. Poisoning (stupefying) fish by means of the *wululu* or *bubwa* pods takes place in June and July.

The word *Chiwinda* has been used above for " hunter," but I am informed (F.V.B.M.) that among the Alunda *chiwinda* is only a general name for hunter and that one of the real hunters, of the hunters' guild, is called *Chiyang'a*. When a *chiyang'a* dies he must always be buried with his head above ground, and two holes must be left in the mound to enable him to see the surrounding country. A dead bird is placed in each hand prior to burial. Also before the burial, one of his canine teeth is taken out and handed to his successor, who uses it as a hunting fetish and must also feed the tooth on blood.

I have no knowledge of similar custom or belief among the Ba-Kaonde, though such may exist.

LIST OF GAME AND OTHER ANIMALS

English.	Kaonde.
Elephant	*Nzofu*
Bull elephant	*Nkungulu*
Cow elephant	*Chikumbe, Ching'ombe*
Tuskless elephant	*Ng'ungwa*
One-tusk elephant	*Chipekwe*
Rhinoceros	*Chilangwa*
Hippopotamus	*Chovwe*
Buffalo	*Mbo*
Bull buffalo	*Ng'ombe*
Cow buffalo	*Inang'ombe*
Eland	*Nsefu*
Bull eland	*Mpundu*
Cow eland	*Kakombe*
Roan	*Ntengu*
Hartebeeste	*Nkonzhi*
Wildebeeste	*Chimfulwe*
Sable	*Mfumbu*
Sable (old bull)	*Kanshije*
Waterbuck	*Mukambi*
Puku	*Nsewula, Nchila*
Mpala	*Mpala*
Lechwe	*Honge, Nja*
Bushbuck	*Ngulungu*
White-backed duiker	*Chikunji*
Duiker	*Kashya*
Oribi	*Katung'u manyika, Katung'unyika*
Kudu	*Nsontwa*
Bushpig	*Nguluwe*
Warthog	*Mpengi*
Zebra	*Mbishi, Ngolo, Chingalika*
Klipspringer	*Kashya mitumba*

English.	*Kaonde.*
Sitatunga	*Mbundu*
Bluebuck	*Kabuluku*
Reedbuck	*Kawazhi, Mbazhi*
Stembuck (?)	*Ching'omba*
Lion (or any large carnivore)	*Bokwe*
Lion	*Ntambo*
Leopard	*Chisumpa*
Cheetah	*Chisekesa, Chisengantambo*
Hyena	*Mungolwe*
Jackal	*Lubwala*
Hunting dog	*Musuka*
Crocodile	*Chiwele, Ng'andu*
Porcupine	*Nungu*
Otter	*Mushingo, Chibawe*
Serval	*Muzuzhi*
Civet	*Katumpa, Mfungwe*
Lynx	*Mbwang'ong'o*
Wild cat	*Kabonzo*
Genet	*Nshimba*
Honey badger	*Kambole, Kankwa*
Ant bear	*Mpumpa*
Tree cony (*Procavia mima*)	*Chibila*
Grey lemur	*Mpongo*
Lesser lemur (" bush baby ")	*Katonto*
Flying squirrel	*Lumembe*
Grey squirrel	*Luyeye*
Small mongoose	*Mumbuluma*
Barred mongoose	*Nkala*
Baboon	*Mpombo*
Grey monkey	*Nsoko, Nkolwe*
Blue monkey	*Mbere*
Colobus	*Mpulumba*
Land monitor	*Mubulu*

English.	Kaonde.
Water monitor	Nsamba
Snake (generic)	Murovu
Python	Lumwengo
Black mamba	Mvubushi
Puff adder	Chipiji, Makata

CHAPTER XXIII

WARFARE

WARFARE is a somewhat grand name for the petty scrimmages in which the Ba-Kaonde and their neighbours used to indulge; but for lack of a better word it will serve. As a rule wars were not tribal. The Kaonde tribe, if it can be so called, never appears to have fought as a tribe. Sometimes sections of the tribe fought against sections of other tribes, but quite as often they fought among themselves. Kasempa and his people fought against the Balamba of Mulonga and of Kalilele; and, as has been recorded under HISTORY, Mushima fought against Ilunga of the Alunda. The Alunda fought the Valuena; but there were more fights between chiefs of the one tribe as when Jing'amba (the present Kapiji Mpanga) fought against Katutamwiulu Mulimanzovu. So far as I can ascertain all these fights were on a small scale and the casualties were very few.

The stronger party, or the party considering itself the stronger, attacked. The defenders generally took position on a hill—if they had time—and round the hill the issue would be fought out. Attack would take place at dawn, and surprise would be effected if possible. The cause of the fight would be either greed—for the spoils of war, women, ivory, guns—or the desire to get back captured slaves, inherited wives taken by someone else, and so on. A few simple prayers preceded the attack, but otherwise there would seem to have been no ritual, unless the decapitation of dead enemies can be so called.

The following general remarks are largely from notes by Mr. Woods. " I have come," he says, " across the remains of old earthworks encircling the former site of a village, thrown up—it is said—as a means of defence ; and I have seen in the bush not far from Kasempa similar remains of a fortified camp. In the latter case man-holes or dug-outs had been made on the inside of the breastwork every dozen yards or so from which the de-fenders would emerge and discharge their guns, retiring again into the pits to reload.

" A prominent hill appears to have been regarded as a stronghold for defensive purposes. Chief Kasempa and his people were besieged in an isolated kopje for some days, close to the site of his village at the time. Chief Chinsengwe is said to have successfully resisted the Ba-Chikunda natives from Ndola about a score of years ago by taking refuge in a similar rocky outcrop on the Kaungashi stream. In both cases there was water at the foot of the hill." (Chimale Hill within sight of Solwezi Boma was similarly used by Kapijimpanga.)

" As regards reconnaisance, spies were sent out, and went openly to the village which it was proposed to attack, and saluted the inhabitants in the ordinary way, asking for beer and tobacco. While they were being hospitably entertained they made observations on the enemy's position, strength and so on. Having gained this information they would rejoin the attacking party, con-cealed a few miles away, and would inform them of their discoveries. If the prospects seemed good a stealthy night march followed and a surprise attack at dawn.

" All the villages were (in pre-European days) stock-aded : the stockades being of considerable height and strength. This was necessary as these raids were frequent, and (apparently) so unjustified in many cases that no one knew when to expect one. Small boys, girls and women of marriageable age were not killed, but such of the male defenders as could not escape were put to death. Escape

" BY THE POWER OF THE SWORD "

Chief Kapiji Mpanga Mwandwe, formerly Jingamba, was a usurper, and won his chieftainship by fighting. He was a great friend of the author.

was not difficult as a rule; and women and children would not be abandoned if it could be avoided. During a retreat these non-combatants marched in front, the males providing the rear guard. There appears to have been no strategy, no effort to cut off the retreating enemy, possibly due to the casual nature of all the fighting."

I think that with these few preliminary remarks the best way to give a picture of native warfare in these parts will be to describe an actual " war " as described to me by the chief actors therein.

Scene of the Fighting. N.E. of the Kaonde country.
Date. Probably at the close of the nineteenth century.
Principal Chiefs.

Ba-Kaonde : Kapijimpanga, Kafitwe.
Balamba : Mutwali, Mulonga, Kalilele.
Bayeke : Mutipula.
And a party of Baluchaji from Angola.

Many years ago when Jing'amba (Kapijimpanga) lived at his grandfather's (Kapoa Mulimanzovu) the people of Mulela, a Lamba chief, lived on the Luamala. Later on when his grandfather died Jing'amba rebelled against his successor, Katutamwiulu Mulimanzovu, and separated from him, coming to live on the Chimale Hill (E. of the Chifubwa), where Chiwanza was. Here he settled, and was known as Kapijimpanga after his victories over his cousin. Having no cultivations he bought his food from the people of Mulela, the neighbouring Lamba chief. At this time the Bayeke (Msiri's people) came from the north, fought against Mulela and killed him. His people thereupon left the Luamala and came near to Chimale Hill to be under the protection of Kapijimpanga. Later, when things had quieted down, they returned to their home. At this time one of these Lamba headmen, Mutwali, went to Chief Kalilele, of the same tribe, and Kalilele took the wife and one sister of Mutwali and kept them, killing another of Mutwali's sisters. The enraged headman set out for Kapijimpanga's to invoke his aid, but on the way he found an elephant lame, and nearly dead, at which his young men fired two arrows. After this diversion the party continued its march and soon met Kapijimpanga, whom they informed of the incident. He supplied them with a horn of powder and two guns, and one or two of his young men to strengthen the party; thus fortified they went after the wounded elephant and killed it. Mutwali gave one tusk to Kapijimpanga for his assistance, and promised him the other if he would help him to recover his wife and sister from Kalilele.

Soon after this a brother Lamba chief, Mulonga, asked Mutwali to let him have this tusk since he wished to give it as tribute (or bribe) to the Bayeke to keep them from attacking him. Mutwali refused, saying that he wanted it to pay Kapijimpanga if he gave him assistance against Kalilele; and to satisfy Mulonga handed him a woman, whom the latter took and gave as a slave to the Bayeke. A little later one Chifumpa came to Mutwali and said to him:

" Chola, your wife, has sent me asking me to deliver this message to you : that you should make haste and save her from Kalilele. If you come to see her it will help, for she will find some means of communicating with you."

Thereupon Mutwali went to Kalilele's and stayed on the edge of the village, where his wife, Chola, met him.

" Go," she said, " and hide in the bush close by at the place I indicate, and there await me. I will collect my things, and then I will escape and join you ; and we can go away together."

But she was treacherous, and instead of doing as she had said she went to Kalilele and told him where Mutwali was hiding, showing how easy it would be to surprise him since he was unsuspecting. Kalilele did as

Chola suggested and killed Mutwali. When his people
heard of his death they went to Kapijimpanga and told
him. That chief collected his people and got ready
to make war on Kalilele. Mutipula, one of the chiefs
of the Bayeke, joined forces with him. On the way they
met Swana Mutwali (=the successor of Mutwali), who
said to Kapijimpanga :

" See here : we did but send to report to you the
death of Mutwali : we did not ask you to make war
upon Kalilele : to do so might stir up a hornet's nest
about our ears."

Thus talking they reached Mulonga's, and Kapijimpanga gave Mulonga some advice, especially telling him
that he should stockade his village since it was not wise
to live in an open unprotected village. Mulonga gave
food to the visitors, and also placed a tusk on the food
of Kapijimpanga and another on the food of Mutipula—
as " a present." (The same kind of " present " that
Ethelred the Unready, used to give, only Mulonga seems
to have been giving these *douceurs* on both sides of
him !)

Although nothing happened at the time the idea of
a war against Kalilele was obviously not abandoned, for
Kafitwe (a Kaonde and a relative of Kapijimpanga) went
to the Bayeke to ask for further assistance in the matter :
he returned, joined by Sompwe, Mulenga and Mushia.
By this time Mulonga's stockade was built ; and when
he saw Kafitwe with his new strength arrive he thought
well to give him a present too, and handed him a tusk
weighing about 15 lb. Reinforced by Kafitwe and his
allies Kapijimpanga said, " Well, now let us go and
fight," and he told Mulonga to contribute to the army
too. Mulonga had no choice and gave him ten men
and five guns. Chipempere and the new Mutwali (all
Lamba) had to join too. Mulonga got a little suspicious
at the way things were turning out, seeing so many
Balamba impressed into this fight, and tried to draw

back, and take away his quota; but Kapijimpanga would have none of it, and set out accompanied by Mulonga's contingent. A few miles out Mulonga's suspicions were fully justified, for the Ba-Kaonde attacked his people and killed three of the men and two women who accompanied them. Mulonga then felt he must fight, so he attacked Kapijimpanga; but, though one man of importance on the other side (Sompwe's son) was killed, Mulonga was decisively beaten and fled with his people.

Kapijimpanga gave chase and demanded tribute from the conquered Mulonga, naming especially a widow of Mutwali's, whom he coveted. Mulonga offered him all Mulela's widows and one other woman instead, but Kapijimpanga was obdurate. That night Mulonga felt that discretion was the better part of valour, and ran away again, leaving behind him all the women, who were seized by Kapijimpanga.

Mulonga then sent to sue for peace, saying he had but fought on account of the treacherous killing of three of his warriors. He offered a tusk as a peace offering, which Kapijimpanga graciously accepted, saying that he bore no ill-will; and that it was Sompwe and not he who had arranged the treacherous killing of Mulonga's men.

By this time Mulonga seems to have been anxious that Kapijimpanga should resume the original offensive and attack Kalilele, urging him to do so, and promising that if he would do as requested he would " live with " (? be subject to) his great ally. Kapijimpanga agreed, but once more something occurred to postpone the great war on Kalilele.

A party of Baluchaji arrived from the West—from some way in what is now Portuguese Angola—bringing with them cloths to trade. They visited Kapijimpanga, having known him of old. After a sojourn with him some of them went further afield with their goods:

one party going to Msaka, another to Mulonga, and a third as far as Luambula's (to the east of Kalilele's).

Now it came to pass that at Luambula's one of the leaders of the Baluchaji was slain, whereupon the rest of the party came back to Kapijimpanga and asked their host's assistance in an attack on Luambula.

Kapijimpanga agreed readily enough, and with the Baluchaji (who were in some strength) he started off, and called upon the young Mulonga (the old one had died, and a successor reigned) to join, which he had no option but to do. When they got to Msaka's the Baluchaji seeing that this headman was a man of substance suggested that they should attack him meanwhile : Kapijimpanga refused, saying that Msaka was the father of his nephews Mwanakatema and Chitondo, so that he could not do this, but he got Msaka to pay a tusk of ivory in consideration for this clemency ! They continued their march and at last they arrived at Kalilele's. Kalilele was nothing loth to fight and came out to meet the enemy ; and early in the fight succeeded in killing Pandanya, the son of Nyundu (one of Kapijimpanga's chief supporters) ; Mulonga wounded himself in the right eye—the hammer of his gun causing the damage, owing to the recoil. The casualties appear to have alarmed Kapijimpanga, and in the evening, when fighting was over for the day, he called on his brave ally Mulonga, and directed him to pray carefully to his family spirits for victory. Mulonga did so with fervour.

The following day the battle was resumed. There seems little doubt that the generalissimo placed his Baluchaji allies in the place of honour, for the casualties on the attacking side seem to have consisted solely of Baluchaji : killed two, wounded one. In spite of these losses the aggressors were victorious and Kalilele admitted defeat. He paid five slaves and four tusks of cow-ivory to the victors. Kapijimpanga and the Baluchaji divided these, Mulonga got nothing. The nominal reason for the expedition, namely, the chastisement of Luambula, was not proceeded with.

It is noteworthy that whereas it may at first sight appear that this series of "scraps" are disconnected there is one main thread that runs right through them. It seems that Kapijimpanga was desirous from one cause or another of fighting Kalilele. Now Kalilele was a great fighter and feared no one. To the date of his death (1921) he remained an indomitable old man. Opportunity after opportunity arose, and the "war" was decided on, allies collected—voluntary and otherwise—but doubts appear to have arisen in Kapijimpanga's mind as to whether he had sufficient margin of strength, so that the war was postponed time after time. The arrival of the Baluchaji, well armed and numerically strong, and the fortunate accident (let us suppose it *was* an accident) of a quarrel with Luambula, who lived beyond Kalilele, gave him the long-sought opportunity *plus* the necessary strength. Thus at last he came to grips with Kalilele and won : whereupon he proceeded no further against Luambula, but disbanded his army.

Mulonga's people had more vicissitudes before the coming of the white man. Some fled to the Bayeke, some to Katanga, some to Shikunda's. . . . They reunited and returned to the Luamala : they were attacked by the Alunda under Shamarenge, but their chronicles are of insufficient interest to record here. The above —in which they feature, frequently if ingloriously—is given as a typical example of the " warfare of the Kaonde and their neighbours "—from the *casus belli* to the treaty of peace. Such examples could be multiplied, but very little variety would be found.

[NOTE.—I have visited the " battlefield " of the fight between Kalilele and Kapijimpanga : but, though it was no surprise attack, there were no earthworks such as those seen near Kasempa by Mr. Woods. The fight took place with natural cover such as is afforded by anthills and trees.]

CHAPTER XXIV

PROVERBS, SONGS, DANCES

I REGRET that I have no fables transcribed: some of them are quite good, especially those of the Alunda. These last have a distinct " moral," which is, as a rule, quite lacking in Bantu fables. It is to be hoped that someone will publish some of them at some future date.

In this chapter I owe thanks to J.H.C.G. and R.E.B.W. for the Kaonde proverbs, to J.L.K. for the Lunda proverbs, to T.R.W. for the songs, and to R.E.B.W. for notes on dances.

KAONDE PROVERBS (*vishimi*). These are given with a translation and paraphrase when necessary. Archaic words often occur.

Luwilo wa nkovu, kwiwangijizha.

The speed of the tortoise is to start early.

Chikunyi, chitemela wingi (not *vingi* as one would expect).

Much firewood blazes readily. (" Many hands make light work.")

Mushindwa jiwiji mupampula kalowa.

One who asks twice is he who turns aside (ceases) from complaining. (The man who shouts loud and keeps on shouting gets what he wants.)

Pachinkila nkulo pamwawa.

Where the waterbuck frequents (lit. touches) it is shallow. (Possibly meaning one returns again and again to a good thing.)

Wakulako kitsi kwaiya boya.
You have inserted a stick (e.g. into a hollow trunk) and
some hair adheres. (R.E.B.W. suggests, " Acts
are followed by their natural consequences.")

Pavundamila nguruwe pa minyemvu.
Where the bushpig turns his back there is green grass.
(A man rejects a superficial advantage, knowing
privately where he can lay his hand on something
better.)

Chanswe chiimanekumo.
Let bad luck stand on one side. (" Don't tempt
providence.")

Chanswe chiimana kumo.
Bad luck stands on *one* side (only).

Uchila mwandalo tsiuchila viwi ne.
You leap over a log, but not over a warning.

Kanwa kalowele mutwi.
The mouth accused (brought trouble to) the head.

Pachawila lukunyi lwanyingulwilwa.
Where firewood has been dropped, chips will lie about.

Kuya nshimba kukeya mambo.
Where the genet goes a case will come therefrom (or
trouble will ensue). (? Does a genet bring bad
luck? or does it mean that a genet entering a
hole means a fight inside as it would with a
stoat?)

Mukulu kavwale mbulu jilombelo ja chisewa.
The old gaffer wears a lizard skin, thereby begging a
decent one.

Mukulu kamone jikasa ja nkalamu.
An old man will not look at lion's spoor. (Possibly
only means old age breeds discretion, and an old
man prefers safety to sport ; but it may mean
" The aged expect short shrift in witchcraft
accusations.")

A Chisungu Girl and Her Boy Husband.

After the unveiling of the former, as shown in the picture underneath.

A Woman Unveiling a Chisungu Girl.

She has been completely covered by a blanket, which is now being pulled away. Her
" supporter " is visible behind her with bangles on her left wrist.

Wawakapo wishi muvilo wamusha.
You snatch at the smoke and leave the fire. (Snatching
at the shadow and leaving the substance.)
Pemba pemba wapemba na vingi.
Wait, wait on ! you wait for ever ! (Procrastination
is the thief of time.)
Kawandaula china chulu nacho chulu chikuchine.
The small anthill fears the big one, so the big one
may fear you. (Respect for elders **advo**cated ;
or, everyone in every station of life has his own
troubles.)
*Ulonda mu mukazhiambwa tsiulonda mu ulumeyambwa
ne.*
Follow as a bitch follows, not as a dog. (A woman is
wiser than a man.)
Mulala nkovu mwapakana.
Where the tortoise sleeps it is narrow. (? It takes two
to make a quarrel.)
Mukishi wa mukwena ke ulajilwa panje ne.
Just because your companion is lucky is no reason
why you should sleep outside. (Cheer up !
There's as good fish in the sea as ever came out
of it !)
Wafya kambala ne muchima-ko.
You have hidden (left) your *chimbala* (cold porridge
left from overnight) and your heart with it.
(Used of a man who has divorced or deserted a
wife and longs to return to her.)

LUNDA PROVERBS. Given in English only, after the
first two, but it may be noted that they all have in the
original a neatly balanced rhythm, the first part being
equal to the last.
Chilemesha cha ngonga, mukatchi u di mafumpa.
" The pouch is heavy, but inside are rings." (Used of
a boastful fellow.)

Kutumba ku nyaba komana manyini, kutemba ku wusoku komana ulumbu.

" To fall out with the ford, there are deep pools."
(To fall out with one's relatives is trouble.)

" The talking bird was master, he scattered his following." (A headman, or other, who nags will soon find himself alone.)

" The cock died in the village, the chicks remain· d clucking." (When there is no chief, there is no order in a village or country.)

" The *nchila* returns from the ford many times, but later will cross."

" The old man is dead to-day. The hyena's droppings have white hairs."

" To ask for water to cook is like building one's village with other people's relatives."

SONGS. T.R.W., in placing his notes on songs at my disposal, writes : " I have put down the music in the way I used to write it for my own record (incredible as it may seem this sometimes helped me to remember a tune) " ; and I think that, while it would have been better if one could have had the music properly transcribed, this is very much better than nothing. I regret that I am unable to improve on it.

Carriers in the Kasempa district sing mainly songs learnt at Lubumbashi (the smelter works in Katanga), and they have got these from the Wawemba. *Lwimbo lwa chibaru* (songs of native labourers on contract) is what they call them. But, as they are sung by Ba-Kaonde, they are worth recording briefly :—

This is very common :—

1 2 3 4   5 6   7 8 9 10 11   12

1. *Twende, tu mu twale, bwana wa lila kwawo.*

" Let us walk, let us take him : the *bwana* is crying for his home."

(Sung by carriers taking their master when he is going on leave.)

Another :—

1   2 3 4   5 6 7   8   9   10   11   12   13

2. *Kawango, mwana wa Bulaya, ngo ngo ngo, ngo ngo ngo,*
14 15 16   17 18 19
Kawango, Kawango.

Kawango, child of Europe. Hey diddle diddle, etc.

The following is probably the commonest, and one hears infinite variations, some apparently nonsense, some obscene. It is a part-song, for one leader and a chorus.

First the leader sings very fast :—

1 2 3   4 5 6   7 8 9

3. *Wunda wa matako Chikongo* (How big are Chikongo's
buttocks,

1 2 3   4 5 6   7 8 9
Wunda wa matako Chikongo How big are Chikongo's
buttocks,

1 2 3 4 5 67 8
Wa tentakanya milesu   He wears calicoes one on
the top of the other).

Then the rest sing in a lower key, and slowly—with unction :—

4. *Wunda wa matako Chikongo, Wunda wa matako Chi-kongo.*

Then the leader :—

5. *Chikongo chowayeriye.*

Then all :—

6. *Chikongo-we.*

Some other verses are :—

2. *Wa tu pereshe chibaya* (You make us grind mealies,
   Bwana TA TU pero   Bwana does NOT give us
   wunga   meal !)

3. *Wa sa nj' iyaya Kaponda* (Kaponda nearly killed me
   Pa ku mwewo wulamba   for calling him a Mulamba).

4. *Wa pishyo munyo kum-* (You expose yourself in the
   wela   wind.
   Wa n'dangurusho bulanda You make me feel like an
                          orphan).
                          (i.e. miserable with jealousy)

The most interesting are the songs sung at dances : some may be alien, all are very hard to follow ; and, I think, the language is often so archaic that even the singers cannot translate it into everyday forms. (Whereby it may be the more interesting ethnologically.) This is a very pretty one, heard on the upper Dongwe (south-west Kaonde, bordering on Mambwera).

7. *Aba bakamwali shibeshiko*
Twa ku ba lumbo wukyewukye
Ne nsoniekwa ba lwimbo baya wurro-o-o.

The time for the second line is the same as for the first. The two first lines mean, " The girls are nowhere, we have called their names very gently."

The last line I cannot translate.

Then follows a chorus to the same tune :—

Mama werere wa yuno
Mama werere wa yo werere
Mama werere wa yo wurro-o-o.

This next I have never heard at dances, but by way of welcome at villages in Mushima's country and on the Lalafuta. I have heard it just recognisably the same sung by women (as welcome too) in the Barotse country.

The words sound like :—

Tomboka ngwenene   The mosquito does a war-dance,
Ngwenene kunana   The mosquito is fat,
Tomboka ngwenene   The mosquito does a war-dance.

But those were only what I could guess : the real words may be quite different.

(Some mourning songs will be found in Chapter VI, etc. ; but only the words unfortunately. I have heard some very pretty Lunda songs, but have no record of them.)

There are some delightful " nursery rhymes," adds T.R.W., which I cannot remember in full (like the writer, he, too, is no longer in the Kaonde country). One begins :—

Mungomba, chinka muroma panshi
(" The hornbill striking its bill on the ground "),
and proceeds with other animals according to their type.

There is a little recitation giving names to all the ten fingers, and another which recounts for children all the parts of the body and what is the function of each, very amusing and quite innocent : just like " This little pig went to market."

I fear that the above is not much more than a clue to Kaonde songs, but it may possibly stimulate someone on the spot to further research.

DANCES. The most interesting dance is the *Bwilandi*, or rather it would be if we could find out more about it. There is something very secretive about the native attitude as regards this dance, and an obvious fear exists that it is a thing that might be prohibited. It is more common in the north of Kaondeland than in the south, and may be of Luba origin. The name comes from the *bwilandi* drug which the dancers take beforehand, a drug that produces a kind of ecstasy. This drug does not grow (not in any quantity anyhow) south of the Luma. The chief feature of the dance is that the dancer simulates, either voluntarily or involuntarily, a lion ; and goes about as a lion. But, and this is really remarkable if it is only made-up, he does not imitate the lion's roar. If anyone were to start " playing at lions "

the roar is the first thing that would be imitated. Another
feature of the drug is that the natives state it gives
wonderful endurance, so that a man under its influence
can travel a hundred miles in a night—all the time " as
a lion." The drumming at the *bwilandi* is distinct from
other drummings, and a Kaonde hearing it in a village
at a distance can identify it without difficulty.

Like most dances it takes place at night. The early
stages may be in the daytime, and are quite innocuous.
The attached illustration shows the " overture." The
dancer has twenty genet skins as a kilt, and the proper
chalk marks on back and chest. The latter stages, with
the ecstasy and the lion performance I have not seen,
nor do I know of any white man who has. If one did
see it I fancy it would be distinctly " modified." Whether
it has any religious significance, or any significance at all,
I do not know.

The *mbwera* dance (of Mambwera origin) is thus
described by R.E.B.W. :—

" I witnessed recently the *mbwera* dance at Ingwe's, in
which Ingwe (a chief living north of Kasempa) himself
took the leading part, and which he took some pains to
stage. The drumming was unusual, and the dance consisted largely of acting. It represents the hunting and
killing of an elephant. The principal dancers were only
two. Ingwe was the elephant and gave a most realistic
show in his part, acting the wounded elephant in its
death agonies trying to get at the other chief actor, the
hunter, who made repeated dashes at him. It is an old-
time *mukurumpi's* dance, and the youngsters had to be
coached by Ingwe as to their parts and the words of the
chorus.

There is a dance called *kasewa*, a snake dance. In this
a drugged (or frenzied) witch-doctor hypnotises (?) the
audience and causes them to see a *mulombe* (see Chapter
XVI) in some old person's hut (R.E.B.W. says " old
woman's hut," but I fancy women do not keep *mulombes*,

so that would be rather pointless). This is probably part of the stock-in-trade of the witch-doctor.

There are *chisungu* dances, and funeral dances, and dances for most events, including dances for no particular reason ; but on the whole the Ba-Kaonde are not great dancers. The Ba-lamba and the Alunda are both more expert.

DRUMMING. There appears to be no method of signalling by means of drums, except the one signal of loud staccato drumming from a chief's village, which is a summons to assemble only, and does not indicate the nature of the news that will be imparted when the assembly meets.

The late Katotola Mukumbi had three drummers who carried small double-ended barrel-shaped drums on which they used to make a very fair imitation of a lion roaring. This they used to do as a show : it was a stock performance. It is said that this was audible for fifteen miles.

CHAPTER XXV

MISCELLANEOUS

IN this chapter I have brought together a few odd notes that do not group themselves naturally under any other headings. I have kept them as short as possible, for the book has already grown somewhat unwieldy. One has to realise that there is no natural " end " to such a book as this, and that an end must be made somewhere. Even if one had the knowledge one could not include everything, but I hope that sufficient has been written to give those interested a true impression of these tribes, and to furnish those who live among them with a good groundwork whereon each, according to his individual tastes, can add further detail. Apart from the fact that fables are untouched, all the subjects in the preceding chapter would reward further study, while many subjects such as diseases, native remedies (herbs, etc.) are entirely omitted. The languages have not been mentioned except incidentally ; but Mr. Griffiths has written a useful little grammar of the Kaonde dialect and Mr. Woods is at work on a dictionary. The Reverend C. S. Foster is also translating the Gospels into the same tongue ; while Mr. Singleton Fisher has written grammars of the Lunda language and is, I believe, translating the Bible into Lunda.

KAONDE BELIEFS ABOUT BABOONS (C.H.H.). Baboon: sing. *mpombo ;* plur. *bampombo.*

" According to the Ba-Kaonde, baboons are extremely human in many ways. Sometimes, it is said, the ' chief '

of a ' village ' of baboons grows old and becomes bald
like a human being. Possibly he is so decrepit that he
cannot climb on to a tree to sleep at night as is (*query*)
the usual habit. If he is as feeble as this the ' young men '
of the ' village ' collect pieces of bark and branches and
build a comfortable shelter[1] wherein the aged ' chief '
can sleep. These shelters resemble closely those that
men build when obliged to spend a night in the bush.
Although the baboons thoroughly understand how to
build these shelters, none but the aged will sleep in, nor
even enter, one.

   " The greatest enemy of the ' village ' is the leopard,
who is very fond of their flesh ; ' and truly,' add the
Ba-Kaonde, ' it is good to eat.' The leopard will stalk
them when they are feeding on the ground, and often
gets to close quarters in spite of the vigilance of the
' watchmen.' He rushes in at the end of his stalk and
sometimes kills as many as three, each with a single blow,
before it is realised that the enemy is among them. Then
they stampede, but collect again at no great distance and
curse the leopard as he begins to eat his kill. He knows
that though they threaten and curse volubly they will not
attack him ; and they, for their part, know that they
need not fear him so long as they keep in close formation.
A leopard will at times hang on to a ' village,' taking toll
of the baboons daily ; which exasperates them exceedingly
and makes them talk the matter over. Planning retalia-
tion they search for and find their enemy, and attack him
in a body. The leopard flees and may escape ; but if the
baboons corner him they then advance fearlessly in mass
formation, overpower him and tear him to pieces.

   " Baboons frequently attack and ill-treat a human if
they can catch one unawares in the bush, but we (it is a
Kaonde talking) know of no case in which they have
purposely killed a man. Certainly he sometimes dies
afterwards from the effect of maltreatment, but they
do not appear to aim at killing him. Once a man is

captured, the baboons tear branches from convenient trees, bark them and bind his wrists together with the bark. His cloth is torn from him and he is placed on the ground, prone upon his back. Then ' the women of the village' approach and consort with him, one after the other. Then they beat him with heavy sticks,[2] and (in some cases) mutilate his parts, tearing them with their nails before departing. A woman falling into the power of the baboons is treated similarly, being raped by the ' men.' I knew of one young girl, living now, who was thus treated by the baboons. She was, at the time, a young girl with her breasts just formed (*kamwale*). After the ' men ' had had their will they made no attempt to mutilate her, nor even to beat her, but left her to find her way home.

" A dog when caught is treated in a similar way, but at the end the baboons deliberately kill it.

" In one case a man carrying a gun was overpowered by baboons who captured him as he was walking alone along a forest path. Some held him while others went to get bark to bind him. One sat down and examined the gun which was loaded and had the cap on the nipple. Whilst carrying out his examination he cocked and fired the gun which scared the whole ' village' and made them stampede. So the man escaped and went on his way in safety.

" We Ba-Kaonde are well acquainted with baboons and know their ways. As a rule, of course, they run away from humans, but there are many alive to-day who have been maltreated in this way. Also they are most destructive to gardens ; and, after eating much and destroying yet more, they carry away bundles of mealies for future consumption. These they carry in their arms (some say tied to either end of a stick) and walk away erect as a man walks."

Kapezhi's " Folly " (R.E.B.W.). Kapezhi told me (writes Mr. Woods) a story of his grandfather, whose name I forget (for brevity I call him Kapezhi, too, F.H.M.). He lived many years ago on or near to the Kabompo; and, being a trifle mad, he was smitten with the desire to seize and pull down the moon. So he directed his people to build him a great *chitala* (scaffold) of massive poles. On this they built another *chitala*, slightly smaller; on this yet another and so on, storey by storey until his tower reached to an immense height. At last Kapezhi thought that it was high enough for him to achieve his desire, and he climbed to the top. The structure, however, was either top-heavy, or had rotted, for when he reached the summit it collapsed; and the old chief falling with it, was killed.

NOTES ON ALBINOS (LUNDA). Albino: sing. *mwabi ;* plur. *amiabi.*

The birth of an albino is considered an auspicious event: the parents are to be congratulated and envied. It is said that Nzambi (God) must love them to bring such happiness into their lives. In this matter, be it noted, Nzambi is considered more powerful than the *akishi* (spirits) and it is Nzambi who is supposed to be responsible for the unexpected good luck (*kutokwa*). It is presumed that the *akishi* get Nzambi to do this, since they cannot bring it about themselves.

After the birth the parents do not thank Nzambi directly, but thank the *akishi* for being instrumental in bringing about this birth.

When the albino child grows, people come to the mother with offerings (a shilling, maybe, or some salt or a few beads) and beg for even a single hair from the *mwabi's* head. This hair is carefully preserved, and when the owner invokes the help of a *mukishi*, no matter in what connection, he mixes the hair with a little dust—taking care not to injure the precious possession—and then rubs the dust that has been in contact with it on his face as he offers up his prayer. In olden days if anyone saw an albino child alone he would steal hair from its head ; and if such a theft were proved against him it would be a serious case, that would call for heavy damages, such as a slave. (The hair is also used as an ingredient in certain specific charms. F.H.M.) One who lived at Murunda village grew up and married, and had children and grandchildren of the ordinary hue. (V.R.A.)

HUMOURS OF ETHNOGRAPHICAL STUDY. In the course of the work which is embodied in these pages, I have, naturally, found a few humorous incidents. One intelligent old man, talking to me about the Creation, solemnly assured me that he believed that muzzle-loading guns were among the gifts from *Lesa* to the first couple on earth : a slight misconception as to chronology !

In another case, while checking my notes on the *mulombe* (Chap. XVI), I detailed what I had heard to a keen helper. When I had finished he said : " That is right in every detail ! The man who told you had one himself, all right. No one who had not got a *mulombe* could possibly know so much about it, all the details of its creation, and habits." It did not seem to occur to him that thereby he, who had the knowledge to confirm the details, himself stood self-convicted as a *mulombe* owner !

A native clerk at Kasempa trying with much zeal to help by compiling some notes on his own (it was he who first unearthed the custom of *lubumboshi* described under TOTEMS, Chap. XXI) headed a page of notes

" KAONDE CUSTOMS-RAPE."

Rather a libel to class it as a " custom "! Of course, he only referred to the native customs in dealing with cases of rape.

I have frequently been asked if the natives do not mind one delving into these intimate customs and beliefs ;

and I can emphatically state that so long as one asks questions sympathetically they like it. (The scoffer can ask his questions in vain, he will but meet with denials or made-up yarns.) Natives have frequently expressed their pleasure at the interest shown in these researches ; and are particularly delighted when they find that the white man's people have something similar in the way of ideas or superstitions. An effort to understand the native mind, however limited may be one's success, not only facilitates the task of ruling them, but it is a sure way to their hearts. One of my best friends, Chief Kapiji Mpanga Mwandwe, is one to whose help I owe much. When I left the district and he came to say " Good-bye," he touched me by calling me " My father who begat me " : a testimonial I shall always value.

¹ H. G. Wells says the chimpanzee makes itself a sort of tree hut by intertwining branches. (*Outline of History*.)

² Darwin (*Descent of Man*) represents baboons as striking with sticks.

CHAPTER XXVI

THE FUTURE OF THE NATIVE

[The following chapter is taken from a paper read by the author at the triennial Missionary Conference at Kafue, July, 1922. It seems apposite to include it, for as I have sketched the past and the present of these tribes the question may occur to many : " What is to happen to the natives now ? "

That is a question I cannot answer and which I do not attempt to answer. The nature of the answer rests not only with us out here, but with every member of the electorate at home. That is where the responsibility for the future lies.

The paper is partly recapitulary, but I have not re-drafted it as this characteristic seems a useful one in a final chapter. In reading it I expanded many of the points, but that is unnecessary here, with twenty-five chapters preceding it.]

INTRODUCTORY

I WOULD like to make it clear at the beginning that I have no intention of trying to forecast the future of the native : suffice it to say that I do believe he has a future, if we help him wisely. My object is, rather, to try to get you to consider whether we have not been working so far without any due consideration for our goal, whether we are not still doing so, and whether it is not time that we did consider what future we are aiming at for the Bantu races in this country, who are our wards, and how best to achieve our aim.

Secondly, may I say that although I am but a layman I have the real moral welfare of the native as much at heart as any missionary ; and that, therefore, I trust you will bear patiently with me when I disagree with you, as I naturally must at times, seeing that I approach these problems from a different angle, and view them from a different standpoint. I read recently an account of three old gentlemen discussing politics and " agreeing fiercely with each other." I think that such discussions—familiar enough to all of us—are rather a waste of time ; and that one gains more by hearing, and trying to grasp, another point of view.

1. General

We have been in this country for, roughly, a quarter of a century ; and, as regards the natives, I think that the result of our presence has been disappointing. The impression which we have made on ordinary village life is inappreciable : our progress towards elevating the rank and file is negligible. If we are to progress, if we are to influence the future of the natives—and to influence it for good—it seems to me that we must study seriously the causes of our comparative failure hitherto. This problem is going to be still more important in the next twenty-five years than it has been in the last : there is a big leavening of mal-educated natives (by which I mean natives who have acquired, unguided, some superficial knowledge of our civilisation) and a growing feeling that they—the natives—are, in the mass, being considered as a commodity to be used for the benefit, or convenience, of the white races.

2. Why Have We Made So Little Progress ?

Many of your supporters at home, and possibly some of you, think that you have come here to convert the heathen. I would like to take that as a text, because I believe that it is the key to our problem. Personally I have never met any heathen in Africa[1] (except for a few civilisation-spoilt individuals to whom I will refer later). I take the definition of " heathen " to be " one without the knowledge or fear of God," which excludes these

CHIEF KATUTA MWINLU MULIMANZOVU.

An aged Kaonde Chief· he died 1922. He succeeded Kapoa Mulimanzovu, but owing to the rebellion of Jing'amba (now Kapiji Mpanga) lost must of his power. Note the shells on forehead and long string of beads suspended from his beard, also the battleaxe over right shoulder.

natives as it excludes Buddhists and many other non-Christian believers. As a matter of fact Buddhism, which in some such points as reincarnation resembles these Bantu faiths, is more atheistical than they are: for while the natives here recognis: a God, the Buddhists worship and pray to Buddha, who himself never claimed to be more than a man.

If the natives of this country had been heathen, you as missionaries, and we as administrators, would have had probably a simpler, and certainly an entirely different, task from that which has confronted us. But the natives, as I will try to explain briefly, have not only a very real religion, but—in a way that cannot be said of European races—they LIVE their religion : it is their life.

The few heathen (or atheists) can be described easily. You know—even better than I do—the common objection to " Mission boys." You know, also, that this bad name has been caused by natives who have attached themselves to some Mission or other for a short time for material ends : have got a veneer, and have left—entirely unconverted to Christianity. Why have they got (and earned) such a bad name ? Not only because they were not Christians, but because they have lost their own religion and have become heathens.

Precisely the same thing applies (in a slightly different degree) to the natives who have worked for long at secular industrial centres and have become detribalised. Tribalism is part of their religion, so in losing that they too have become heathens.

I believe that we will find in this class—the natives heathenised by contact with us—a most valuable finger post, and a most salutary warning if we will but take it. Let us beware that we do not turn the devoutly religious natives of Africa into heathens. There is a risk of this. Every centre of European employment provides this risk : every Mission centre also provides it.

Luckily I believe that if we realise it, it is an avoidable risk.

3. WHAT IS NATIVE RELIGION?

This may seem out of place under the title of this paper; but I assure you it is not. One cannot consider any aspect of native affairs without considering native religion. Of course, I have no time here to touch on it except in a very sketchy way, and in sketching what seem to me to be the salient points of native religion, I allow for the fact that in each tribe there are differences, greater or less.

In *Nuttall's Dictionary* Religion is described as "a habitual, all-prevading sense of dependence on, reverence for, and responsibility to, a higher power." This seems to me an admirable definition of native religion. I venture to affirm that this sense is more habitual and all-pervading with the average Bantu than with the average European. We say "God is everywhere : God knoweth all, seeth all . . ." but what proportion of our race LIVES that belief? All natives in their natural state LIVE this belief : the belief in the omniscience and universal presence of the " spirits."

The natives believe in a God-the-Creator. A few (e.g. the Ba-Kaonde) pray directly to God for rain : the majority do not approach Him directly at any time ; but they believe that all living things have " life," which is conceived as a shadow ; and that this " life " came from God-the-Creator. The shadow ("shade" or "soul") leaves the body after death and becomes a family spirit. These souls having departed from the human shell exist eternally, and every living man is but an emanation from a departed soul; so that all natives to-day, so far as the breath of life in them is concerned, are but emanations from the dead. Thus a tribe consists of the souls departed and the souls living—the latter proceeding from the former. " The dead," wrote Lafcadio Hearn, " are the real rulers of Japan." And this is equally true of these Bantu races. One must grasp this fact and respect

this belief if one is to get any confidence from the
natives : for slighting anything connected with the dead
(and all is connected) to them seems blasphemy.

The family spirits having lived on earth for some time,
and having their own ideas on human affairs, impose on
the living the duty of following the tradition of their
elders. Law and Custom proceed from the elders (i.e.
from the spirits). It is this that gives the moral force to
native religion—and the force is the greater owing to the
fact that the spirit displeased is supposed to be able to
remind the sinner very forcibly of his sins of omission or
commission. This seems to be the basis of all native
custom, and the guiding principle of every considered
act. Marriage, birth and death customs, initiation
ceremonies, circumcision where practised, arts and
industries, the legal code in all its branches, and every
other ceremony and custom of local life is more or less
dependent on the will of the spirits. The elaborate code
of " shame " which influences native life greatly, the
general relations between individuals—conversation,
eating, greetings, respect for elders, outward relations,
private relations, sex relations, prohibited degrees in
marriage, are all controlled by this religion-ruled custom.
Breaches of any part of these codes are believed to be
punished by death (especially of the sinner's children),
sickness, bad luck, sterility and other penalties. Among
other things a wrong done to an individual, if not properly
settled, will turn his spirit into one adverse to the evil-
doer. Natives say, " If we listen to tradition (considered
by them to be divine) all will be well ; if we do not, *we
hurt ourselves* "—a really high moral idea : in fact, the
more one studies native religion the more one realises the
value it has as a moral check throughout their lives.

4. The Difficulty of our Task

If the reality and the universal application of native
religion be grasped it shows us, I think, that missionaries

in their work of conversion, and administrators in their work of governance, have a far harder task than is realised by the uninitiated. For both of us our calling is a serious profession, and, like all professions, needs a long and patient preparation. It seems to me (believe me, I speak with reverence) that to rely entirely on Divine guidance, without preparing yourselves by studying deeply and sympathetically the natives to whom you have come, is wrong ; as it is wrong for us to rely on British justice and so on without similar study. No one appreciates more than I do the fact that many missionaries and many officials know and live up to this ; but in both classes some do not. When religion, custom, morals, the social fabric are all intertwined, as they are with the natives, any " new " religion, or " new " law or procedure has an uphill fight. We only handicap ourselves if we class native religion incorrectly as " devil worship," and if we fail to realise the considerable elements of good that there are in it. Such attitude by us—be we missionaries or administrators—creates a spirit of antipathy in the devout natives ; and, so long as antipathy exists, we will fail in our mission to help them and raise them.

[NOTE.—Since writing the above I have read the following in an article entitled " Administrators and Anthropologists " by Arthur Grimble, in *United Empire*, December, 1921. It seems so apposite that I hope you will excuse me quoting it.

" If our social prejudices weigh heavily against us, those of a native are supreme to him. A native who offends against one article of his social code·is generally considered impossible in all directions ; he has insulted the custom of his ancestors, who are usually gods, and therefore he has violated his religion. Primitive peoples have not yet reached our stage of isolating groups of prejudices into separate compartments ; their rules of life, art, religion and handicraft are thoroughly dependent

one upon another : profane one and the shock will be
serially transmitted."]

5. The Need of Caution

We must be careful in tampering with any portion of
the social fabric of these natives, lest, being all connected,
it all falls together.　We need to build, and to build
thoughtfully, before we demolish, for these native
customs (all based on religion) are the sole restraining
factor—moral, legal and general—in their lives.　If we
destroy this factor before the natives are ready to assimilate
anything better, we will be causing them to degenerate
instead of elevating them :　a serious responsibility.
*We have, as a matter of fact, to a certain extent, done this
already.*　Can we not build on what they have got, instead
of trying to give them an entirely new set of ideas ?　Is it
beyond our power to build on and purify the existing
system and codes ?

We have taken upon ourselves the responsibility for
the welfare and the future of these natives.　Therefore
to us, as representatives of our race, and as representatives
of Christendom (let us not forget that we represent
both) the problem of the natives' future is of supreme
importance.　Those of our race and faith at home have
not done much to solve this problem—though it is their
duty as trustees ;—but we, out here, have done little
better than those at home ;　and our responsibility is
greater, our negligence more culpable.

6. Our Aims ; And An Idea As To How We May Attain Them

I am sometimes asked to what state of life I want to
raise the native.　I aim at no state of life : there is no such
thing.　The expression is a contradiction in terms, for
static equilibrium is death.　Growth is the essence of
life ;　and I aim at growth—a process and not a state.

The process that is my aim may be summed up as Elevation.

We call the natives the backward races; and rightly so in my opinion. We need first to find out what is the cause of this backwardness.

There are many contributory causes: climate, physiology, fertile soil, sparse population and so on: certain aspects of the communal idea have retarded progress also; but I am by no means alone when I assert that superstition has been the chief retarding influence. Let me, please, emphasise the necessity for separating religion from superstition: witchcraft is NOT a part of native religion. It is a common belief that it is—just as many people think that a witch-doctor is a witch—but it is not; and witchcraft is the chief enemy of Africa. A most religious tribe (the Alunda) have a proverb: "Leave witchcraft alone and the children will multiply."

Almost as bad a bar to advancement is dogma.[2] Speaking of Africa generally, while we have done next to nothing to remove superstition, there has been a tendency to replace it by dogma. This Conference is a welcome testimony to the fact that this danger is realised.

If a man—even a black man—is to live aright he must find strength and guidance in himself. He must trust his own nature, with its infinite possibilities. He must trust it and use it. But, if he is to do this, the shadow of the supernatural must cease to chill and darken his life. Our very first step is to kill the overpowering belief in witchcraft, which is stifling the country. This we can only do by Christianity and education. (The victory against superstition has been greatly handicapped by this confusion in the minds of many between native religion and superstition. To the natives their religion is sacred: witchcraft is an abomination. Ignorant contempt of their religion has handicapped our work against superstition, and will continue to do so.)

I will come to education later. First, I will take
Christianity ; and, though I speak as a layman, I nevertheless speak as a Christian. If Christianity is to save
Africa it seems to me that it must be the Christianity
of Christ in its simple form : shorn of dogma.
Dogmatism really means that certain propositions are
really true ; but unfortunately these propositions mean
different things to different minds ; and the assumption
that the particular reading thereof is necessarily true is
a constant source of separation and strife : of hatred,
malice and all uncharitableness. Dogma in the mental
sphere is as disastrous as in the moral and social : it
divorces reason and intuition . . . so let us avoid all
dogma. One needs to be fairly complacent to be satisfied
with the progress we have made here; and, if the result
be poor, let us be quite honest and admit that there has
been a fault. The fault, as regards conversion, is not in
our Faith, so it must be in our methods. Dogma is
probably one cause : misunderstanding and slighting
native religion and the native point of view is another.
Lack of a definite goal, of a plan, of co-operation, are
contributary causes.

If we have failed as regards conversion we have failed
just as badly in the non-spiritual way. Eighty per cent,
or more, have been untouched by our rule. Let us say
that we have elevated ten per cent in any way by our
occupation (a generous estimate), we have also done the
opposite for at least as many, leaving eighty per cent—
the man in the village (which includes women and
children)—untouched. What a record ! Wherein lies
the fault ? Failure to provide education : lack of any
effort to elevate—to help the native on and up. And the
reason for that fault ? While not forgetting the essential
fact that funds have been lacking I think the chief
reasons are our habit of treating the native as a commodity
at the disposal of the white, our fetish of orderliness and
the entire absence of any co-operation between us and

the people most concerned—the natives themselves. The result is stagnation. Law, order and discipline are not progress. They are foundations excellent as such but as useless in themselves as are the foundations of a house that is not built : in fact one only destroys more or less good ground by digging foundations which are valueless *per se*. Yet in any African protectorate (eastern half) the authorities point proudly to these foundations— law, order, discipline : as if they had some intrinsic value. As for building on these foundations, we have not yet got the plans for the edifice. If we go on thinking thus we vote for stagnation—and stagnation is death.

[If you will forgive a short historical digression, I would like to show that I am not merely theorising. One of the best of many examples provided by history of the blind worship of law, order and discipline is to be found in old Peru, and there is no more perfect example of the stagnation of a people than that. One more example : one of the most close parallels to our rule in tropical Africa is furnished by the rule of Rome in Britain. For some time the Romans thought of nothing but law order and discipline: result, stagnation . . . and re-bellion. Boadicea's rebellion taught Rome a lesson, and under a more enlightened policy—associated largely with the name of Agricola—the Britons were taught to build houses instead of huts, to cultivate, to start industries, develop mines, export their produce, and so on: result, progress and peace. Though a terrible set-back occurred when the Romans left (for reasons irrelevant in this connection), that Roman policy laid the foundations of a progress that made those despised savages advance further than any advance dreamt of by the Romans.]

We come to this, therefore ; unless we change our ideas and methods the natives have no future. Without growth there can be no future. Are we to perpetuate this ? And, if not, how are we to assure that the native shall have a future, and what is to be the nature of that future ?

This is where the need for thought and co-operation comes in. We all need to pull together and pool our ideas. I think we must all agree that we want the natives to have a future, and we cannot deny that we have taken on ourselves the responsibility for looking after them. What we need to do is to get at the masses ; to get at village life : instead of converting or educating a small percentage and leaving the majority to stagnate or worse, to aim at raising the whole morally and mentally and materially. We would do better to raise the hundred by ten per cent than to raise the ten by a hundred per cent, though, in practice, the latter would be a corollary of the former. If the masses be raised a little, more would be raised considerably than otherwise. We need to bring Christianity to their doors, to educate them at home, to teach them home industries : here, as in all else, to build up and improve what is already there, adding a little—by degrees—and avoiding anything " revolutionary." We want to show the villager how to develop : how to trust and make the most of his own nature : to help him to rise and expand.

I consider that we, as the governing race, have a special obligation to provide the natives with this home education. It is we who have introduced the destructive element into their society : it is because of us that many natives get detribalised (and therefore irreligious). The miscalled " mission boy," the worker on the mines and on farms, the house boy (all equally anathema to the chiefs and headmen), pick up bits of knowledge, lose their old tribal and religious checks and become a disintegrating, destructive element. As long as we occupy the country we cannot prevent that—natives will always be attracted to centres of civilisation, and increasingly so unless we give them interest, occupation and money-earning power at their own homes. In such centres they

become " educated "—largely in evil—for all contact
with the white man educates the native and expands his
ideas. Since we cannot prevent this we should counteract it by sound and elevating village education ; incidentally encouraging all to keep the fifth commandment,
which is the first point in the native code that the mal-
educated native forgets. We should do this partly for
the selfish reason that, if we do not, our house will fall
about our ears ; but also from the higher motive that,
having introduced the destructive element, we—as
trustees—ought also to introduce the constructive
element. In my opinion there should be no further
delay in starting this—every year's delay will add
enormously to the difficulties of the task ; and a day will
come when regeneration will be impossible, because we
will soon have nothing whereon to build, nor will co-
operation with the natives be possible. *At present* we
would get a considerable amount of support for any
tactful advance on these lines from village headmen and
elders if we could strengthen the " village aristocracy "
against the element of *nouveaux riches.*

To do this we must use all the knowledge we have
acquired and can acquire of the native's beliefs and
customs, so as to enable us to get him on our side instead
of alienating him. We simply must have his co-operation
in his own elevation or we are foredoomed to failure,
and also to enable us to see what parts are best worth
retaining and building on. We *must* use his tribal
structure, and even buttress it by some such means as
guilds ; and, of course, to do this means some recognition
of his religion. I fear this last is a hard thing to some of
you, but I would ask you to consider it carefully. We
cannot support tribalism and deny native religion *in
toto*, for tribalism is part of it. I believe we will be getting
the native nearer to Christianity this way than in any
other way—for to break down his own religion hastily
will tend more to make the native heathen than Christian.

Look, as I said before, at those who have been robbed of their old moral guide and have not found one to replace it.

In other ways we can help the future of the natives. It lies with us to remedy one of the contributory causes of backwardness which I enumerated : the sparse population. By careful investigation in my own district I have found native infant mortality to vary from sixty per cent to about seventy-five per cent. The Rev. E. W. Smith says that among the Ba-Ila it varies between seventy-five and ninety per cent! In a quarter of a century what have we done to remedy that? (That it can be remedied the reduced mortality in the neighbourhood of any Mission proves.)

Again, we can do something with native laws. African natives are unique among primitive races in the richness of their judicial codes. We could straighten them out and purge them of vicious excrescences. In all the East Central African protectorates (I am ignorant of West Africa) I do not know of any law promulgated by us *for the natives*. All our laws here, for example, are either for the whites, for the relations between white and black, or for the government and taxation of the black : not one for the blacks themselves.

Whenever we have done anything direct we seem to have started at the wrong end : chiefly by trying to cure ideas and beliefs with a penal code, forgetting that education must come first, e.g. we legislate against and hang the witch-doctor—who is *essential* in native life—instead of realising that the only cure for him (i.e. in his harmful rôle, for he has an innocuous side also) is to eradicate the belief in witchcraft, and so make him no longer essential. We punish women for killing children who cut the wrong teeth first, or who cannot walk in due time, without considering that if they do not do so they will be—in native eyes—guilty of constructive murder on a big scale . . . instead of trying to teach them better, or even of trying to save the lives of thousands of healthy, normal children every year. We tell natives that certain customs are contrary to natural morality, and send them to prison because of them, instead of teaching them better : thereby behaving very much as the Romans did when they sent the Christians to the lions : i.e. failing to realise that we are asking the native to deny his religion for fear of gaol—a thing that no one has the right to do. Moreover, native religion (like any other) will flourish if it be proscribed ; and penal codes alone will never cure the evils in it.

We claim to be a superior race and to have a superior Faith. I believe both claims are justified ; but let us not " rub it in " quite so much to the natives. Let us not be too arrogant and derisory. Let us not assume our superiority as proven to them in every way. Above all, let us try to think less of what WE are doing, of what WE can do. "WE" don't count. What is of importance is what *is being done* for the natives, and what *can be done* for them. WE are nothing but agents. OUR point of view does not matter,

> " The game is more than the players of the game ;
> And the ship is more than the crew."

Then, I believe, we will make a start. Then we will begin to see daylight, and the natives whose welfare our representatives at Versailles called " a sacred trust " will have some chance of a future.

---

[1] The Wakwa, by L. Rukwa (Tanganyika territory) are practically pagan.

[2] I use the word in its colloquial sense.

INDEX

To Marry A Succubus

Dustin Midnight

First Edition Published 2023

To Marry A Succubus

First Hardcover/paperback/kindle published 2023

ISBN: 9798850656089 Hardcover
9798850656072 Paperback

DEDICATION

Sometimes it's hard to find a way to dedicate these books. There are so many people out there that deserve a dedication to. So since I need to make one. This book is dedicated to the writers who helped forge the path that brought me to loving stories, and shined the light to the road that began my journey of writing.

DUSTIN MIDNIGHT BOOKS

BORDELLO BOOK SERIES
Bordello of the Moon
Bordello of the Sun
Bordello of Desire

MONSTEROTICA SERIES
The Genies Desire
The Amazon Queen

SUCCUBUS SERIES
To buy a Succubus
To Marry a Succubus

GODDESS SERIES
Married to a goddess

SUPER ANIMALS SERIES
The Descent of Orpheus Barns into Super animals

To Marry a Succubus

CONTENTS

To Marry a Succubus

ACKNOWLEDGMENTS

This book Acknowledges those searching for love and just haven't found it yet. I'm sure one day you will find the love of your life. It just takes time .